'Civil Disorder is the Disease of Ibadan'

'Ijo Igboro Larun Ibadan'

DATE DUE

Western African Studies

'Civil Disorder is the Disease of Ibadan'

Chieftaincy & Civic Culture in a Yoruba City

RUTH WATSON
Lecturer in History
Birkbeck College, University of London

Ohio University Press
ATHENS

James Currey
OXFORD

Heinemann Educational Books (Nigeria)
IBADAN

James Currey
73 Botley Road
Oxford OX2 0BS

Ohio University Press
Scott Quadrangle
Athens, Ohio 45701

Heinemann Educational Books
(Nigeria) Plc
1 Ighodaro Rd
Jericho
PMB 5205, Ibadan

British Library Cataloguing in Publication Data
Watson, Ruth
    'Civil disorder is the disease of Ibadan' : chieftaincy &
    civic culture in a Yoruba city. - (Western African
    studies)
    1. Ibadan (Nigeria) - Politics and government
    I. Title
    320.9'66925

ISBN 0-85255-459-1 (James Currey cloth)
IBSN 0-85255-454-0 (James Currey paper)

Library of Congress Cataloging-in-Publication Data
Watson, Ruth.
    'Civil disorder is the disease of Ibadan': chieftaincy and civic culture in a Yoruba city
    / by Ruth Watson.
        p.cm.-- (Western African studies series)
    Includes bibliographical references and index.
    ISBN 0-8214-1450-X (alk. paper) -- ISBN0-8214-1451-8 (pbk.: alk paper)
    1. Ibadan (Nigeria)--Politics and government. 2. Political
    culture--Nigeria--Ibadan--History. I. Title. II. Western African studies

DT515.I2.W38 2002
303.6'2'0966925--dc21   2002074827

ISBN 0-8214-1450-X (Ohio University Press cloth)
ISBN 0-8214-1451-8 (Ohio University Press paper)

Typeset in 10½/12 pt Monotype Ehrhardt
by Long House Publishing Services, Cumbria, UK
Printed in Great Britain
by Woolnough, Irthlingborough

Ibadan kure
Ibadan bere ki o too wo o
Ibadan Mesi ogo nile Oluyole
Nibi ole gbe e jare olohun
Ibadan kii gbonile, bi ajeji
A ki waye ka ma larun kan lara
Ija igboro larun Ibadan

Ibadan, greetings
Ibadan, bow down before you enter it
Ibadan Mesi ogo is the home of Oluyole
Where the thieves get the better of the property-owners
Ibadan never blesses the natives as much as strangers
No-one comes to earth without some disease
Civil disorder is the disease of Ibadan

An *oriki* of Ibadan

Contents

List of Maps & Photographs

Acknowledgements

This book is a revised version of my D.Phil. thesis, submitted to the University of Oxford in 1998. Financial support was provided by an Oriel College/University of Melbourne Mayer Scholarship, a Commonwealth Scholarship and a Beit Senior Research Scholarship. Oriel College also kindly helped me out of financial difficulties at a crucial time. The Beit Fund and the Association of Commonwealth Universities financed two fieldwork trips to Ibadan. I am grateful for all these sources of funding, which made the research possible.

In Ibadan, the generosity of numerous people made two visits there both successful and enjoyable. The Department of History at the University of Ibadan kindly granted me research affiliate status for the duration of each of my fieldwork trips and provided vital administrative assistance. I am grateful to Professor Omoniyi Adewoye who, as Head of Department in 1995, helped to arrange accommodation at Tafawa Balewa Hall with the assistance of the Warden, Dr. Ewete. In 1997, Subash and Veebha Garde provided a welcoming home. I am also much obliged to Chief (Dr.) Raymond Zard for his hospitality and enthusiastic interest in my work, as well as for assisting with the practical difficulties of transport between Lagos and Ibadan. Margaret and 'Agbo Folarin, as well as Bolaji Olarinsoji, remained the supportive family who I first adopted during my childhood years in Ife. For their interest and valuable advice I thank Dr. 'Tayo Adesina and Professor Akin Mabogunje, as well as Professor Bolanle Awe who kindly gave access to a useful primary source. I am also warmly grateful to Dr. LaRay Denzer who introduced me to a vibrant social network and generously supported my research in all sorts of ways.

The staff of the National Archives in Ibadan, especially Mr. Michael Ehmadu, assisted me greatly in their expert retrieval of sources. Mr. Sina Osunlana and Mr. Sam Odularu of the Maps and Manuscripts Collection in the Kenneth Dike Library were extremely helpful and tolerant of my demands on their time. I am also grateful to the staff of Rhodes House and Queen Elizabeth House Libraries in Oxford and to the custodians of the CMS archive at the University of Birmingham.

Acknowledgements

Exploring the history of Ibadan was made even more of a pleasure by the people who so generously shared their knowledge in interviews. I am much indebted to my research assistant, Mr. Raufu Yesufu, who accepted my ignorance and patiently suggested ways to improve my research method. Raufu's deeply layered understanding of the Ibadan past and the politics of history-telling taught me an enormous amount and shaped the way this book was written. I am also deeply appreciative of the welcome extended to me by Raufu's family, who went out of their way to be helpful and supportive.

Without the expert supervision and friendship of Gavin Williams, this book would not exist. His enthusiasm for the project has been relentless from the day I first met him in 1994, when he handed over his entire notes on the diaries of Akinpelu Obisesan as well as the advice that I contact Raufu Yesufu, who was his research assistant in 1971. Gavin's incisive criticisms of my writing and his intuitive engagement with the arguments I sought to develop were an inspiration, helping me through times of confusion and doubt. Gill Williams accepted my disruption of her family's life and provided much needed support.

The task of converting a doctoral thesis to a book predictably took much longer than I expected. A first draft was completed while I was Kirk-Greene Junior Research Fellow at St. Antony's College, Oxford. I continued revisions whilst teaching in the School of History, Classics and Archaeology at Birkbeck College, where thanks are due to Emma Dench and Hilary Sapire, who convinced me to declare the book finished. I also appreciate the help of Emmanuele Curti, who improved my amateurish maps enormously. At James Currey Publishers, Douglas Johnson and Lynn Taylor patiently waited and endured my numerous delays. Of the several friends and colleagues who read versions of the book at various stages of completion, I am especially grateful for the advice and encouragement of Natalie Adamson, Karin Barber, Wayne Dooling, Paulo Farias, Maureen Malowany, Sharon Musher and John Peel. I owe special thanks to Helen Verran for her imagination and for teaching me so much.

Finally, thank you to my parents, Max Watson and Helen Verran. Apart from their constant support for my academic ambitions, it was they who took me to Nigeria in 1979. The origin of this book is a childhood spent in Ife.

Copyright Acknowledgements

Abbreviations

BAP	Bishop Akinyele Papers
CMS	Church Missionary Society
DC	District Commissioner
HMP	Herbert Macaulay Papers
IAP	Isaac Akinyele Papers
IDU	Ibadan Descendants Union
INAS	Ibadan Native Aboriginal Society
IPA	Ibadan Patriotic Association
IPU	Ibadan Progressive Union
KDL	Kenneth Dike Library, University of Ibadan
NA	Native Authority
NAI	Nigerian National Archives
OP	Akinpelu Obisesan Papers
WD	Revd Williams Diaries

A Note on Orthography

All Yoruba words in the text have been italicised. Diacritical marks are not given. When quoting from sources I have followed the spelling used. Otherwise I have used standard Yoruba spelling. Thus *Alaafin* sometimes appears as Alafin, an anglicised version of the same word.

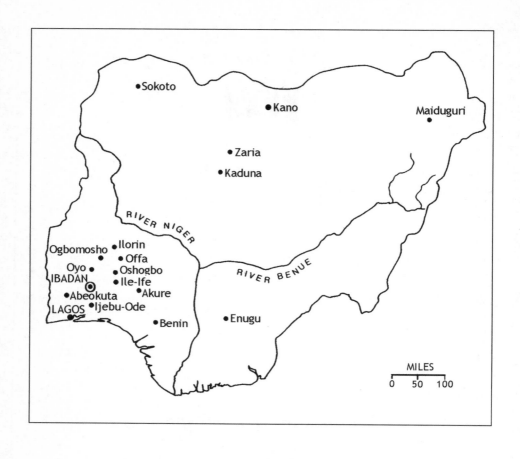

Map 1 Nigeria, showing location of Ibadan

1

The Civic Ibadan
& the War of Pen

'Ibadan – a model of historical facts.'[1] So proclaimed the editors of *Ibadan Mementoes* in January 1995, commemorating the first year anniversary of Emmanuel Adegboyega Adeyemo's installation as *Olubadan*, the most senior chieftaincy title in the city. *Ibadan Mementoes* includes articles about the life and chieftaincy career of Adeyemo, as well as short biographies on some of the city's leading personalities. It seeks 'to demonstrate that Ibadanland … is a reservoir of creative minds in many human endeavours'.[2] A glorified description of the city is included, in addition to an 'Ibadan City Anthem'.

Ibadan Mementoes celebrates a civic Ibadan. It presents a puzzle. What does the claim that Ibadan is 'a model of historical facts' mean? It depends on how the term 'model' is defined. The editors of *Ibadan Mementoes* do not specify their definition but, given the eulogising tone of their text, they probably intend 'exemplar'. There is an alternative: 'Ibadan – a conceptual representation of historical facts'. This second reading is one starting point for the analysis of political culture developed in this book.

This conceptual model was used during an interview I conducted during October 1995. Lawuyi Ogunniran, a local historian, was anticipating publication of his Yoruba text, *Ibadan Mesiogo Ninu Ogun Ile Yoruba, 1829–1893*. Also present was *Mogaji* Olugbode, a friend of the historian and head of the compound I was visiting. I asked Ogunniran about the focus of his research. He replied:

> There are certain things which made Ibadan to be great – that was the focus of my attention in that book.… Ibadan was a republican democracy, where every man born in Ibadan has the potential to be *Olubadan*, if he wants it enough.… Those who were the founding fathers believe that the chieftaincy belongs to them, but it is not the case. It is a democracy and everyone has the right to representation.[3]

[1] *Ibadan Mementoes: Oba Adeyemo's Noble Past, Glorious Present and Progressive Future X-Rayed. Historical Perspective on Ibadanland* (Ibara, 1995), p. 19.

[2] *Ibid.*, p. 5.

[3] Lawuyi Ogunniran and *Mogaji* Olugbode interviewed, 19 October 1995, Ibadan.

1

At this, *Mogaji* Olugbode interjected: 'It is not anyone, it has to be one of those who fought for the town. These men founded the town by blood, and their descendants are the chiefs. Their blood cannot be bought by money.'[4] Ogunniran did not respond to his friend, but turned instead to me, explaining, 'This man is aggrieved.'[5]

Subsequently, an impassioned debate ensued between the historian and the *Mogaji*:

> *Mogaji*: I am not happy with what you said. We should cry for chieftaincy in Ibadan but we must fight it out. I have been *Mogaji* for twenty years and still I have no title. Twenty years!

> *Ogunniran*: We have a responsibility to collect materials and facts and look at them objectively to reveal the past. If we do this we will see that chieftaincy in Ibadan was never settled. … I am not saying that anyone can become a chief, but anyone who fights for the town can. There is no single founder of Ibadan, therefore the chieftaincy cannot be with just one family. It is a democracy. Anyone who is a citizen can aspire to a title.

> *Mogaji*: You are fighting war of pen! War of pen! That is not my war, mine is war of blood, this is blood spilled for the town of Ibadan by its founders and they must be honoured. I will say it, I will even write it on paper. Ibadan is founded not by one man but by a group of people. The chieftaincy does not belong to one man. But this does not mean it can belong to anyone.[6]

The protagonists held different views of Ibadan chieftaincy. For Ogunniran, a history where 'everyone has the right to representation' meant that access to titles remained open. For *Mogaji* Olugbode, although titles were not restricted to a single family, they belonged to the descendants of those who had gained recognition for their military exploits during the previous century. Both men, however, took for granted that chieftaincy titles ascribed civic status.

Challenging this normative view – that chiefs speak for and exercise authority within a civic community – the central contention of this book is that a civic political culture is made, not given. Exploring over a century of Ibadan history, it is a study of both the pre-colonial and colonial city. We begin with its foundation as a war camp in 1829 and end with its hosting of the 1939 Conference of Yoruba Chiefs, a political forum invented by the colonial policy of indirect rule. The focus of the book is on the relationships between chieftaincy and city politics. It argues that an examination of the ways in which Ibadan people and, after 1893, British administrators conceived and expressed these relationships reveals the making of Ibadan as a civic community. Through the course of the century, this process of making political community shifted from the battlefield to a discursive field – a 'war of pen'. Associated with this shift were institutional forms of rule that entangled various cultural symbols and practices. The aim of my study is to explore how and why this historical shift occurred and what it meant to the people who made it happen.

---

[4] *Mogaji* Olugbode, *ibid*.
[5] Lawuyi Ogunniran, *ibid*.
[6] Lawuyi Ogunniran and *Mogaji* Olugbode, *ibid*.

Civic culture in politics and history

A proud Ibadan citizen explained his city's constitution to me this way:

> We set up a sort of republican system of government. And that is basically where we are different from all the others in Nigeria ... we don't care from where you come, if you come and distinguish yourself – you assimilate yourself with the interests of Ibadan, then you can rise up to any position. Secondly, if you are born in Ibadan here, you are entitled to become the head or the traditional ruler of Ibadan. In other words, just the system that is obtaining in most of the civilised countries of the world, we have been practising it in Ibadan centuries ago.[7]

On another occasion, *Osi Olubadan* Durosaro declared that the government of nineteenth-century Ibadan 'was like what used to happen with Greek city-states'.[8] Both men assume that Ibadan chieftaincy is and has always been a civic institution.

How are we to understand the term 'civic'? A classic text of comparative politics, *The Civic Culture*, defines its subject as 'a set of orientations toward a special set of social objects and processes'.[9] A later, influential book on democratic government in modern Italy identified particular characteristics of a civic community: active participation in public affairs; equal rights and obligations for all; respect and trust between members and, finally, the embodiment of these qualities in voluntary associations.[10] But for an historian, this focus on political attitudes as a starting point is problematic. Here, the 'norms and values of the civic community' are assumed; a foundation for qualitatively measuring the 'civic-ness' of a society. Where these norms and values came from and how they developed over time is not explained.

In these political science texts, fairly predictable conclusions are reached. For example, Putnam compared the workings of political institutions in different geographical regions of Italy. He found that 'institutional performance' was determined by social context, particularly the degree of 'civic traditions' in each region.[11] This finding was no doubt valid and Putnam's appreciation of the relevance of history to contemporary social contexts is important. Yet his analysis ultimately fails to explain the motivations of the people responsible for the institutional performance he measured. Focusing solely on how people pursued political objectives was not enough to identify 'the conditions for creating strong, responsive, effective representative institutions'.[12] Putnam also needed to question what people's objectives actually were, how these objectives changed in different situations, and why they pursued them.

A more revealing approach is found in recent scholarship on the Greek *polis*. 'Instead of constituting familiar references all ready for use', writes François de Polignac:

---

[7] Chief Adisa, interviewed 20 January 1996, Ibadan. Chief Adisa is a solicitor who holds an honorary title; he is not a member of the *Olubadan*-in-Council.

[8] Chief Durosaro, *Osi Olubadan*, interviewed 7 November 1995, Ibadan.

[9] Gabriel Almond and Sidney Verba, *The Civic Culture: Political Attitudes and Democracy in Five Nations* (London, 1989 [1963]), p. 12.

[10] Robert D. Putnam, *Making Democracy Work: Civic Traditions in Modern Italy* (Princeton, 1993), pp. 86–91.

[11] *Ibid.*, p. 15.

[12] *Ibid.*, p. 6.

The notions of city and citizen can, on the contrary, only be properly understood once the social formation that gave rise to them has been elucidated. We must make an effort to forget the institutional image of the Greek city if we are to understand the true nature of a historical phenomenon yet to be defined.[13]

Following de Polignac's emphasis on history as generative, this book will show how a civic community is an outcome of politics and, at the same time, a shifting foundation that gives meaning to politics. That is, in Ibadan, making history and doing politics were mutually constitutive processes. The civic Ibadan was a continuing emergent polity and, as it emerged, so too did the institution of Ibadan chieftaincy that in turn shaped the forms and practices of city politics. My objective here is to develop a perspective that uncovers the implicit expectations and cultural symbols that were both made by and embedded in certain modes of political action. Today, I argue, to explore the civic Ibadan is to read contesting models of historical facts.

'The London of Negroland'

The historical genesis of a civic Ibadan is in the city's military origins. *Ibadan Mementoes* celebrates this paradox in its recitation of the third verse of the 'Ibadan City Anthem':

Ibadan, ilu jagunjagun	Ibadan, city of warriors
Awon to so o d'ilu nla	They who made it into a great city
Awa omo re ko ni je	We its children will not allow
K'ola ti ogo won run.[14]	That their honour and glory perish.

From the 1820s onwards, the area that is today south-western Nigeria was beset with intense political turmoil. A combination of events – the collapse of the Oyo Empire as a result of internal dissent; the expansion of the Sokoto Caliphate to the north; and the prohibition and consequent disruption of the Atlantic slave trade – produced a climate of near-continuous violent upheaval throughout most of the nineteenth century. Wars ensued between various rival polities and refugees flooded into the area. About 1829, in the aftermath of one of these wars, a group of soldiers occupied the deserted Egba village of Ibadan.

Within just twenty years, this war camp had grown into a large city. Population estimates range widely. In 1851, the Anglican missionary David Hinderer suggested a figure between 60,000 and 100,000 people;[15] six years later, his Baptist counterpart

---

[13] François de Polignac, *Cults, Territory, and the Origins of the Greek City-State*, trans. Janet Lloyd (Chicago, 1995), p. 3.

[14] *Ibadan Mementoes*, p. 6. I am grateful to Karin Barber for her help with this translation.

[15] Church Missionary Society Papers, Special Collections, Main Library, The University of Birmingham, Yoruba Mission (cited hereafter as CMSB) CA2/049/104: David Hinderer, 'Journey and visit to Ibadan, a Yoruba town two days journey from Abeokuta', Quarterly Journal Extract, 23 October 1851. David Hinderer was a Swiss-German, ordained to the priesthood in 1848 and sent to Abeokuta the following year as an agent of the London-based Church Missionary Society (CMS). After his 1851 visit to Ibadan he returned two years later with his wife, Anna, and established a mission station at Kudeti. By the time of his departure in 1869 there were two more missions in the city, namely, Aremo and Ogunpa.

4

T.J. Bowen proposed 70,000.[16] In 1890, Assistant Colonial Secretary Alvan Millson was sent on a 'peace mission' to Ibadan, a visit that was part of a wider imperial project to end the regional wars. The following year, at a meeting of the Royal Geographical Society, he described the city:

> The London of Negroland...: Surrounded by its farming villages, 163 in number, Ibadan counts over 200,000 souls, while within the walls of the city itself at least 120,000 people are gathered. Its sea of brown roofs covers an area of nearly 16 square miles, and the ditches and walls of hardened clay, which surround it, are more than 18 miles in circumference.[17]

Evidently, Millson viewed Ibadan as an impressive urban centre. Apart from farming, he identified slave raiding as the other occupation of city residents. Emphasising that raids were undertaken to acquire slaves for domestic purposes, Millson made reference to Ibadan's bellicose society, where control over people was militarily and politically vital. This internal demand also related to Ibadan's agricultural base, since slaves were generally put to work on the farms surrounding the settlement.[18] It was an arrangement that enabled the city to feed itself, despite being constantly at war with neighbouring polities.

The Ibadan economy was not solely dependent on farming and 'warlike pursuits'. According to Hinderer, there was 'a good deal of industry to be seen in & about the town'. He referred to male-dominated crafts such as weaving, tanning and black-smithing, as well the manufacture of oil and soap (from palm produce) by women.[19] Furthermore, 'trade routes radiated from Ibadan in virtually all directions'.[20] The nodal position of the city enabled it to develop rapidly into a commercial hub where local textiles and primary produce such as yams, beans, corn, kola-nuts and palm oil were exchanged for imported goods. From the south came firearms, European cloth and salt; while the north provided slaves, livestock, swords, ivory and onions.[21]

Ibadan was more than an urban centre – it was also a powerful military polity. By the mid-1870s, the city war chiefs claimed jurisdiction over towns almost two hundred miles east from their base (see Map 2). Most conquests were achieved by a huge army marching on foot; few warriors used horses. In 1878, many towns in the eastern part of the empire revolted to fight for their independence. The addition of this war to ongoing conflicts with the Egba and Ijebu to the south and Ilorin to the north meant that Ibadan was eventually forced to fight on five fronts. These battles dragged on until the imposition of British colonial rule in 1893.[22]

[16] Although T.J. Bowen visited Oyo, Ogbomoso and Ilorin, he never went to Ibadan. He proposed the Ibadan population figure in a chapter titled 'The Geography of Yoruba' but did not name his source. See *Central Africa: Adventures and Missionary Labours in the Interior of Africa, 1849–1856* (London, 1857), p. 221.

[17] A.W. Millson, 'The Yoruba country, West Africa', *Proceedings of the Royal Geographical Society* 13 (1891), p.583.

[18] *Ibid.*, p. 578.

[19] CMSB, CA2/049/104: Hinderer Journal, 23 October 1851.

[20] Bolanle Awe, 'Militarism and Economic Development in Nineteenth Century Yoruba Country: the Ibadan Example', *Journal of African History* 14 (1973), p. 71.

[21] *Ibid.*

[22] See Bolanle Awe, 'The Rise of Ibadan as a Yoruba Power in the Nineteenth Century' (Oxford University D.Phil. thesis, 1964); Toyin Falola, *The Political Economy of a Pre-Colonial African State: Ibadan, 1830–1900* (Ile-Ife, 1984); S.A. Akintoye, *Revolution and Power Politics in Yorubaland 1840–1893. Ibadan Expansion and*

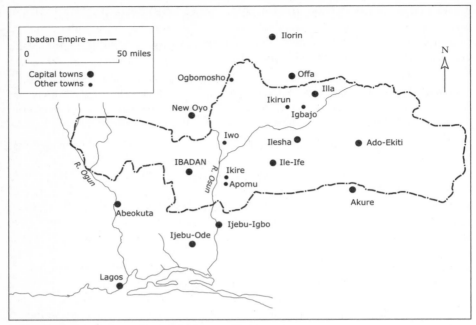

Map 2 The military polity of Ibadan, c. 1874 (after Akintoye, 1971)

The nineteenth-century past is present in *Ibadan Mementoes* and in the argument between Ogunniran and *Mogaji* Olugbode. The term 'Ibadanland' refers directly to the former military empire and the 'war of blood' recalled by the *Mogaji* could hardly be more explicit. Significantly, Ibadan is located in a region known for its historical tradition of urbanism. It is to the extensive literature on this subject that we now turn.

A model of urbanism

The Yoruba are a group of linguistically and culturally related populations, most of whom now live in south-western Nigeria and in parts of the Benin Republic.[23] 'Probably the most distinctive feature in the spatial expression of this culture', suggests Wheatley, is the tendency of its people to live in 'large, permanent, compact aggregations'.[24] Some of these communities, which were generally bounded and fortified by walls, date back to at least the eleventh century. Ile-Ife is said to be the

[22] (cont.) *the Rise of Ekitiparapo* (New York, 1971).

[23] The process by which the name 'Yoruba' came to refer to this group of people is detailed in J.D.Y. Peel, 'The Cultural Work of Yoruba Ethnogenesis', in *History and Ethnicity*, eds Elizabeth Tonkin, Maryon McDonald and Malcolm Chapman, (London, 1989), pp. 198–215.

[24] Paul Wheatley, 'The Significance of Traditional Yoruba Urbanism', *Comparative Studies in Society and History* 12 (1970), p. 396.

oldest – certain accounts of origin claim it as first, the 'navel' of humankind and second, the cradle of Yoruba urban culture.[25]

During the late colonial period, Yoruba towns became a subject of interest for Western academic scholars. Among them was William Bascom, an American anthropologist who sought to use the settlements as test cases for a Wirthian model of urbanism.[26] By proving that 'the Yoruba had cities even before European penetration' Bascom sought to rank their urban development on a par with more industrialised societies.[27] Importantly, the scholarship on Yoruba urbanism that he pioneered challenged narrow definitions of the term 'urban' by introducing a cross-cultural perspective. But radical as it was in its conception, this model of Yoruba urbanism is a timeless ideal. It is a model of assumptions – *not* historical facts.

According to Bascom, the Yoruba town was constituted by two levels of social/spatial structure. The 'primary group' was a patrilineage that he assumed was 'the residential unit'.[28] This kin-group inhabited a confined household space known as the compound: a physical structure which comprised a large, rectangular building of rooms facing inward onto a verandah that, in turn, surrounded a courtyard. The next social/spatial structure was the quarter – a group of lineages and their compounds which, via the 'exercise of authority' by a chief, were integrated into an administrative unit.[29] Chieftaincy titles were claimed on the basis of lineage membership; particular titles belonged to specific lineages. For those lineages who had titles, succession was hereditary within the lineage.[30]

Bascom argued that Yoruba towns were urban because they had 'a formalized government which exercises authority over the primary groups and incorporates them into a political community'.[31] Incorporation was taken as given; an automatic result of the appointment of each quarter chief to a town council. The rule of an *oba* over the other council chiefs further consolidated this unity. Peter Lloyd, another influential exponent of the ideal, put it thus: 'The ruler is ... in some respects a divine king, a personification of the whole town.'[32] An *oba* gained the right to his position by professing membership of the royal lineage – a group who claimed descent from a town founder who was usually associated with a past migration from Ife.[33] Later scholars contended that the power of the *oba* was also expressed by the central position of his palace in the town layout.[34]

This lineage-based model of Yoruba urbanism was challenged by Jeremy Eades in his book, *The Yoruba Today*. Eades argued it was ahistorical and proposed that

---

[25] J.A. Ademakinwa, *Ife, Cradle of the Yoruba Part II* (Lagos, n.d.), p. 3. See also M.A. Fabunmi, *An Anthology of Historical Notes on Ife City* (Lagos, 1985).

[26] Louis Wirth, 'Urbanism as a Way of Life', *The American Journal of Sociology* 44 (1938), pp. 1-24.

[27] William Bascom, 'Urbanization Among the Yoruba', *The American Journal of Sociology* 60 (1955), p. 453.

[28] *Ibid.*, p. 451.

[29] *Ibid.*, p. 450.

[30] Bascom did not explain how chieftaincy titles were allocated. See Peter Lloyd, 'The Yoruba Lineage', *Africa* 25 (1955), p. 249.

[31] Bascom, 'Urbanization', p. 451.

[32] Lloyd, 'Yoruba Lineage', p. 250.

[33] *Ibid.*, p. 239.

[34] Eva Krapf-Askari, *Yoruba Towns and Cities* (Oxford, 1969), p. 55.

'Yoruba urbanism only assumed its characteristic form as a result of the 19th-century wars.'[35] Outlining a two-stage process of urban development, he maintained that settlement patterns before this period were much less centralised. He also adopted a more flexible perspective on Yoruba kinship and questioned the view of lineages and compounds as coterminous. In practice, compounds rarely contained a single lineage; usually, members of two or more descent groups lived in the household. Eades referred to earlier work by Yoruba scholars and pointed out that their accounts focused on *ile*, translated as 'the compound', as an unit of analysis. They did not disguise internal complexity in favour of a model of unilinear descent groups.[36]

In this way, Eades showed that the households and physical spaces where people lived did not simply reflect a static lineage group. Yet he assumed that the residential principle was paramount and implied that people's identity as compound members overrode their identity as members of lineages. Consequently, Eades's model simply replaced 'the lineage' with 'the compound' as the basic building block of urban social structure and sustained the implicit assumption of Bascom's original presentation of Yoruba urbanism. Political community remained a given; a predetermined result of the mechanical exercise of authority over territorial administrative units. Eades and Bascom differed only in their conceptions of how these units were constituted.

Studies of particular towns have shown that this model is empirically and conceptually flawed. Barber explored the past of Okuku through the Yoruba language genre of *oriki*, a fragmentary, highly complex form of oral praise poetry. Her research undermined the assumption that the lineage was a unitary, clearly demarcated social unit. In doing so, she demonstrated that the descent group was rarely equivalent to the residential group. At the same time, neither were the residents of any particular compound formed into an unchanging, homogenous entity. By contrast, social boundaries in the town were: 'continually redefined according to the circumstances, giving rise to different "groups", differently recruited in different situations, so that no single definition of a primary social unit was in the end possible.'[37]

Peel posed a conceptual objection to the model in his study of Ilesha, focusing his criticism on its reductive understanding of political community. The primacy given to 'the lineage', he argued, presented kinship as somehow anterior to politics. Yet in daily social life, accounts of kinship were shaped by political needs and, simultaneously, political needs were influenced by competing accounts of kinship. Lineages were produced by the politics of the town, not just by norms of descent.[38] Unless one considered the numerous forms of this politics, one would not understand Ilesha history.

[35] J.S. Eades, *The Yoruba Today* (Cambridge, 1980), p. 38.

[36] *Ibid.*, p. 45. Eades referred to Johnson's *The History of the Yorubas* and a University of London PhD thesis completed by N.A. Fadipe in 1939. The author died in 1944 but his book was later edited and published as *The Sociology of the Yoruba*, eds Francis Olu. Okediji and Oladejo O. Okediji (Ibadan, 1970).

[37] Karin Barber, *I Could Speak Until Tomorrow*: Oriki, *Women and the Past in a Yoruba Town* (Edinburgh, 1991), p. 158.

[38] J.D.Y. Peel, *Ijeshas and Nigerians. The Incorporation of a Yoruba Kingdom, 1890s–1970s* (Cambridge, 1983), p. 10.

Yoruba language vocabularies also indicate that a rigid view of social structure in Yoruba towns is unsustainable. For example, the term *ilu* can refer to 'town', 'community' or 'council'. Since there is no distinct term to denote the polities of which they were the centres, *ilu* can also mean 'state' or 'society.'[39] A related term, *araalu*, means 'citizen.' This is sometimes distinguished from *ara oko*, which signifies contempt for a 'farm yokel.'[40] However, *oko* (farm) can also be used as a metaphor for any place of productive, 'civilising' work. For example, a trader goes to *oko owo*, the 'farm' of trading – that is, a trading trip.[41]

The ways in which Yoruba people identify their 'towns' and their own statuses as 'citizens' are not always the same. How these terms are defined depends on the context and on the interests at stake. This suggests that attention should focus on the shifting social situations that make them have meaning. If we are to understand what Yoruba towns have in common, we need a rigorously comparative approach that explores the history of each town in its own terms by investigating the actual practices of town life.

In this context, we should note that a 'town' or 'city' and a 'civic community' are also not necessarily coterminous. Residents living in the same city might not necessarily identify an allegiance to a civic community. It is particularly a social relationship with the political institutions of urban life, in this case chieftaincy, which differentiate a city from a civic community. In Ibadan, debates over residents' inclusion or exclusion from this political institution are the substance of making civic community. Why this should be the case is the central question of this study.

The argument

This book argues that the making and re-making of a civic Ibadan community between 1829 and 1939 is best understood through the ways that city residents perceived Ibadan politics and their shifting roles as social actors within it. By adopting this perspective, the analysis reveals civic culture as a contentious historical process, rather than as a fixed set of political attitudes. At the same time, it unveils the multiple ways that Ibadan people and, later, British administrators intervened in and debated this process. Significantly, in both the pre-colonial and colonial periods, these interventions and debates struggled to define the institutional form and constitutional practices of Ibadan chieftaincy in ways that were simultaneously symbolic and material. As a result, civic discourse in Ibadan could be as much ideology as it was actual things, such as buildings, monuments and cloth.

The book is ordered chronologically. The following chapter investigates the early development of Ibadan and the origins of its chieftaincy system. It examines how the city was established and the means by which it expanded, both socially and spatially, in a context of regional warfare. By doing so, it suggests that the structural account of

---

[39] *Ibid.*, p. 9.
[40] R. C. Abraham, *Dictionary of Modern Yoruba* (London, 1958), p. 305.
[41] Barber, *I Could Speak*, p. 316.

political community developed in the model of Yoruba urbanism does not explain the nature and form of civic collectivity in Ibadan. This point is taken up in Chapter 3, which explores political culture in nineteenth-century Ibadan. It contends that the making of civic community is best understood through an analysis of Ibadan militarism that rejects a false dichotomy between 'external' warfare and 'internal' civil disorder.

A transitional period in Ibadan politics, characterised by the end of regional warfare and the incorporation of the Ibadan military polity into the British Empire, is the subject of Chapter 4. It examines how, in the absence of the battlefield, warrior chiefs reconfigured their material and symbolic bases of political mobilisation to maintain their civic power. By closely examining civil unrest and a controversial murder trial, it elucidates strategies of defining and exercising legitimate authority that were an outcome of interaction between two political institutions - Ibadan chieftaincy and colonial administration.

Governor Lugard and exponents of the ideology of Indirect Rule viewed this type of interaction as destructive of 'Native Custom' in Ibadan. As a result, wide-ranging constitutional reforms were devised and imposed after 1912. These reforms, explored in Chapter 5, entailed specific discursive political practices that materialised in the form of chiefly depositions and colonial pageants. This political epoch was closed in 1931 by the appointment of Governor Cameron and a related project to modernize 'Native Administration' in Nigeria. In Chapter 6, I analyse the experience of this project in Ibadan as one of 'breeding civic pride'. The project was enthusiastically developed by particular groups of city residents, politically excluded by the previous colonial regime, who sought to increase their civic status. Finally, Chapter 7 exemplifies and draws together the argument of the book as a whole, by examining a controversy over the design of a particular cloth intended to be worn at the Conference of Yoruba Chiefs during 1939. It contends that this conflict is best understood through an historical reading of political culture in the city that focuses on the simulataneously material and symbolic form of the civic Ibadan.

The sources

The approach taken in this research necessitated a rigorous use of varied sources. Throughout the study, it was not always possible to distinguish between primary and secondary material or between historical and political discourse. All sources provided information about events and people's actions in the past. Simultaneously, sources re-told these events and actions in ways that offered a commentary on the social context in which they were produced.

For example, *The History of the Yorubas* by Reverend Samuel Johnson is an invaluable eyewitness account of the pre-colonial Ibadan past. It is also a written record of oral narratives which reflect upon that past and make it serve particular cultural objectives. Another example is a book that has come to be the definitive history of Ibadan, which exists in three different versions. It began as a transcription of oral accounts collected by Isaac Akinyele. He recounted the nineteenth-century past to assert his own political agency in the twentieth. Like Johnson's book, his text reveals not only how history was made but also how it has been remembered and how it is lived.

Government correspondence between colonial administrators offers a further historical perspective. Their ambivalent position as outsiders needing to assert and legitimate their authority affected not only what they saw and did but also the ways in which they represented themselves and others. Such official documentation is complemented by the private papers of both British officials and Ibadan citizens. These letters and diaries enable a daily monitoring of people's actions and their reflections upon them. Today, historical re-telling continues in the recounting of oral narratives. These sources validate alternative versions of the Ibadan past by selectively drawing upon Johnson's and Akinyele's texts. In other contexts, they ignore or challenge the written accounts.

For the historian attempting to interpret a past that actually happened, such tensions within and between sources create difficulties. On the one hand, 'distortions' should not be ignored. On the other, they cannot simply be identified and set aside in the hope of uncovering a pristine historical truth. Distortions not only locate and implicate sources in social and political action, they also give them meaning. Removing them is a practical as well as a theoretical impossibility. My approach has been to read Ibadan history through its distortions and ambiguities. I do this by juxtaposing different sources against each other and by adopting different vantage points on their layered re-tellings. Witnessing the contested dialogue in which sources were made and continue to be engaged enables a richer account of historical experience.

2

A Composite Band of Marauders
Urban Settlement & Chieftaincy

'The history of Ibadan has many versions to it' proclaims a recently published popular text.[1] This variability is characteristic of the historiography of Yoruba traditions, which perpetually renew rivalries between two contesting centres of power – ancient Ife and imperial Oyo.[2]

The Ife-centred account of the foundation of Ibadan claims that the city was established by Lagelu, an ambitious Ife warrior who led his followers to a forest inhabited by 'fugitives, outlaws, rascals and criminals'.[3] A *babalawo* ('father of secrets') was summoned to consult the *Ifa* divination system about whether the site was approved for settlement; he was directed to make an offering of two hundred snails. They were scattered and told: 'Creep as far as you can, over a very wide area.' The snails travelled far and wide in all directions – that is why, the legend goes, Ibadan has been expanding ever since.[4]

A variation maintains that Lagelu was accompanied by his brother, Labosinde. Today, those who profess descent from Labosinde assert rights to the title of *Oluwo*, a chief who is responsible for installing Ibadan's ruler, the *Olubadan*.[5] By making a direct and sustained link between Ife and Ibadan pasts, this version of origins legitimates a claim for Ibadan sovereignty. As Apter has pointed out, similar Ife-centric traditions exist in the foundation narratives of other Yoruba towns such as Ilesha and Ondo, providing 'an ideological foil to Oyo revisionism'. These narratives are maintained by the political oppostion of Ife's successor states to the hegemonic claims of Oyo, rather than by 'traditionalistic piety for Ife's past grandeur'.[6]

---

[1] Bamiro Aofolaju, *Landmarks in the History of Ibadan* (Ibadan, 1996), p. 5.

[2] Andrew Apter, 'Traditions Reviewed: Ancient Ife and Old Oyo', in *Black Critics and Kings: The Hermeneutics of Power in Yoruba Society* (Chicago, 1992), pp. 13–34.

[3] Kemi Morgan, *Akinyele's Outline History of Ibadan, Part One*, (Ibadan, n.d.), p. 29.

[4] E.B. Idowu, 'Religion in Ibadan: Traditional Religion and Christianity', in *The City of Ibadan*, ed. P.C. Lloyd, A.L. Mabogunje and B. Awe (Cambridge, 1967), p. 236.

[5] Chief Akanwo, *Oluwo* of Ibadan, interviewed 6 February 1996, Ibadan.

[6] Apter, *Black Critics and Kings*, p. 34.

Lagelu's settlement is said to have been known as *Eba Odan* meaning 'near the savannah', referring to a location at the edge of the forest belt.[7] The name Ibadan, some scholars suggest, derives from this geographical description.[8] Tales go on to tell of the town's destruction by other polities in the region after an *egungun* was exposed in the market-place: 'for what mortals could withstand the wrathful indignation of the spirits of the ancestors?'[9] Lagelu and his children sought refuge in a nearby forest and lived by plunder. On one of these raids: 'a daughter of Lagelu captured a crown belonging to a neighbouring ruler, and, after showing it to her father, she ripped it to pieces in anger.'[10] The lack of a city-crown in Ibadan is explained by this story.

Subsequently, we are told, the refugees moved to live on a hill; they survived on *igbin* (snails) and *oro* (wild mangoes) collected there. A commonly recited *oriki* (appellation) commemorates this practice:

Ibadan, omo ajorosun,	Ibadan, child of one who ate wild mangoes for supper
Omo aje igbin yo,	Child of one who took snails for a main meal
Omo afi ikarahun fori mu.[11]	Child of one who drank from snail shells.

The 'second Ibadan' was founded when Lagelu and his people came down from this hill to a place called *Ori Yangi*. It is said that this area is now the site of *Oja'ba* (a main city market), a claim which asserts the antiquity of Ibadan by establishing the historicity of present-day urban landmarks.[12] The hill which had provided for the settlers was later believed to accommodate an *orisa* (deity); they called her *Okebadan*. Other accounts maintain that Lagelu was buried in *Okebadan* hill; they suggest it is his spirit which remains there.[13]

The male priest of this cult today holds the title of *Aboke*. On the occasion of the annual *Okebadan* festival, he makes offerings and sacrifices to her shrine. Dressed in women's white clothing, he leads a procession into the city, where residents participate in the dancing, druming, singing and feasting.[14] Chief Ayorinde, a prominent oral historian, described the festival as a 'Remembrance Day' for the survival of Lagelu and his people.[15] Parrinder suggested it was 'a day of licence in which repressed feelings come to the surface', associated with rites of fertility and agricultural production.[16] Other commentators have described it as an infusion of endurance and the 'war spirit'[17] or a day of 'lampooning without fear of reprisals'.[18]

---

[7] I.B. Akinyele, *The Outlines of Ibadan History* (Lagos, 1946), p. 1.

[8] Bolanle Awe, 'Some Ibadan Place-Names: A Source of Historical Evidence', *African Notes* 6 (1970–71), p. 85.

[9] Morgan, *Akinyele's Outline*, p. 37. *Egungun* are ancestral masquerades usually associated with particular households.

[10] *Ibid.*, p. 38.

[11] This *oriki* was often heard during interviews. The translation is my own.

[12] Akinyele, *Outlines*, p. 3.

[13] *Ibid.*

[14] George E. Simpson, *Yoruba Religion and Medicine in Ibadan* (Ibadan, 1991 [1980]), p. 56.

[15] Chief Ayorinde, *Asipa Olubadan*, 'Oke'Badan Festival'. I am grateful to Chief Ayorinde for giving me a copy of this useful pamphlet.

[16] Geoffrey Parrinder, 'Ibadan's Annual Festival', *Africa* 21 (1951), pp. 54–8.

[17] Bolanle Awe, 'Ibadan, Its Early Beginnings', in *The City of Ibadan*, p. 18.

[18] R. C. Abraham, *Dictionary of Modern Yoruba* (London, 1958), p. 265.

The Oyo-centred account of Ibadan's origins relates the foundation of the city to the Owu War, an outcome of the political crisis which engulfed the region after the fall of the Oyo Empire. During the early 1820s, the polities of Ife and Ijebu joined arms against Owu, a city state attempting to prevent their slave-raiding expeditions. The allied armies were at first defeated by Owu and, retreating, they sought refuge at Ibadan, a deserted village. Egba people from the surrounding area and Oyo refugees fleeing from the north moved into the temporary camp. These groups augmented the ranks of the defeated soldiers and subsequently, the war recommenced.[19]

The allied armies besieged Owu for five years; it was ultimately famine which caused its *oba*, the *Olowu*, to flee. His departure marked Owu's surrender and the town was ruined, never to be rebuilt. Afterwards, the soldiers did not disband but went on to overrun and plunder other towns. They eventually sought a resting place:

> Ibadan alone they found not destroyed by fire, and so this marauding band hastily occupied it, the war-chiefs taking possession of any compound they chose, and their men with them and thus Ibadan was again re-peopled but not by the owners of the town, but by a composite band of marauders, consisting of Oyos, Ifes, Ijebus and some friendly Egbas.[20]

By contrast, the Ife-centred account stresses continuity between mythological and historical Ibadan pasts by incorporating a tale of two Owu wars. It recounts that, after the first war, the *Olowu* was invited to settle in Ibadan where he married the daughter of the *Olubadan*. This assertion establishes a relationship with Lagelu, said to have been the first *Olubadan*. The second Owu War resulted from the *Olowu* sacrificing his wife to *Osun* (an *orisa*); the *Olubadan* retaliated by summoning 'six famous warlords' to fight Owu people. After their victory, the Ibadan army and their allies resettled the deserted town.[21]

This foundation of the 'third Ibadan' has been dated *c*. 1829.[22] Rivalry amongst the marauders was so prevalent that it was not long before an insurrection led to the departure of many (but not all) from the Egba group. They first camped just outside Ibadan and then moved further south to occupy the village of Abeokuta, a settlement which expanded rapidly to become one of Ibadan's military rivals.[23]

Warriors, compounds and lineages: settling people in Ibadan

The early growth of Ibadan is revealed in oral histories (*itan*) of contemporary household/compounds (*ile*). These accounts often contradict each other and their chronologies are not reliable. In fact, they are purposely partial and selective; they seek to recount the past of a particular group of people, not the past of the Ibadan community as a whole. However, *itan* remain important historical sources because, at

---

[19] Rev. Samuel Johnson, *The History of the Yorubas from the Earliest Times to the Beginning of the British Protectorate* (London, 1921), p. 209. The publication date is misleading – the work was actually written during the nineteenth century.

[20] Johnson, *History*, p. 224.

[21] Morgan, *Akinyele's Outline*, pp. 49–54.

[22] Akin Mabogunje and J.D. Omer Cooper, *Owu in Yoruba History* (Ibadan, 1971), p. 62.

[23] Johnson, *History*, p. 225.

Photo 2.1 Mr Raufu Yesufu standing in front of the meeting house of *ile* Delesolu, Oje, Ibadan in 1995 (*Photograph by the author*)

the very least, they describe *how* Ibadan expanded, both socially and spatially. Each account encapsulates the form of urban settlement by simultaneously affirming internal diversity and a shared social project of joining a new town.

In this chapter we will view settlement and political practices in early Ibadan through a focus on the contesting pasts of a particular household, *ile* Delesolu. The last chief of this compound, *Asipa Olubadan* Yesufu Ekanoye, died in 1965. Since then, competing histories have so dominated the *ile* that a replacement *mogaji* (head of an *ile*) is yet to be installed. On 12 May 1989, the Supreme Court of Nigeria upheld a 1985 judgement of the High Court which empowered certain members of Delesolu's compound to prevent a Mr Oseni from 'parading himself as Head of Delesolu Family'.[24] It was hoped that a *mogaji* would then be installed, but *Olubadan* Ashinke refused to acknowledge the Supreme Court ruling. The *Olubadan*-in-Council is now being sued in yet another pending court case.[25]

The court record of the *mogaji* dispute is constituted by 'traditional evidence'. This is oral testimony of Delesolu history, presented to the court by the plaintiffs, the defendants and their witnesses. Our exploration will draw on this material as well as other *itan* of the compound.[26] These will be contextualised with *itan* from different *ile* in addition to documentary sources.[27]

[24] Latunde v. Lajinfin, Supreme Court of Nigeria, 1989. A copy of the court record (cited hereafter as CR) was loaned to me by Raufu Yesufu.
[25] Alhaji Lawal Ekanoye interview, 2 October 1995, Ibadan.
[26] I am grateful to Raufu Yesufu of *ile* Delesolu, Oje, Ibadan for supplying most of the sources used here. Without his generosity and help it would never have been possible to explore Delesolu history. Thanks also to Gavin Williams for introducing me to Mr Yesufu.
[27] These are Samuel Johnson's *The History of the Yorubas*, eyewitness reports from Yoruba and European

A Composite Band of Marauders

'A military headquarter'

Some *itan* assert that the founder of an *ile* was among the first group of soldiers to come to the war camp; they narrate how he occupied a place and subsequently used it as a military base. Such histories do not usually refer to compounds being appropriated, although it is implied that Ibadan was a named and pre-existing settlement.[28] For example, although other *ile* dispute the time of Oluyole's arrival in Ibadan, there is general acknowledgement that he was one of the early settlers:[29]

> The founder of the present Ibadan *Iba* Oluyole come from Oyo-Ile. This was around 1820. You know in those days war was here and there. He come to Ibadan as a warrior, as somebody very strong, a leader and a soldier.... All was just like a forest. So he have to land at a place called Itabalailai, just very near to this our own area here. It is from there now, another war started, he went.[30]

Subsequently, when returning from military raids with followers, slaves and booty, warriors like Oluyole secured more land on the war-camp outskirts. Claims were established by an area being cleared, occupied and then cultivated. Thus when the missionary David Hinderer visited Ibadan in 1851, he commented that Oluyole was remembered to have had thousands of slaves working extensive farms for him before he died.[31]

Once these first compounds and farms were established, Ibadan became 'a military headquarter for marauding and other expeditions'.[32] A turning point was the *Gbanamu* War, which took place *c.* 1830, after the Oyo settlers turned against Maye, an Ife soldier who had assumed dominance over the rival factions in the war camp.[33] Following his expulsion from Ibadan on grounds of his oppresive rule, Maye arranged alliances with other towns and prepared 'to crush Ibadan by an over-whelming force'.[34] According to one history of *ile* Delesolu, which I shall call the 'Olajinfin sons' version, it was at this time that the warrior Oluyole sent to Ogbomosho where the brothers Delesolu and Olajinfin joined him.[35] They lived in

---

[27] (cont.) missionaries and I.B. Akinyele's Ibadan histories. Of these, Johnson's text is the most important. Its use as a primary source is discussed in the next chapter. Akinyele published his *Iwe Itan Ibadan* about 1916; it has since been reprinted four times. The author translated it into English during the 1930s and it finally appeared as *The Outlines of Ibadan History* in 1946. During the 1970s, Akinyele's niece, Kemi Morgan, undertook another translation of the work and published it in three parts under the title: *Akinyele's Outline History of Ibadan. Revised and Enlarged*. See Toyin Falola, 'Kemi Morgan and the Second Reconstruction of Ibadan History', *History in Africa* 18 (1991), pp. 93–112.

[28] Apart from examples cited below, *ile* Oderinlo, *ile* Kure, *ile* Fadaya, *ile* Ibikunle and *ile* Fijabi narrated their settlement histories in this framework.

[29] Two *ile* who claim that their founders arrived before Oluyole are *ile* Oluwo and *ile* Jenrinyin. The former claims a hereditary religious title in Ibadan.

[30] Chief Akanbi, *Lagunna Balogun* (*Mogaji* Oluyole), interviewed 14 February 1996, Ibadan.

[31] CMSB, CA2/049/104: Hinderer Journal, 23 October 1851.

[32] Johnson, *History*, p. 244.

[33] *Gbanamu* means 'grasping fire'. Johnson, *History*, pp. 238–42. See also Kemi Morgan, *Akinyele's Outline History of Ibadan, Part One* (Ibadan, n.d.), pp. 61–4.

[34] Johnson, *History*, p. 240.

[35] Delesolu Alabelahon, *Itan* (translated English text) collected by Gavin Williams, 1970. Cited hereafter as Delesolu *Itan* (GW).

16

Ijeru, about five miles from Ogbomosho. A variation claims that Delesolu and Olajinfin came to Ibadan from Ijeru immediately before the war and joined the retinue of Oderinlo, a warrior from Ajagba near Ilorin.[36]

According to the historian Samuel Johnson, when the victorious Ibadan forces returned home, they held a public meeting. He continues, 'it was resolved that as they now intend to make this place their home they should arrange for a settled government and take titles'.[37] Oluyedun, a veteran of the Owu War, assumed the military title of *Are-ona-kakanfo*. He claimed to be a son of Afonja, the *Are-ona-kakanfo* of Ilorin who had rebelled against *Alaafin* Aole of Oyo, an event which had contributed to the disintegration of the Oyo Empire. Lakanle and Oluyole, also both Oyo men, took the titles of *Otun Kakanfo* and *Osi Kakanfo* respectively.

Six other installations were carried out by Osun, who was installed as *Sarumi* by Labosinde, one of the few Ife people allowed to remain in the settlement.[38] Labosinde's presence in this account goes against the alternative claim that he was Lagelu's brother, but nonetheless enables Ibadan chieftaincy to be rendered more 'authentic' through a connection to Ife, the centre of pan-Yoruba cosmology. Labosinde was himself honoured as *Baba Isale* ('the father underneath'), in recognition of his skill at disbanding fights between rival soldier factions. Johnson makes an analogy with the civic culture of ancient Rome by recounting that Labosinde's 'token of authority' was a bundle of whips carried in front of him, 'as used to be done before the Roman Tribunes of old'.[39]

In contrast to Johnson's appropriation of Roman civic livery, Kemi Morgan states that Osun placed *akoko* leaves on the heads of the chiefs when installing them and thus 'started Ibadan on a municipal life'.[40] This is a reference to the symbolic significance of *Newboldia laevis* in Yoruba chieftaincy installations; it is not only in Ibadan that they have been (and still are) used. Interestingly, the tree from which these leaves are harvested is one of those used to worship Ogun: 'The *orisa* ['god'] of war, of the hunt and of all pursuits in which iron or steel is used'.[41] It could be speculated that the use of *akoko* in Ibadan is related to their link with Ogun and, as such, has more to do with warfare than with municipal life. However, as will be shown in the next chapter, it is questionable to oppose these practices – there is a powerful sense in which a 'civic Ibadan' *was* warfare. Whether or not *akoko* featured in this first installation of Ibadan chiefs, the important point is that there was no attempt to confer royal or divine privileges on *any* of the incumbents. All titles, excepting that of Labosinde, were military.

There was also no defined 'ruler of Ibadan'. Although Oluyedun was ostensibly the head, he was too old to engage in battle. Leading independent expeditions, Lakanle and Oluyole eclipsed his authority. Their rivalry eventually culminated in

---

[36] *Mogaji* Oderinlo interview, 20 November 1995, Mapo, Ibadan.
[37] Johnson, *History*, p. 244.
[38] *Ibid.*, p. 244.
[39] *Ibid.*, p. 245.
[40] Morgan, *Akinyele's Outline Part One*, p. 66.
[41] Simpson, *Yoruba Religion*, p. 29. On p. 66 he writes: 'the *akoko* tree is sacred to Ogun'.

'repeated civil fights at home, until nearly the whole of the important war-chiefs perished one after another'.[42] Oluyole led a plot against Lakanle and, in the face of it, the latter committed suicide, 'not wanting the town to be spoilt because of him'.[43] As an early example of a political practice of intrigue and betrayal amongst Ibadan chiefs, this incident was historically significant and will be returned to in the next chapter. For now, the key point is that, despite Johnson's claim, the government of Ibadan's marauders was certainly *not* settled.

Settling Oje

Having asserted his political authority, Oluyole's next military engagement was the disastrous *Eleduwe* War between Oyo and Ilorin which culminated in the desertion of Oyo-Ile, sometime between 1837 and 1839.[44] Atiba assumed the Oyo throne and established a new capital at Ago-Oja, conferring the title of *Ibasorun* on Oluyole. Following his own installation, Oluyole allocated titles at Ibadan. The warrior Oderinlo was granted the title of *Balogun* and, around the same time, Delesolu was installed as *Areago*.[45] Both these men were among those reportedly involved in the conspiracy against Lakanle.

It was after Lakanle's death that Delesolu established his own compound – all histories date his move to the rule of Oluyole. A recent oral account put it thus: '*Iba* Oluyole is the landlord of Ibadan by then. He is the only man given power to give land to anybody that came to Ibadan by then.'[46] Rival histories of Delesolu's move are the basis of the long-running political dispute in the compound. They can be set out as follows:

Olajinfin Sons Version	Delesolu Sons Version
After the end of *Gbanamu* War both brothers [Delesolu and Olajinfin] remained at Ibadan and stayed with Oderinlo. Delesolu had two female issues namely: Adeola and Oyinkanola. Both Adeola and Oyinkanola died childless. Due to infantile mortality both brothers approached Oderinlo to allow them to settle at outskirt or around Ibadan. At that time the size of Ibadan was very small.... Oderinlo then settled Delesolu and Olajinfin in his farm near Odo Elegun. On getting to the place Delesolu gave the area where he settled Oje which is a name taken after his town from where he came. The original town of Delesolu	Delesolu came from Abeokuta with his brother Olusenmo during the reign of *Bashorun* Oluyole. When he came to Ibadan he settled at Oja'ba near *Balogun* Oderinlo's compound with other chiefs like Ojuolape [who] came from Ogbomosho.... Oja'ba was the main area of Ibadan when Delesolu came. It has not been extended.... As a result of inter tribal wars Oluyole and *Balogun* Oderinlo decided to put.... Delesolu, Olusenmo and Ojuolape at the gate which was Oderinlo's farm. Delesolu, Olusenmo and Ojuolape then went to settle at Oderinlo's farm. After their settlement, Delesolu was the leader of the

[42] Johnson, *History*, p. 256.
[43] Akinyele, *Iwe Itan Ibadan*, p. 34.
[44] Johnson, *History*, pp. 263–8.
[45] *Ibid.*, p. 283.
[46] Raufu Yesufu interview, 10 May 1997, Ibadan. It was actually *Balogun* Oderinlo who allocated land to Delesolu; this statement aims to emphasise Oluyole's political dominance.

is Oje but he finally came to settle at Ijeru in Ogbomoso. ... When Delesolu got to his present house he created a market there called Oje market Ibadan. He also built a house in his new site given him by Oderinlo where he became a chief. He was made *Areago Iba Oluyole*.[47]

team. He named the settled area as Oje in memory of his place at Abeokuta. A flowing water was named Yemetu in remembrance of his mother. The two names are existing in Abeokuta.[48]

Competing genealogies of political office emerge from these two histories. According to the 'Olajinfin Sons' account, all of Delesolu's children continued to die after he moved to Oje. When Delesolu himself died, he was survived only by his brother Olajinfin, who subsequently took over the compound, as well as his property and wives. After Olajinfin died, he was succeeded by his son Adeoye; since then, those who claim to be descended from Olajinfin also assert rights to the *mogaji* position.[49]

There were two sub-versions within the defendants' account. One stated that Olusenmo, said to have jointly founded the compound, was Delesolu's brother.[50] The other stated that Olusenmo was Delesolu's son, secretly born to him by one of his (Delesolu's) father's wives in Abeokuta.[51] Eventually, the second version was taken as the accurate one and Delesolu's other sons were named as Baiyewu, Latunde and Oseni.[52] Both versions concurred that Olusenmo died before Delesolu and asserted it was then decided that Ojuolape, who lived in the adjacent compound, should inherit Delesolu's property.[53] It is said that Ojuolape refused and instead appointed Olajinfin as a caretaker 'pending the time the children of Delesolu would grow up.'[54] This 'Delesolu Sons' account claimed that Olajinfin was a 'townsmate' of Ojuolape from Ogbomoso, and asserted he was not Delesolu's brother. After Olajinfin died, the story goes, 'his children started to take over the property of Delesolu' and they monopolised the *mogaji* position.[55] The defendants claim descent from Olusenmo and thus suggest they are direct descendants of Delesolu. With this genealogy, they assert authority over Lajinfin's successors.

Both histories of *ile* Delesolu are centred on competing claims to the post of *mogaji*, an Ilorin-Fulani term which identifies the head of an Ibadan *ile*. Before analysing the accounts in detail, it is thus necessary to explore the institutional framework to which they refer.

Compounds and titles

Precisely when the *mogaji* position was adopted in Ibadan is unknown. However, a decision to change the law of inheritance, said to have occurred in 1858, would have

[47] CR: Ayoade, Plaintiff Evidence, 8 October 1976.
[48] CR: Sunmonu, 2nd Defendant Evidence, 18 September 1975.
[47] CR: Ayoade, Plaintiff Evidence, 18 April 1974.
[48] CR: Sunmonu, 2nd Defendant Evidence, 18 September 1975.
[49] CR: Sunmonu, 2nd Defendant Evidence, 16 December 1977.
[50] CR: Sunmonu, 2nd Defendant Evidence, 3 May 1978.
[53] CR: Sunmonu, 2nd Defendant Evidence, 16 December 1977.
[54] CR: Gbadamosi Sanuola Ojuolape, 2nd Defendant Witness, 25 July 1978.
[55] Sunmonu, 2nd Defendant Evidence, 16 December 1977.

encouraged many more households to adopt the rank. On the death of a compound founder, the usual practice was for all property and wives to pass to the founder's brothers. In Ibadan:

> It was proposed to alter this custom… If the children are minors the uncle may act for them until they come of age, otherwise the eldest surviving issue of the founder of a house must succeed as the head of the house in rotation until it comes to the turn of the children of the next generation.
>
> [...] At the time of the succession the personal effects are distributed amongst the nearest relatives, every one having a share of the clothes, slaves, money etc., but the house, inalienable slaves, principal farms, in a word, the real property, and all that goes to make the house what it is, are never to be alienated. These are assigned to the eldest surviving son and successor.[56]

Interestingly, the key point of contention between the two accounts of Delesolu history is whether *ile* property was inherited by a brother or a caretaker. This implies that if this change in practice actually occurred, it was being contested at the very time Delesolu died.

In her pioneering research on nineteenth century Ibadan, Awe suggests that the conferment of the *mogaji* rank was an attempt to reconcile hereditary succession and open competition in town government.[57] During the late 1840s, there were some heads of households who were not related to the family of their predecessor; they gained their position by proving themselves on the battlefield.[58] By contrast, a *mogaji* was usually, or at least claimed to be, an heir of the compound founder. However, a *mogaji* could not claim a chieftaincy title on the basis of his pedigree. He simply joined the pool of candidates seeking political offices in the city. Falola contends that 'the *mogaji*-ship' institutionalised the process of selection for a title. As such, he argues, it was a strategy by certain Ibadan familes 'to perpetuate the names of the earliest leaders as well as their lineages.' The appointees were usually promising young soldiers, he writes, 'rather than, as in most Yoruba towns, the eldest males'.[59]

Both these arguments are supported by David Hinderer's description of Ibadan chieftaincy in 1851. He names warriors as the 'respectable class' and continues, 'their mode of government might not improperly be called a military aristocracy, the mighty man of valour being a nobleman'. However, he does not mention a tendency for particular families to monopolise chieftaincy appointments through nominating *mogaji*.[60]

In my view, Ibadan *ile* adopted the *mogaji* position for both practical and strategic reasons. Individual military merit was the means by which social status was established among men in the city. This status – proven by a large number of followers – had to be achieved before one could gain a chieftaincy title. No-one held prior claim to political office because of the reputation of his predecessor; he had to establish his own. However, if he succeeded to head an *ile* which was militarily

---

[56] Johnson, *History*, p. 327.

[57] Bolanle Awe, 'The Rise of Ibadan as a Yoruba Power' (Oxford University D.Phil. thesis, 1964), p. 108.

[58] The best known was Ibikunle, who took over *ile* Toki and later became *Balogun*. Akinyele, *Outlines*, p. 61; *Mogaji* Ibikunle, interviewed 24 November 1995, Ibadan.

[59] Toyin Falola, 'From Hospitality to Hostility: Ibadan and Strangers, 1830–1904', *Journal of African History* 26 (1985), p. 61.

[60] CMSB, CA2/049/104: Hinderer Journal, 23 October 1851.

successful and prosperous, he would gain a substantial retinue. By virtue of 'having people' he was more likely to become a chief. Thus, if an *ile* was to sustain or develop a presence in the chieftaincy ranks, it had a vested interest in holding itself together as a large household. A specific rank that identified the leader of the compound was essential.

At the same time, there was a problem of competition for leadership between the brothers and sons of a compound founder. These tensions had to be minimised if the people who constituted an *ile* were to be maintained as a collective. The 1858 law attempted to achieve this. However, it was an unsatisfactory solution because it only postponed the problem for a generation. Although leadership was initially restricted to the 'eldest son', on his death it became open to his brothers. By that time, the sons of the eldest son of the compound founder might also consider themselves eligible. Despite such limitations, similar pragmatic, short-term political compromises were to become an enduring characteristic of Ibadan chieftaincy.

Contrary to Falola's suggestion of a restrictive, institutionalised policy there is evidence that, as late as the 1870s, the men appointed to titles were not always *mogaji*. Johnson mentions those who 'rose into prominence by heading a band of young men for exploits' as well as the occasional 'old and experienced veteran'.[61] Titles were allocated by the highest-ranking chiefs; selection depended upon the available vacancies and the personal interests of those in positions of influence.

The number of positions in use was not constant. New offices were adopted on particular occasions while others were dropped, sometimes to be revived later. There was, nonetheless, a steady increase in the number of titles made available through the course of the nineteenth century.[62] To generalise, it appears that there were four main lines by the 1850s. Titles in those of the *Balogun*, *Seriki*, and *Bale* were taken by male *ologun* ('brave warriors'). The *Iyalode* was a successful female trader. An *ologun* was initially appointed to a junior post; he then competed for promotion to a higher position on his line or to another line altogether. There was no definite order.

The *Balogun* led the senior military men on war campaigns, accompanied by the *Seriki* and his subordinates, who were less experienced soldiers. Another junior military office was that of the *Sarumi*, the chief of the cavalry. The *Bale* was a veteran who had previously distinguished himself in battle; once installed, he did not usually leave the town. Several scholars have incorrectly asserted that the *Bale* chiefs were a 'civil line' of retired soldiers.[63] However, Johnson refers to 'the Bale's principal war-chiefs' and also describes their involvement in numerous military engagements.[64] In 1886, the missionary William Allen reported that 'knockers' had arrived in Ibadan

---

[61] Johnson, *History*, p. 380; p. 387. These men (Ajayi Ogboriefon and Lawoyin respectively) might have been *mogaji*, but Johnson does not describe them as such.

[62] See Appendix I.

[63] Awe, 'Ibadan, Its Early Beginnings', p. 19; Toyin Falola, 'The Political System of Ibadan in the 19th Century', in *Evolution of Political Culture in Nigeria*, ed. J.F. Ade Ajayi and Bashir Ikora, (Ibadan, 1985), p. 108; George Jenkins, 'Politics in Ibadan', (Northwestern Univ. Ph.D. thesis, 1965), p. 48; Toyin Falola and Dare Oguntomisin, *The Military in Nineteenth Century Yoruba Politics* (Ile-Ife, 1984), pp. 49–50.

[64] Johnson, *History*, p. 310. See also descriptions of *Ajiya Bale* Abayomi, p. 323, pp. 343–4, pp. 358–9, p. 366, pp. 370–1 and *Otun Bale* Sumala, p. 358.

town from the battle front. These messengers warned that if *Otun Bale* Tajo and his soldiers did not return with them to the battlefront, the *Otun Bale* would have to commit suicide.[65]

If the Ibadan army was at war when a *Bale* died, his position was left vacant until it returned.[66] Alternatively, a chief might postpone taking the post until he had completed another successful military campaign. Thus from 1867 until 1870 Ibadan had no *Bale*, whilst *Balogun* Akere led the Ibadan army against Ilesha.[67] This was again the case from 1880 until 1893.[68] Both the *Bale* and the *Balogun* operated their own courts, where they heard cases between the chiefs under their jurisdiction. Thus *Bale* chiefs would take their disputes to the *Bale* and vice versa.[69] However, the *Balogun* was usually more powerful than the *Bale*.[70] This was because of his ongoing involvement in warfare, which enabled him to continue to amass booty and slaves.

A woman who was a wealthy market trader in Ibadan could compete to be elected *Iyalode*. Anna Hinderer, the wife of David Hinderer, called on *Iyalode* Subuola in 1854 and described her as 'a person of much influence and looked up to with respect'. She reported that the female chief was 'surrounded by her attendants and people, in great order, and some measure of state' during her visit. The *Iyalode* mediated disputes between women in the town and took them before the *Bale* if necessary.[71] She also involved herself in Ibadan military campaigns by supplying her fellow chiefs with credit to purchase firearms and ammunition. In addition, she contributed her own corps of armed slaves to the war effort, appointing an experienced soldier to lead them.[72]

Nominations for junior titles, as well as promotion within the ranks, were influenced by the personal interests of the senior chiefs. At different times, some groups were favoured over others. For example, Johnson writes that during 1870 *Bale* Orowusi attempted to prevent titles being awarded to prosperous *mogaji*, preferring instead elderly, comparatively poor men.[73] Orowusi himself belonged to the latter category, being overshadowed by his more popular son, Akeredolu.[74] As *Bale*, his policy was probably intended to hinder Akeredolu from usurping his authority.

Are-ona-kakanfo Latosisa, who was Orowusi's successor, adopted a different

---

[65] Maps and Manuscripts Collection, Kenneth Dike Library, University of Ibadan (cited hereafter as KDL), Private Papers of I.B. Akinyele (cited hereafter as IAP): William Stephen Allen, 1886 Diary, 25 February.

[66] *Bale* Olugbode died in 1864 when the Ibadan army was still on its way back from the Ijaye War. His successor *Basorun* Ogunmola was installed after their return in 1865. See Johnson, *History*, p. 365.

[67] Akere died at the battlefield and *Bale* Orowusi was installed on the army's return. See Johnson, *History*, pp. 378–9; p. 383.

[68] *Are-ona-kakanfo* Latosisa left Ibadan for the Ekitiparapo front in April 1880 and died there in August 1885. The army did not return to Ibadan until August 1893. Johnson, *History*, p. 447; p. 500; p. 629.

[69] Akinyele, *Outlines*, p. 73.

[70] Ibikunle overshadowed *Bale* Opeagbe (as *Seriki*) and *Bale* Olugbode (as *Balogun*) between 1850 and 1864. *Balogun* Ajobo 'often usurped' the authority of *Bale* Orowusi before both chiefs were removed from power in 1871. On Ibikunle, see Morgan, *Akinyele's Outline History Part Two* (Ibadan, n.d.) pp. 67–75 and Johnson, p. 295; p. 309. On Ajobo, see Johnson, *History*, pp. 383–6.

[71] Anna Hinderer, *Seventeen Years in the Yoruba Country* (London, 1872), p. 110.

[72] Bolanle Awe, 'The *Iyalode* in the Traditional Yoruba Political System', in *Sexual Stratification: a Cross-Cultural View*, ed. Alice Schlegel (New York, 1977), p. 151.

[73] Johnson, *History*, p. 387.

[74] *Ibid.*, p. 379.

political strategy. Rather than attempting to curb the political ambitions of his eldest son Sanusi, he sought 'to perpetuate the administration of Ibadan in his own family.'[75] Thus, at the commencement of his rule, Latosisa proposed that young *mogaji* 'should be advanced to responsible position[s] in order that they might use the means at their command for the public benefit which they would otherwise not do'.[76] 'Means', in this context, refers to people. If a *mogaji* was not recognised for his 'public' feats on the battlefield, he might seek retribution by sending his followers on raids against households of the senior chiefs. Such action would jeopardise Latosisa's political status.

The result of these various levels of political flexibility was that most chieftaincy titles in Ibadan were not exclusive to particular *ile*.[77] If a male chief died, his household could not elect another of their members to keep his rank. They could only nominate a new *mogaji*. The chief's title became available and, in theory, all *mogaji* and militarily successful men in the town were eligible for appointment. If the post was a senior one, junior chiefs added to the competition. The *Iyalode* title was also neither hereditary nor permanent. If an *Iyalode* lost her economic status as a prominent trader, another more wealthy woman would usurp her post.[78] After she died, her *ile* appointed a *mogaji* who competed for titles in the male lines; it did not usually remain headed by a female.[79]

Households and lineages

The *mogaji* post identified the leader of a military Ibadan household and compound. It was also an incentive for individuals to excel in battle. Although a *mogaji* might not be immediately appointed a chief, he could still be recognised as the head of a wealthy and successful *ile*, with potential for a title in the future. This leads us to an important question. Who constituted *ile* in nineteenth century Ibadan?

The simple answer is 'people'. A more complex response must address how these people became a collective. Both Falola and Awe assume that 'the lineage' – a group descended from the male founder of the compound – was the basic corporate body. They describe this core patrilineage as residing in a household made up of other groups – slaves, *iwofa* ('pawns'), 'war-boys' and their wives – who, together, were known as 'strangers'. Falola specifically insists that the division between *omo ile* (patrilineage) and *ara ile* (strangers) was clear-cut and unambiguous.[80]

Competing histories in the current *ile* Delesolu *mogaji* dispute reveal that this view is oversimplified. It is precisely the demarcation of the lineage as a corporate body which is at stake – the boundaries between lineage and strangers are repeatedly shown to be more fluid than fixed. Furthermore, these contests over lineage

---

[75] *Ibid.*, p. 414.

[76] *Ibid.*, p. 390.

[77] The exceptions were the *Oluwo*, *Apena* and *Aboke* titles.

[78] Efunsetan took over from Subuola by this means during the late 1860s. Johnson, *History*, p. 392.

[79] There was an exception to this practice in 1919 (during the colonial period) when Ajisomo succeeded her elder sister Lanlatu as *Iyalode*. See Akinyele, *Outlines*, p. 68.

[80] Toyin Falola, *The Political Economy of a Pre-Colonial African State: Ibadan, 1830–1900* (Ile-Ife, 1984), p. 45.

membership extend beyond the town compound. For example, in March 1994 the Court of Appeal heard a dispute over the ownership of a piece of land at Aladun village. The plaintiffs, Morenikeji family, professed descent from a grandson of Delesolu and charged the defendants with trespass. Conversely, the defendants claimed that *they* were Delesolu family and that the plaintiffs were their tenants.[81]

To close such cases, the courts must rule that one of these lineage histories is more legitimate than the other. In the land dispute, the plaintiffs' claims were termed 'perverse' and dismissed.[82] In the *mogaji* case, the 'Delesolu Sons' group have lost consistently, despite numerous appeals.[83] Exponents of the 'Olajinfin Sons' genealogical account have thus upheld their right to leadership of *ile* Delesolu.

Given this context, it is tempting for historians to abandon the discredited court testimonies altogether. Yet this leaves an intriguing question unanswered. Why do these rival accounts exist? One explanation might be the increased competition for land and political status in present-day Ibadan. Nonetheless, although this indicates why people go to court, it does not explain where their contesting evidences originated. While some accounts seem more plausible than others, the detailed connections between them make it difficult to reject any one as wholly invented. How should historians interpret them?

The perceptive ruling of Judge Oguntade, presiding in the Aladun village case, offers an approach. He writes:

> Each of the traditional histories called by the parties can be likened to a package. The court had to accept one package or the other. Once the court accepted a package, it also accepted fully the contents of the package. A court could not broach the package it had accepted and then reject some of its contents.[84]

Historians are more fortunate in that they are not required to accept either package. It is more revealing to consider each traditional history as 'a model of historical facts'. Oguntade's judgement is useful because it points out that the facts only have meaning in the context of their model. Or, as Barber and Farias put it: 'the textuality of the text is the clue to how meaning is constructed'.[85]

To understand a past which is sedimented in the lineage histories of *ile* Delesolu, historians must pay attention to their literary form. When this approach is extended to *itan* collected from other compounds, the layered history of Ibadan *ile* comes into view. By focusing on the way these accounts tell the past, it becomes evident that they all share a narrative framework centred around repeated historical events of 'settling people'.

Like *ile* Delesolu, most Ibadan *ile* acknowledge that their founder met already established warriors when he first came to the war camp.[86] Newcomers were

---

[81] Morenikeji v. Adegbosin, Court of Appeal, 1994, p. 8. The case notes were loaned to me by Raufu Yesufu.

[82] *Ibid.*, p. 19.

[83] Latunde v. Lajinfin, Supreme Court of Nigeria, 1989, p. 15.

[84] Morenikeji v. Adegbosin, p. 18.

[85] Karin Barber and P.F. de Moraes Farias, *Discourse and Its Disguises. The Interpretation of African Oral Texts* (Birmingham, 1989), p. 2.

[86] For example, *ile* Ojuolape, *ile* Aliwo, *ile* Kofo, *ile* Ogunmola, *ile* Opeagbe, *ile* Olugbode, *ile* Ogboriefon, *ile* Foko, *ile* Alesinloye, *ile* Olunloyo. This is by no means an exhaustive list.

commonly refugees fleeing the war-devastated areas. Alternatively, they might be men who had judiciously managed to join in the rampage at the time of a military raid or women and men who had been captured as slaves. A female refugee usually joined an Ibadan compound through being taken as a wife either by its *mogaji* or chief, or by a successful resident soldier. She could exercise some autonomy in this position and might run her own trading business, a cloth-dyeing operation and/or be engaged in processing palm produce into oil or soap.[87] Women slaves were either appropriated as wives or sent to work on farms outside the city.[88]

Men who came to Ibadan by their own accord (rather than being captured) initially chose a *babaogun* (military patron) and joined his private army as an *omo ogun* (war-boy). The *babaogun* was usually, but not always, a warrior chief; he was selected on the basis of his reputation for generosity and battle success. *Omo ogun* frequently chose patrons who had migrated to Ibadan from their own region. Thus, around Oje today, there are many households who trace their origins to communities in the Ogbomosho area.[89] In later decades, when Ibadan chiefs claimed jurisdiction over several towns, ambitious male inhabitants from these places joined the armies of their overlords.[90] Slaves also became soldiers; but they were not able to exercise as much choice in determining whose army they belonged to.[91] In return for their military services, both groups gained a right of residence in Ibadan and a share of war booty.

Itan then tell how a particular soldier was already, or later became, militarily successful. Success was measured by the number of people he had supporting him, that is, his wives, slaves, war-boys and their families. 'Overcrowding' was usually named as the factor which motivated a group of people to leave a compound.[92] Together with his followers, a soldier approached his *babaogun* and requested a portion of the household farm on Ibadan's outskirts. Although this land grant was not a 'purchase', it might be acknowledged by a material exchange. For example, it is said that Delesolu gave *Balogun* Oderinlo eleven slaves before he and his people departed from the central location of Oja'ba.[93] The name Delesolu gave to his area, which at that time lay beyond the eastern limits of Ibadan, was Oje. Each lineage history maintains that this name recalls Delesolu's place of origin, his *orile*. But where this place actually was remains contested.

Both the 'Olajinfin Sons' and 'Delesolu Sons' seek to prove that the Oje claimed by the other is wrong, an ideological struggle which implies the competing factions have separate *oriki orile*.[94] That is, the groups most likely emphasise that they came from different places because they *did* – the origins of their rival histories are

---

[87] CMSB, CA2/049/104: Hinderer Journal, 23 October 1851.

[88] Johnson, *History*, p. 325.

[89] Chief Ojuolape, interviewed 15 October 1995, Ibadan; Alhaji Giwa (*ile* Aliwo), interviewed 29 December 1995; *Mogaji* Kofo, interviewed 6 January 1996.

[90] Johnson, *History*, p. 406.

[91] *Ibid.*, p. 324.

[92] Of the accounts listed above, eight gave overcrowding as the reason for leaving a host compound. Of the remaining two, one named fire and the other claimed that compound residents quarrelled. Obviously, these latter reasons were also related to high population densities.

[93] Delesolu *Itan* (GW).

[94] Barber, *I Could Speak*, p. 166.

probably *literally* in their origins. Essentially, the historical accounts of both sides are mirror-like transpositions of each other. Each one features a lineage – a set of fathers and sons – living with, or adjacent to, another set of people who are internally linked by friendship or kinship but who are unrelated to the lineage. The narrative structure and the historical characters are the same in the two accounts, but the relationships between the characters and where they came from are not. The point of contention in the court case is who can claim true descent from the group identified in each account as the lineage.

For example, the 'Olajinfin Sons' maintain that Baiyewu was a man from Iwo who came to live with Delesolu as his 'servant'. After Delesolu died, Baiyewu brought his brother Latunde to Olajinfin and sought permission 'to house Latunde anytime he came down from Iwo to sell tobacco'. When Baiyewu later died, Latunde buried him and took over 'the place of his dead brother'. He was then joined by another brother, Oseni, and the two of them 'lived and died in Delesolu compound'.[95]

On the opposing side, the 'Delesolu Sons' claim that the men named above were the sons of Delesolu and were born in Ibadan. They assert that Olajinfin lived in the adjacent compound of Ojuolape as his 'townsmate' and, as evidence of a friendship between the two men, also claimed that Olajinfin's mother, Ariyeke, was buried in Ojuolape's compound.[96] The 'Olajinfin Sons' group did not deny this, but they claimed Ariyeke was Delesolu's mother as well and contended that Ojuolape was a 'war-captain' of Delesolu who came with him from Ijeru.[97]

Thus, although a lineage is represented in *ile* Delesolu histories, it comes into view precisely at the point when it was changing radically. Consequently, lineage history is not recounted as a tale of the establishment and maintainence of a separate and bounded kin-group. By contrast, it is told as a history of contingent connections between numerous people who actively assert their independence from one another. Simultaneously, they make claims to assert authority over each other. The demarcation of lineage boundaries is an assertion of their fluidity within a household's shared past. There is no consensus; instead, histories offer alternative heterogenous groupings. The view is one of various social possibilities – not one of solid and permanent social units.[98]

Considering the turbulent context of town life in early nineteenth-century Ibadan, this view is not surprising. The residential groups of every *ile* were in a constant state of flux. Amidst regional warfare, new groups of refugees and slaves arrived in the town, joined a warrior's retinue and altered the social composition of his *ile*. This readiness to accommodate outsiders is recalled by an epithet of Ibadan *oriki*: 'Ibadan never blesses the natives as much as the stranger'.[99] According to the rival testimonies of *ile* Delesolu, it appears that these people could and did adopt themselves into the lineage of the compound founder. Descent from that 'original group' secured individuals their right of residence. But the claim of descent did not

---

[95] CR: Ayoade, Plaintiff Evidence, 8 October 1976.
[96] CR: Sunmonu, 2nd Defendant Evidence, 18 September 1975.
[97] Delesolu *Itan* (GW).
[98] This analysis was influenced by Barber's description of lineages in Okuku. See *I Could Speak*, p. 159.
[99] *Ibadan kii gbonile, bi ajeji.*

mean that a group gave up the identities which recollected the different places they came from. Rather, they tenaciously retained their separate origins.

This obstinate assertion of independent collectivities within the past of one lineage suggests that Ibadan *ile* were never composed of single kin-groups. Writing in 1967, Lloyd maintained that compounds in the city were inhabited, 'with a few exceptions, [by] the descendants in the male line of one of the more powerful immigrants of the early to mid-nineteenth century'.[100] This assertion is factually incorrect. Although lineages certainly do live in these compounds, as a social category, they are most notable for their heterogeneity, renewed nowadays through competing versions of history. For Barber in Okuku, each *ile*, 'seemed to shift its boundaries whenever you looked at it'.[101] We could easily say the same of *ile* Delesolu.

Importantly, apart from a consistent flow of newcomers there was also a steady loss of people from each *ile*. Falola argues that such 'fissions' occurred when ambitious men aspired to have their own compounds and 'used flimsy excuses just to make sure they became independent ... an *idile* [lineage] tried all its possible best to prevent fissions'.[102] The first of these assertions is partly correct, but the second is false. In fact, the trend seems to have been the opposite:

> When he [Delesolu] got here ... he has many people and all the chiefs of Ibadan by then were sending emissaries, they are sending people to Delesolu to give them land.... So after Oderinlo settled him, then he too began to settle people, about 130, it is about 130 compounds that he settled.[103]

This account names two settled people, Agate and Agidi. Agate was Delesolu's drummer, who, according to the 'Olajinfin Sons' group, was brought from Ogbomosho. 'Agate's section' was built the same day as Delesolu's house, and was strategically located near Oje market so that the drummers could announce the arrival of visitors. By contrast, Kure was an Ibadan warrior chief who sent his oldest son, Agidi, to Delesolu. Once Delesolu was established in his new area, he settled Agidi and his followers nearby.

These fissions offer further evidence of the instability of *ile* in nineteenth-century Ibadan. Neither lineages nor residential groups were immutable social units. From the perspective of the warrior chief who made a land grant, members of a departing party were still, in some ways, 'his people' – he was simply expanding his political jurisdiction by settling them elsewhere. As far as those departing were concerned, they were now autonomous. However, in other social contexts, they maintained political allegiance to their *babaogun*. For example, consider this *itan* of *ile* Olunloyo:

> My great-grandfather first pitched at a place that is now Molete [a suburb in south Ibadan], he was there with his men. In Ibadan, they saw him making fire and they sent to find out what was happening. They were frightened to leave a dangerous man there, he might pounce on the town at any time. In that period there were so many warriors plundering around. Therefore Oluyole invited him and his men to Oja'ba.... But they hadn't been there long when their war-boys had a

[100] P.C. Lloyd, 'Introduction', in *The City of Ibadan*, p. 5.
[101] Barber, *I Could Speak*, p. 158.
[102] Falola, *Political Economy*, p. 46.
[103] Yesufu interview, 10 May 1997, Ibadan.

clash, that is, Olunloyo's and Oluyole's. Two warriors should not stay near each other like that, so Olunloyo decided to move to the present compound. ... It was *Iba* Oluyole and Olunloyo who built the entrance gate to the compound, they had to fence the compound to keep it safe.[104]

Although this account places emphasis on the independence of Olunloyo, it nonetheless indicates the historical event of a land grant. The mention of Oluyole's assistance with the entrance gate might initially seem contradictory given the emphasis on rivalry between the two warriors and their war-boys. However, this assistance encapsulates the memory that Oluyole allocated the land; it manifests a social and political relationship. It shows that, at the very time they were redefined, the social and spatial demarcations of *ile* were blurred.

Ibadan and Yoruba urbanism

Although the warrior-founder of a compound often lived with brothers and sons (as well as wives and daughters) his household was not a patrilineage – it was a hetero-geneous collective, an army, largely made up by the families of war-boys and slaves. This residential group was constantly changing as new refugees arrived, became soldiers, built up their military retinues, and then departed to set up their own *ile*, taking their own group of followers and their families with them. Accordingly, most chieftaincy titles were not reserved by particular *ile* and were neither royal nor hereditary. They were allocated to *ologun* according to pragmatic criteria of military merit and maintenance of a large following. In the case of the *Iyalode*, economic status, judged by her position as a prosperous trader, was the standard.

These characteristics mark Ibadan as an anomaly within the model of Yoruba urbanism. Exponents of this ideal conceived political community as the given production of a formalised government exercising authority over primary groups. In nineteenth-century Ibadan, however, the social/spatial boundaries of lineages, compounds and quarters were so volatile that it is impossible to identify a basic 'primary group'. Indeed, as late as 1952, an exasperated colonial official reported: 'Not only are the quarters undefined; for the most part they are undefinable.'[105] Furthermore, the number of titles was variable and, as we shall see, appointments were extremely contested – it is profoundly misleading to describe Ibadan chieftaincy as 'formalised government'.

The next chapter will show how Ibadan was incorporated into a political community. My starting point is not institutional structure. It is institutionalised suicide.

[104] Chief Olunloyo, *Otun Balogun* (*Mogaji* Olunloyo), interviewed 26 October 1995, Ibadan.
[105] Nigerian National Archives, Ibadan (hereafter, NAI), Iba. Div: 1/1/2910, J.F. Hayley, 'Ibadan Divisional Reforms, Final Report', p. 5.

3

Ibadan Makes History
Civil Disorder, Militarism & the Yoruba Past

On 12 February 1877, *Foko* Aiyejenku 'finally retired to rest, by blowing out his own brains'.[1] This event marked the climax of a month of intrigue between Ibadan chiefs. It also ended the life of Aiyejenku who, forty years before, had reportedly been at the centre of the plot against Lakanle. Aiyejenku's history as a soldier and a chief, pieced together from Rev. Samuel Johnson's *The History of the Yorubas*, reveals participation in the expansion of the Ibadan empire and involvement with the careers of some notorious Ibadan *ologun*.[2] As such, it is a useful entry point into the workings of pre-colonial Ibadan politics.

After Lakanle's suicide, Aiyejenku became *Asaju* in the ranks of *Basorun* Oluyole. Following Oluyole's death, he joined the men of *Seriki* Ibikunle. When Ibikunle was installed *Balogun* in about 1851, he became *Areagoro Balogun*.[3] The two men fought in the Ijaye War between 1860 and 1862, a campaign that is generally regarded as a turning point for Ibadan imperialism.[4] After the fall of Ijaye, the warriors did not immediately return to Ibadan. Instead, they engaged in other wars against allied groups of Egba, Ijebu and Ijaye soldiers.

---

[1] Johnson, *History*, p. 410.

[2] Samuel Johnson (1846–1901) was born in Hastings, Sierra Leone, the third son of Henry and Sarah Johnson who were both freed slaves. In 1857, Henry was recruited by the missonary David Hinderer as a scripture reader and he and his family arrived in Ibadan during January 1858. Samuel completed early education at Kudeti mission school and from 1862–65 he attended the CMS Training Institution in Abeokuta. After his return to Ibadan in 1866 he was appointed schoolmaster at Kudeti; three years later, both the Kudeti and Aremo schools were placed under his control. He became the catechist in charge of the Aremo station in 1875. During 1881–86 he served as a peace negotiatior between the Ibadan war chiefs and the Ekitiparapo confederation on behalf of the Lagos government. He was ordained to the priesthood in 1886 and appointed pastor of Oyo in 1887, where he worked until his death. He completed the manuscript of his monumental history text in 1897, having begun work on it during the early 1880s. Its use as a primary source is discussed later in this chapter. See Michel R. Doortmont, 'Recapturing the Past: Samuel Johnson and the Construction of Yoruba History' (Erasmus University Ph.D. thesis, 1994).

[3] Johnson, *History*, p. 310.

[4] J.F. Ade Ajayi, 'The Ijaye War, 1860–5', Part II in *Yoruba Warfare in the Nineteenth Century*, J.F. Ade Ajayi and Robert Smith (Cambridge, 1964), p. 122. See also Awe, 'The Rise of Ibadan', pp. 161–205.

29

A long-running battle centred around Iperu, during which time *Balogun* Ibikunle fell ill with dropsy. *Alaafin* Adelu intervened to break up the rival camps towards the end of 1864.[5] However, when the Ibadan group was dispersing, the Egba again attacked them and began taking prisoners. In the chaos that followed, the sickly *Balogun* Ibikunle was almost captured: 'Akere the *Asipa* was the only war-chief who waited to protect the *Balogun* besides his own men and body guards.'[6] Eventually, the Egba gave up this particular assault and sought alternative captives. *Balogun* Ibikunle was successfully carried back to Ibadan, where he died in 1865.

Once in their city, the Ibadan warriors began competing for titles. Aiyejenku 'negotiated for and obtained the title of *Fowoko*.'[7] He was a candidate for the *Balogun* title, but it was instead allocated to Akere, as a reward for his protection of Ibikunle. Johnson contends that Aiyejenku's claim was ignored because Ibadan residents were against the giving of senior titles to men from Oyo-Ile. This practice had developed after the demise of *Basorun* Oluyole, who had 'tyrannized over his chiefs so mercilessly'.[8]

A decade later, *Foko* Aiyejenku had become even more unpopular for continually reminding the other Ibadan chiefs about 'the administrations of former distinguished rulers'. *Are-ona-kakanfo* Latosisa resented him and 'was ever on the look out for an opportunity of putting an end to this "historian"'. Johnson continues:

> He had little sympathy even amongst the junior chiefs, who were all affected with the prevailing avarice; for he was said to be of an irritable temper, too bold and pointed in his remarks, and when he reproved, did so without respect of person or rank; and being so capable a warrior there was a latent fear that if this man was backed up and eventually placed at the head of the government he would rule with rigour and become oppressive.[9]

When the *Aregbajo* of Igbajo was deposed by his townspeople in January 1877, the Ibadan warrior chiefs had their chance to humiliate Aiyejenku. In this context, the politics of Ibadan imperialism requires a brief explanation.

The Ibadan Empire was an hegemony over people. After a town was conquered, its residents became 'subject' and an Ibadan warrior chief became their *babakekere* (patron). In this position, he provided them with military protection from rival armies and approved appointments of town rulers. He stationed political representatives called *ajele* to signify his authority. The most important tasks of an *ajele* were to extract tribute payments from town inhabitants and to collect tolls on trade routes to Ibadan.[10] Tribute was paid in slaves, livestock, foodstuffs and manufactured goods; tolls were more often paid in cowries. Both these sums went directly to the *babakekere* – Ibadan had no central treasury. After a *babakekere* died, his fellow chiefs competed to gain control of his former subject towns, in order to collect income. Like most titles, these positions were not hereditary.[11]

[5] Johnson, *History*, p. 357.

[6] *Ibid.*, p. 359.

[7] *Ibid.*, p. 366.

[8] *Ibid.*, p. 367.

[9] *Ibid.*, p. 407–8.

[10] Bolanle Awe, 'The *Ajele* System: a Study of Ibadan Imperialism in the Nineteenth Century', *Journal of the Historical Society of Nigeria* 3 (1964), p. 55.

[11] Falola, *Political Economy*, p. 147.

Igbajo was an Ijesha town north-east of Ibadan (see Map 2) which had been defeated by forces under *Balogun* Akere during 1867.[12] He died on the battlefield in 1869 and, eight years later, *Foko* Aiyejenku was the *babakekere* of Igbajo. On 13 January 1877, the deposed *Aregbajo* came to Ibadan:

> The *Are* and the other chiefs were for reinstating him, but Aiejenku was opposed.... He spoke in his usual authoritative way which offended his brother chiefs and hence ... he was rejected by all the chiefs in the public meeting and that declaration was confirmed by his being deprived of all the towns hitherto tributary to him, including this very Igbajo.[13]

A week later, the chiefs attempted take over the collection of tolls at the Abeokuta gate.[14]

Aiyejenku accepted the confiscation of his tributary towns but he bitterly objected to losing his toll payments. He re-established control over the gate and armed himself for a confrontation, 'resolved upon civil war, come what may.'[15] However, a few days later the other Ibadan chiefs 'won over all the chiefs who were his personal friends, and to his subordinate chiefs they offered titles and ranks and tributary towns, and then decided to attack him in a body'. At this point, many of Aiyejenku's slaves fled his compound, seeing 'the impossibility of their being able to resist the whole town opposed to him'.[16] The chief himself then departed and sought refuge with a neighbouring chief. Immediately afterwards: 'The whole town in arms swooped down upon his quarter of the town and sacked every house, removing everything ... leaving the whole place in desolation and ruin.'[17]

Aiyejenku was then permitted to go back to his compound. On 30 January 1877, Samuel Johnson was among a group of Church Missionary Society (CMS) agents who visited him. Johnson quoted Aiyejenku's explanation of why he did not prevent the ransacking of his compound: 'I was unwilling to shed a drop of blood in a town of which I was among the foremost of the settlers, and where I built houses, and where I was blessed with wives and children.' Subsequently, some of Aiyejenku's slaves returned. His rival chiefs retaliated, resolving 'that he should not receive them again but that each should return permanently to their temporary masters'. On 12 February, messengers arrived to tell him that he should die. This time, no-one would accommodate him and he chose to kill himself.[18] With no supporting people, *Foko* Aiyejenku had neither social identity nor political status. He completed his annihilation by suicide.

Aiyejenku's life history is a microcosm of the complex political connections between chieftaincy and warfare in pre-colonial Ibadan. This chapter will review the extensive historiography on this subject to show how the city was conceived as a political community. It concludes with the beginnings of Ibadan's incorporation into the British Empire.

[12] Johnson, *History*, p. 370.
[13] *Ibid.*, p. 408.
[14] *Ibid.*
[15] *Ibid.*
[16] *Ibid.*, p. 409.
[17] *Ibid.*, pp. 408–9.
[18] *Ibid.*, p. 410.

Chiefs, spoils, people and conspiracy

The majority of chieftaincy titles in Ibadan were 'open' – only three offices were held exclusively by particular *ile*. Once titles were gained, promotion was not guaranteed. Only chiefs who had continuing military success and hence, material resources could sustain their political careers. The missionary David Hinderer regretted the conspicuous consumption which resulted, commenting that the 'headmen'

> [had] an idea as if it was utterly impossible for great men, as they consider themselves, to live according to their stations without war and kidnapping. Nor will they be convinced to the contrary as long as they have to feed every day their hundreds of soldiers ... [who] when at home, spend their time in feasting and parading about almost day and night.[19]

Apart from daily expenses, a chief also had to pay huge costs for his installation. For example, when the warrior veteran Lawoyin became *Seriki* in 1870, Johnson reports that the wealthy *Balogun* Ajobo gave him '800 bags of cowries, a horse, a sword, gowns etc [to] defray the expenses incidental to his taking office'.[20] Johnson does not state who received these goods. The most likely beneficiaries were the already-installed senior Ibadan chiefs; a portion might have been sent to the *Alaafin* in Oyo.

As Hinderer remarked, war spoils were commonly used to cover this expenditure. Indeed, military campaigns were often extended and sometimes even instigated to accumulate a booty of agricultural produce and, most importantly, slaves. For example, after an Ibadan expedition against Ijesha towns during the early 1850s 'Some of the minor chiefs who were not satisfied with what they got asked leave to make incursions in other directions; they were allowed to do so.'[21] Ambitious soldiers used war as a personal economic enterprise:

> Slave-raiding now became a trade to many who would get rich speedily, and hence those who felt themselves unlucky in one expedition, and others who quickly spent their ill-gotten gains in debauchery and all excesses would band together for a raiding expedition.[22]

'Rich' in this context connotes both people and money.[23] Most slaves were retained and trained as soldiers. Johnson states that by the late 1850s 'it has become the law and custom that soldier-slaves are never to be sold under any circumstances; they are to remain permanently as members of the house'.[24] Alternatively, slaves worked outside the city as farmers. Their produce was used to feed military households and to supply the Ibadan markets: 'So that a military state though Ibadan was, food was actually cheaper there than in many other towns.'[25] By this means, the cost of meeting the daily needs of soldiers was not as onerous as Hinderer implies.

Apart from a body of soldier slaves, a powerful warrior chief also had a group of

---

[19] CMSB, CA2/049/104: Hinderer Journal, 23 October 1851.

[20] Johnson, *History*, p. 390. These goods have a massive economic value. Although the amount could be exaggerated, Johnson was living in Ibadan during 1870 and probably witnessed the installation.

[21] *Ibid.*, p. 312.

[22] *Ibid.*, p. 321.

[23] Barber, 'Money, Self-Realization', p. 213.

[24] Johnson, *History*, p. 324.

[25] *Ibid.*, p. 325.

'freeborn' soldiers who served under him. A freeborn was sometimes an immigrant or, more commonly, a former soldier slave who had purchased his freedom. This was achieved by a slave capturing one or two others and exchanging them for himself. However, Johnson admitted that this transaction was at the discretion of the chief – he could keep all three men as slaves if he wished. Those who succeeded in emancipating themselves moved away for a short time 'to publicly make known their freedom'.[26] They afterwards frequently returned to the same *ologun* as an *omo ogun* (war-boy) or 'subordinate chief'. The latter category described prominent soldiers who gained titles within a private army. For example, Aiyejenku held such an office as the *Asaju* of *Basorun* Oluyole's men.

As was shown in the previous chapter, a successful *omo ogun* did not usually stay indefinitely in a large *ile*. When he had built up a retinue, he led his people to establish their own compound. After they left, this group might still pay allegiance to their former *babaogun*. This factor introduced another level of complexity to social/ spatial boundaries in Ibadan – an influential chief could claim subordinate chiefs and followers in smaller *ile* that were geographically distant from his own quarter.

An *ile* expressed political loyalty to a *babaogun* in three ways – by re-joining his private army at the time of a military campaign; by supporting his claim for promotion in the chieftaincy ranks; and, occasionally, by offering him a small tribute.[27] In return, the chief represented their interests to other *ologun*. He also arbitrated internal disputes within the compound, as well as those between households under his jurisdiction. The *babaogun* usually received payments for carrying out these duties, most often in the form of agricultural goods. Should these quarrels not be resolved, they were taken before the court of either the *Bale* or the *Balogun*, depending on the line to which the *babaogun* himself belonged.[28]

The obligations of *babaogun* and *babakekere* were similar and several of the powerful Ibadan warrior chiefs held both statuses. Although not all subject towns were conquered, freeborn people in the city exercised considerably more autonomy than their counterparts in the empire because they could choose their patron.[29] Most *ile* that did not accommodate a chief were under a *babaogun*. They usually selected a patron who had previously granted them land or who was resident nearby. Alternatively, their *babaogun* might come from, or be *babakekere* for, the same town as the person named as the founder of their *ile*. To gain and maintain the allegiance of smaller households, a *babaogun* needed to head a militarily successful and prosperous compound.

Ibadan chiefs aimed to be *babaogun* of as many *ile* as possible. Each client *ile* contributed to the group of people whom a chief could claim as followers; they enabled him to enhance his social status and to achieve his economic and political ambitions. Falola points out that apart from *ile*, there were also numerous groups of hangers-on who had no fixed compound. These people joined the following of a wealthy chief

[26] *Ibid.*, p. 326.

[27] Falola, *Political Economy*, p. 138.

[28] Akinyele, *Outlines*, pp. 72–3.

[29] During the first two decades of Ibadan's existence, several communities became subject towns by accepting the military protection of Ibadan war chiefs. CMSB, CA2/049/104: Hinderer Journal, 23 October 1851.

or trader (who might be a woman) and left him or her as it suited them.[30]

An *ile* or set of hangers-on could desert their *babaogun* at any time. Political loyalty was contingent on a senior chief maintaining his status through mastery in battle as well as on a degree of favour amongst his *ologun* companions. Should he lose the latter, he would almost certainly lose his client *ile*. Once this happened, a chief had difficulty asserting a prominent social status in the town – he lacked a body of supporting people. His claim to political authority was subsequently nullified and his deposition was confirmed. The response of the chief concerned was usually to leave Ibadan or commit suicide. His title then became available to junior chiefs and *mogaji* seeking titles on the chieftaincy lines.

Throughout the nineteenth century, this potential for political turnover fuelled an intense and violent power struggle between Ibadan chiefs. As a phrase of Ibadan *oriki* recalls: 'No-one comes to earth without some disease; civil disorder is the disease of Ibadan.'[31] Such 'civil disorder' characterised political life both within and without the city.

In the following section, we will examine several incidents of deposition as a way of gaining insight into how Ibadan politics worked. The principal primary source for this chronological account is Samuel Johnson's *The History of the Yorubas*. As Peel points out, 'its chief glory as a history lies in how it treats the politics of Ibadan, where Johnson lived for most of his life, from mid–century onwards'.[32]

The disease of civil disorder, *c.* 1830–80

The targets of civil disorder were chiefs perceived to be too powerful. Following the expulsion and defeat of Maye in about 1830, the first major case was that of *Are-ona-kakanfo* Lakanle. *Basorun* Oluyole recruited his favourite war-boy, Aiyejenku, by giving him the title of *Asaju*. When Lakanle realised he had lost the support of 'he whom he liked so much and who knew all his secrets' he gave up his life and his title.[33]

The demise of Eleepo through the late 1830s was more drawn out. He was a key player in the plot against Lakanle; *Basorun* Oluyole acknowledged his role by offering him the *Balogun* title. However, he refused it and the post was given instead to Oderinlo. Afterwards, Eleepo accompanied *Balogun* Oderinlo on his first military expedition. Johnson admits 'no town at this time gave any cause of offence for an attack, all the same the *Balogun* was sent against Ede – a town under their own protection'.[34] He explains this irony as a consequence of 'the custom at Ibadan that a newly created *Balogun* should ... prove his worth to the title and thereby commend himself to the respect of the soldiery'.[35] Eleepo, nevertheless, prevented the destruction of Ede and, throughout the expedition, 'he ruled the army according to his will'.[36]

[30] Falola, *Political Economy*, p. 45. The term *babaogun* only refers to males.

[31] *Aki wa aiye ki a ma l'arun kan lara; ija igboro larun Ibadan.*

[32] J.D.Y. Peel, 'Two Pastors and Their Histories: Johnson and Reindorf', to appear in *Basler Afrikanische Bibliographie*. Thanks to John Peel for providing an advance copy.

[33] Akinyele, *Iwe Itan Ibadan*, p. 33

[34] Johnson, *History*, p. 284.

[35] *Ibid.*

[36] *Ibid.*

When the Ibadan army returned to the town after their unsuccessful campaign, Eleepo 'was accused to his face of usurping the rights of the *Balogun*'. The chiefs demanded that he apologise and prostrate before Oderinlo. Since he refused, 'his humiliation was there and then decided upon':

> The next step taken was to deprive him of his principal subordinate war-chiefs by conferring town titles on each of them, making them members of the town council with equal votes.... [N]one of his subordinate chiefs called at his house as before, and all matters in his quarter of the town were taken straight to the *Balogun*. Thus Eleepo saw himself isolated.[37]

The siege of Oshogbo by Ilorin forces distracted attention from this dispute. In 1840, the Ibadan army again took to the field; Eleepo was not allowed to proceed with them. Since they were initially intimidated by the horse-mounted Ilorin soldiers, *Basorun* Oluyole proposed to send Eleepo to join them: 'The Ibadan war-chiefs hearing this were fired with jealousy lest the honour of the victory might be his and hence were resolved to risk a battle at all costs.'[38] Their triumph became known as the battle of Oshogbo; it was the first serious defeat of the rival Ilorin-Yoruba forces.[39]

Undaunted, Eleepo organised his own private expedition, 'and returned home with many captives and much booty by which he satisfied the cravings of his war boys'.[40] In this way, he augmented and maintained the body of people supporting him. However, returning from Oshogbo, the Ibadan army was resolved on his expulsion and 'threatened a civil war'.[41] *Basorun* Oluyole joined their plotting; when Eleepo learned of his deceit, he finally 'left the town with about 1,000 followers'. He later joined the rival military forces of Ijaye and was killed in battle during 1846.[42]

Shortly after Eleepo's departure, a group of chiefs raised an insurrection against *Basorun* Oluyole and 'the whole town was soon in uproar'.[43] When the insurrection leader was shot dead, Oluyole's men gained the upper hand and the rising failed. Johnson subsequently reflects on this incident, as well as the defeat of Ilorin at Oshogbo, in one of the key passages of his text:

> After the events narrated above, the history of the Yorubas centred largely at Ibadan which, down to the time of the British Protectorate continued to attract to itself ardent spirits from every tribe and family all over the country, who made it their home, so that while the rest of the country was quiet, Ibadan was making history.[44]

These depositions occurred before the Ibadan Empire had developed. By 1871, the first stage of conspiracy was to deny the victim his *babakekere* status; such was the fate of *Balogun* Ajobo. Ilesha was conquered by the Ibadan army in 1870 – consequently, the Ibadan chiefs assumed the power to select its ruler. Ajobo's fellow *ologun* were outraged that he took this role for himself alone and 'appropriated all the presents'. There was a fear of civil war, 'but Ajobo had not the courage to

---

[37] *Ibid.*, p. 285.
[38] *Ibid.*, p. 286.
[39] Robert Smith, 'The Yoruba Wars, *c*. 1820–93', Part I in *Yoruba Warfare*, pp. 33–36.
[40] Johnson, *History*, p. 289.
[41] *Ibid.*, p. 290.
[42] *Ibid.*, p. 302.
[43] *Ibid.*, p. 291.
[44] *Ibid.*, p. 293.

attempt one; on the contrary he spent largely to purchase his pardon.'[45] Nevertheless:

> The desire to encompass his fall [was] very strong especially with Ajayi the Osi and Lawoyin the Seriki, who were under great obligation to him for the means of attaining their present position. To them his fall would mean one lift upwards in their titles, and an obliteration of their feeling of obligation to him.... Consequently, there was another explosion engineered by these two chiefs; he was deprived of all his tributary towns, was forbidden to attend Council, and was rejected by the chiefs.[46]

Ajobo's response was to order his coffin to be made and his grave to be dug. On 6 July 1871, it was heard he had escaped from Ibadan. He was pursued by *Seriki* Lawoyin, riding the horse that Ajobo had given him.[47]

The chiefs and war-boys who had plotted against Ajobo visited *Bale* Orowusi to stake their claims for titles. Nonetheless, Orowusi 'saw at once through the scheming of the war-chiefs who would get rid of a chicken-hearted *Balogun*; but he the *Bale* had no need of a fire-eater for one, and hence he apprehended trouble'.[48] It appears that his suspicions were well-founded – Orowusi's death was rumoured on 15 August. When it was confirmed on 19 September 'his [Orowusi's] people went that same evening and set Ajobo's house on fire'.[49] Subsequently, two young war chiefs, Latosisa and Ajayi Ogboriefon, assumed the titles of *Are-ona-kakanfo* and *Balogun* respectively.

Six years later, just two weeks after Aiyejenku's suicide, 'Iyapo narrowly escaped being murdered.'[50] The *Seriki* had participated in the plunder of the old chief's compound and had acquired a basket of beads and several slaves. He gave these to the other chiefs, but they 'were resolved upon his overthrow for his independent and defiant attitude'.[51] The task was difficult: 'Iyapo was too influential a man to be overpowered suddenly ... he was positively hated by the principal leading chiefs, but none had the courage to face him.'[52]

A few months later, this conspiracy was overtaken by an increasing animosity towards *Are* Latosisa and an unpopular military campaign against the Egba. On 27 August, Robert Oyebode wrote in his diary: 'the chiefs are fighting with the *Are*.'[53] Ten days on, Latosisa 'dashed his chiefs in order to appease them'.[54] Johnson reports a planned insurrection in early October, but the plot was disclosed to Latosisa by *Osi Seriki* Solalu, 'a notorious tale-bearer'. *Osi Balogun* Ilori, a son of *Basorun* Ogunmola, also abandoned the intriguers, 'fearing the consequences to himself in case of failure'.[55]

[45] *Ibid.*, p. 384.

[46] *Ibid.*, p. 385.

[47] *Ibid.*, p. 390.

[48] *Ibid.*, p. 385.

[49] *Ibid.*, p. 386.

[50] KDL, IAP: Robert Scott Oyebode, 1877 Diary, 26 February.

[51] Johnson, *History*, p. 411.

[52] *Ibid.*, pp. 411–12.

[53] KDL, IAP: Oyebode, 1877 Diary, 27 August. For details of Oyebode's professional connections with Samuel Johnson, see Doortmont, 'Recapturing the Past', p. 96.

[54] *Ibid.*, 6 September.

[55] Johnson, *History*, p. 417.

By November 1877, 'Ibadan people was in tumult respecting the *Are*'s conspiracy. The *Balogun* and *Seriki* refused going to the *Are*'s.'[56] Nevertheless, on 2 November, *Balogun* Ogboriefon reconciled with *Are* Latosisa, fearing that *Seriki* Iyapo would betray him. Oyebode reported: 'We went to Salute the Are. We met all the chiefs there except Iyapo. The *Balogun* was pardoned. We heard that all the Seriki's men were placed behind Ilori & Solalu.'[57] Three days later, Iyapo was acquitted at the 'town's meeting day'.[58] However, this was Latosisa's 'ruse to get him [Iyapo] into his power, for he instructed his slaves to shoot him down, when he least expected danger'.[59] Latosisa's slaves warned Iyapo and 'all measures to get at him and kill him suddenly, failed'.[60] In the end, the *Are* deposed the *Seriki*, gave titles to his soldiers and, consequently, 'all Iyapo's clients were forced to brake [*sic*] allegiances with him.'[61] On 11 November, the *Seriki* committed suicide.[62]

Women chiefs were not immune from such malevolent intrigues. A well-known victim was *Iyalode* Efunsetan, the head of the women market traders during the early 1870s. Efunsetan was 'very rich owning some 2,000 slaves in her farms alone exclusive of those at home. She had also her own captains of war and warboys.'[63] Latosisa perceived her political influence and economic power as a threat to his own ambitions. When he returned from his first military campaign as *Are-ona-kakanfo*, he made three accusations against her. Awe suggests that these indictments highlight the duties and responsibilities of an *Iyalode*, at least as Latosisa perceived them.[64] He charged:

> 1. That she did not accompany him to the war. 2. That she never sent him supplies during the campaign. 3. That she did not come in person to meet him outside the town wall to congratulate him on his safe return.[65]

These accusations are to a certain extent contradictory – the first task excludes the successful completion of the others. Nevertheless, on 1 May 1874, Latosisa deposed Efunsetan and installed *Otun Iyalode* Iyaola. Two months later, he paid members of her household to murder her.[66]

A 'responsible man', Omoko, was then appointed as *mogaji* of *ile* Efunsetan.[67] A decade later, Rev. Daniel Olubi reported that her house was 'confiscated'.[68] The

---

[56] KDL, IAP: Oyebode, 1877 Diary, 1 November.

[57] *Ibid.*, 2 November.

[58] *Ibid.*, 5 November.

[59] Johnson, *History*, p. 418.

[60] *Ibid.*, p. 419.

[61] KDL, IAP: Oyebode, 1877 Diary, 9 November.

[62] *Ibid.*, 11 November. Johnson states he killed himself on 17 November. *History*, p. 419.

[63] Johnson, *History*, p. 393.

[64] Awe, 'The *Iyalode*', p. 153.

[65] Johnson, *History*, p. 391.

[66] *Ibid.*, p. 392.

[67] *Ibid.*, p. 394.

[68] KDL, IAP: Daniel Olubi, 1884 Diary, 8 August. Originally from Abeokuta, Olubi (1831–1914) accompanied Rev. Hinderer on his 1851 journey to Ibadan and returned there with him to establish the CMS Kudeti mission in 1853. He succeeded Hinderer as head of the three Ibadan mission stations (Kudeti, Aremo and Ogunpa) in 1869 and was ordained to the priesthood in 1876. See Doortmont, 'Recapturing the Past', p. 21.

compound was attacked, *Mogaji* Omoko was badly wounded and her people were seized. On 9 August 1884, 'Efunsetan's slaves are put in slave stalls.'[69] Since *ile* Efunsetan had been appropriated by *Are* Latosisa after her death, this raid was actually an attack on *his* household. Ten days later, Olubi wrote in his diary (his emphasis): '*Very strong* message came from the camp requesting property of Efunsetan or Omoko to be fully restored.'[70] The *Are* had left for the battlefront in April 1880; he was increasingly unpopular with the townspeople for failing to break the Egba blockade of the Ibadan trade route to Lagos.[71]

Ibadan chieftaincy did not become a centralised form of governing during the decades 1830 to 1880. If townspeople perceived a chief as too influential, they attacked him or her. They worked *against* centralisation, being just as disposed to plunder the material base of institutional consolidation as they were to constitute it. After 1880, warrior chiefs were almost permanently engaged at the battlefield and formal installations in the city ceased. Nonetheless, intrigues continued. As will be shown, conspiracy played a role in the Ibadan chiefs' signing of a treaty with British colonial authorities in 1893.

The question of how Ibadan was incorporated into a political community remains. There is also another. Why was competition for titles so intense? Most historians suggest that the answers to both these questions lie in the connections between politics and warfare in the turbulent social context which ensued after the fall of the Old Oyo Empire. Their explanations introduce another model of historical facts – 'Ibadan militarism'. This model is itself part of another, larger, discursive field to which we will now turn.

Yoruba historiography and Ibadan militarism

Yoruba warfare is well researched. Robert Smith produced the first general academic survey and followed up his work with a more specialised description of weaponry.[72] He later broadened his focus to compare several pre-colonial West African states and investigate foreign relations in the region.[73] J.A. Ade Ajayi wrote a detailed case study of the Ijaye War and argued that the conflict was essentially political rather than economic.[74] He subsequently investigated professional Yoruba warriors as a 'political class'.[75] Falola and Oguntomisin developed Ajayi's project into a wider comparative survey of the relationship between militarism and politics in nineteenth-century Yorubaland.[76]

---

[69] KDL, IAP: Olubi, 1884 Diary., 9 August.

[70] *Ibid.*, 19 August.

[71] Johnson, *History*, p. 447; pp. 457–61.

[72] Smith, 'The Yoruba Wars, *c*. 1820–93', Part I in *Yoruba Warfare*, pp. 9–55; 'Yoruba Armament', *Journal of African History* 8 (1967), pp. 87–106.

[73] Robert S. Smith, *Warfare and Diplomacy in Pre-colonial West Africa* (London, 1976).

[74] Ajayi, 'The Ijaye War, 1860–5', Part II in *Yoruba Warfare*, pp. 59–128.

[75] J.F. Ade Ajayi, 'Professional Warriors in Nineteeth-Century Yoruba Politics', *Tarikh* 1 (1965), pp. 72–81.

[76] Toyin Falola and Dare Oguntomisin, *The Military in Nineteenth Century Yoruba Politics* (Ile-Ife, 1984).

Civil Disorder, Militarism & the Yoruba Past

The contemporary ethnic/political identity of 'Yoruba' is one of the enduring outcomes of Yoruba warfare. Originally, the term was a Hausa word identifying people in the Old Oyo Empire.[77] Today, it encompasses millions of those who live in south-western Nigeria and the Benin Republic – people who also know themselves as Egba, Ijebu, Ife, Ijesha, Ekiti, Ondo, Igbomina, Yagba and Anago.[78] Such diversity brings into view the huge corpus of texts collectively termed 'Yoruba historiography', a literature which was spawned during the mid-nineteenth century and has continued to expand.

The process of Yoruba collective identification began in communities of liberated slaves such as Sierra Leone, where common traits like a shared language became important. Samuel Crowther's *A Vocabulary of the Yoruba Language*, generally considered to be the earliest document of Yoruba historiography, emphasises the point. Published in 1843, the text includes a seven-page historical section. Crowther returned to his homeland in 1841; many other freed slaves followed him. Their distinct social/cultural group became known as Saro and, like Crowther, a great number of them were Christian missionaries.[79]

Saro people were the forebears of the Christian Yoruba intelligentsia. 'That we study a people called "the Yoruba" at all', contends Peel, 'is due largely to them.'[80] These numerous men and women established schools, developed a standard orthography for writing the Yoruba language, translated the Scriptures and produced various studies of traditional religion in both English and Yoruba. From the 1880s onwards, their literary production was also part of a movement of cultural nationalism. Facing racial prejudice and exclusion from colonial and ecclesiastical institutions, this group – who were 'Yoruba' in the modern sense of the word – embarked on a vigorous search for an authentic indigenous culture which could be asserted against the imported European one.[81] Their favoured political tool was writing history.

The History of the Yorubas, a book almost 700 pages long, is without doubt the most outstanding example of this specific type of 'regional nationalist' historiography. Reprinted nine times, the text has variously been described as 'the principal glory of Yoruba historiography' and 'the indispensable foundation for all historical and anthropological work on the Yoruba'.[82] Samuel Johnson completed his book in

---

[77] Peel, 'Yoruba Ethnogenesis', p. 202.

[78] P.F. de Moraes Farias, '"Yoruba Origins" Revisited by Muslims' in *Self-Assertion and Brokerage: Early Cultural Nationalism in West Africa*, ed. P. F. de Moraes Farias and Karin Barber (Birmingham, 1990), p. 110.

[79] Robin Law, 'Early Yoruba Historiography,' *History in Africa* 3 (1976), p. 71.

[80] Peel, 'Yoruba Ethnogenesis', p. 198.

[81] Farias and Barber, *Self-Assertion and Brokerage*, p. 2.

[82] Robin Law, 'Early Yoruba Historiography', *History in Africa* 3 (1976), p. 72; Peel, 'Yoruba Ethnogenesis', p. 198. For other analyses of Johnson's *History* see B.A. Agiri, 'Early Oyo History Reconsidered', *History in Africa* 2 (1975), pp. 1–16; Doortmont, 'Recapturing the Past'; Toyin Falola, 'Ade Ajayi on Samuel Johnson: Filling the Gaps' in *African Historiography: Essays in Honour of Jacob Ade Ajayi* ed. Toyin Falola, (Harlow, 1993), pp. 80–9; Robin Law, 'How Truly Traditional is Our Traditional History? The Case of Samuel Johnson and the Recording of Yoruba Oral Tradition', *History in Africa* 11 (1984), pp. 195–221; Robin Law, 'Constructing "A Real National History": A Comparison of Edward Blyden and Samuel Johnson', in *Self-Assertion and Brokerage*, eds. Farias and Barber, pp. 78–100; P.F. de Moraes Farias, 'History and Consolation: Royal Yoruba Bards Comment on Their Craft', *History in Africa* 19 (1992), pp. 263–97; Ato Quayson,

1897, but it did not appear in print until 1921.[83] By this time, Doortmont suggests, it represented a view which was already quite out of date – the new trend was 'ethnic provincialism'.[84] This more local approach to history-writing was fostered by educated elites seeking greater social and political influence in their own communities. I.B. Akinyele's *Iwe Itan Ibadan*, originally published about 1916, stands out as the Ibadan example.

Decades later, the development of academic Yoruba historiography was closely associated with the foundation of Nigeria's first university at Ibadan in 1952. Opened initially as a college of the University of London in 1948, Ibadan University admitted Ph.D. candidates in history from its earliest days. The focus of Yoruba studies shifted once again, becoming part of a larger project of nationalist historiography. This enterprise gained further impetus with independence and the launch of the Ibadan History Series during the 1960s.[85] For Peel, the result was: 'a sort of Whig history, an account of how the fittest representatives of the African people – mediators and modernizers – have risen within the bounds of colonial society'.[86]

Yoruba history was different, in that there were several monographs which focused solely on the nineteenth century. Biobaku's Ibadan Ph.D thesis, published in 1957 as *The Egba and their Neighbours, 1842–1872*, is usually identified as the pioneering work. His focus on a specific community sustained the earlier trend of conceiving 'Yorubaness' in provincial terms. The dominant narrative remained local history, placed within a social and political context of continuity and change in a wider Yoruba nation.

Given Ibadan's rise to prominence during the nineteenth century, many of these works covered some aspect of the city's history. Mabogunje and Omer-Cooper investigated the history of Owu and how its destruction led to Ibadan's establishment.[87] Akintoye argued that Ibadan was one of the main protagonists in the 'power revolution among the Yoruba' through the latter half of the nineteenth century.[88] He concentrated on Ibadan's imperial conquests of the Ekiti, Ijesha, Akoko and Igbomina. Biobaku discussed both Egba and Ijebu relations with Ibadan insofar as they competed for the control of trade routes.[89] Akinjogbin and Law contested issues

---

[82] (cont.) *Strategic Transformations in Nigerian Writing. Orality and History in the Work of Rev. Samuel Johnson, Amos Tutuola, Wole Soyinka and Ben Okri* (Oxford, 1997).

[83] Rev. Johnson sent his book to the London-based Society for the Promotion of Christian Knowledge (SPCK) in 1898. Publication was refused and Johnson was asked to write a shorter history in the Yoruba language for use as a textbook in mission schools. He requested the return of the manuscript but, by the end of 1899, it was evidently lost. When Samuel Johnson died two years later, his brother Obadiah took on the task of reconstructing the text from notes and finally succeeded in having it published 24 years after its original completion. Since then, it has reprinted nine times. Doortmont, 'Recapturing the Past', p. 50.

[84] Michel R. Doortmont, 'The Invention of the Yorubas: Regional and Pan-African Nationalism versus Ethnic Provincialism', in *Self-Assertion and Brokerage*, p. 106.

[85] Paul E. Lovejoy, 'The Ibadan School of Historiography and its Critics', in *African Historiography: Essays in Honour of Jacob Ade Ajayi* ed. Toyin Falola, (Harlow, 1993), p. 198.

[86] Peel, *Ijeshas and Nigerians*, p. 11.

[87] A.L. Mabogunje and J.D. Omer-Cooper, *Owu in Yoruba History* (Ibadan, 1971).

[88] S.A. Akintoye, *Revolution and Power Politics in Yorubaland, 1840–1893. Ibadan Expansion and the Rise of Ekitiparapo* (New York, 1971), p. xxi.

[89] S.O. Biobaku, *The Egba and their Neighbours, 1842–1872* (Oxford, 1957).

of chronology, particularly as they concerned the disintegration of the Oyo Empire and consequent foundation of Ibadan.[90]

The work of two scholars – Awe and Falola – is of particular interest to this study.[91] They described the enormous importance of Ibadan for Yoruba political and economic development in research that remains invaluable for its historical detail and conceptual insight. Like most work on 'nineteenth-century Yorubaland', however, both authors used the category 'Yoruba' anachronistically. This tendency is something of an irony, given that one of the major achievements of the literature to which they contributed was to document the diverse and contested histories which brought the modern concept of Yoruba into being. Yet, each study took the certainty of a 'Yoruba nation' for granted and then read it back into the past.

Ibadan imperialism and the Yoruba nation

Bolanle Awe outlined her pioneering D.Phil. thesis as 'an examination of the factors which contributed to its [Ibadan's] growth and led to its eventual ascendancy'.[92] The first of these factors, she argued, was the political vacuum that resulted from the disintegration of the Oyo Empire. She emphasised the aggression of the Ilorin-based Fulani as the major cause of its collapse and contended that there was a need for a rival military force.

Awe then set out an incisive analysis of how Ibadan became a 'republic of warriors', stressing the influence of external political instability on the city's growth and expansion.[93] She also pointed out that the Ibadan warriors recognised the *Alaafin* of Oyo as their suzerain so as to legitimate the absence of hereditary succession in Ibadan.[94] Describing town politics as 'the background to Ibadan's emergence as a Yoruba power', Awe documented Ibadan's imperial expansion up until the 1860s. This was the period when Ibadan chiefs developed the '*Ajele* system' as a way of extracting resources from the inhabitants of towns brought under their control. Although this system was closely intertwined with chiefs' competitive struggles to build up their material base of political power, Awe placed more importance on its function as a mode of empire-building.[95] She pursued this theme in subsequent chapters, describing three distinct phases of militarism: the Ijaye War (1859–62); campaigns over control of trade routes (1862–72); and, finally, a renewed imperial offensive under *Are* Latosisa and the outbreak of the Ekitiparapo War (1872–86).

---

[90] I.A. Akinjogbin, 'A Chronology of Yoruba History, 1789–1840', *Odu* 2 (1966), pp. 81–6. R.C.C. Law, 'The Chronology of the Yoruba Wars of the Early Nineteenth Century: a Reconsideration', *Journal of the Historical Society of Nigeria* 5 (1970), pp. 211–22.

[91] Awe and Falola are both on the fringes of the 'Ibadan School'. Neither studied at Ibadan, although Awe joined its History Department after submitting her D.Phil. to the University of Oxford. Unlike most of her colleagues, she did not publish her thesis in the Ibadan History Series, producing instead a number of articles. Falola belongs to the second generation of Ibadan historians; he has published prolifically since submitting his Ph.D. thesis to the University of Ife. See Lovejoy, 'The Ibadan School', p. 199.

[92] Awe, 'The Rise of Ibadan', p. *i*.

[93] *Ibid.*, pp. 76–120.

[94] *Ibid.*, p. 100–1.

[95] *Ibid.*, pp. 121–60.

Awe argued that Ibadan's military success through these three decades enabled the warrior chiefs to act independently of the *Alaafin*. The problem was that their assumption of regional political control led to estrangement from the *Alaafin* and further strained relationships with neighbouring polities. Consequently, the Egba and Ijebu stepped up their efforts to frustrate the flow of trade. The Ekiti and Ijesha dependencies rebelled by establishing the Ekitiparapo military alliance against Ibadan. Other battles with Ilorin to the north and Ife to the east also flared up. Since these five forces were unable to effect a final defeat on Ibadan, a military stalemate resulted.[96]

It was this final factor which, in Awe's view, involved the British in Ibadan's external relations.[97] During 1881, they attempted to broker a ceasefire in the Ekitiparapo War and thus reduce the disruption of trade between Lagos and the interior. Although these negotiations collapsed the following year, a second initiative during 1886 was more successful. In September, the contesting parties ratified a 'Treaty of Peace, Friendship and Commerce'. The Ekitiparapo–Ibadan front, as well as the war with Ife, were eventually quitted and the camps were dispersed.[98]

Ibadan's other conflicts with the Egba, Ijebu and Ilorin continued. The British allied with Ibadan to open trade routes and, in 1892, Governor Carter authorised a military expedition against Ijebu. Defeat forced both Egba and Ijebu submission; subsequently, Carter visited and broke up the Ilorin–Ibadan war camps. Awe contended it was fear of a military attack which finally forced the Ibadan chiefs to capitulate to British rule in 1893.[99] Summing up, she posited: 'Ibadan's rise to power in the Yoruba country cannot be explained in terms of its economic development.'[100] She concluded that an aggressive, politically motivated imperialism was the main cause of the city's growth.

In contrast, Toyin Falola sought 'to bridge the gap in Ibadan history by focusing on its economic aspect'.[101] As part of this project, he analysed Ibadan warfare as economic imperialism; thus augmenting Awe's emphasis on political factors. He pointed out that material wealth, especially having people, was closely intertwined with assertions of power and status in the city.[102] More broadly, he described the various forms of labour organisation in Ibadan and the different productive activities of its inhabitants, such as farming and manufacturing.[103] He also documented Ibadan's external trading network and contended that it was this resource which stimulated British imperial interests in the region.[104]

Falola described nineteenth-century Ibadan chieftaincy somewhat misleadingly

[96] *Ibid.*, p. 285.

[97] *Ibid.*, pp. 293–336.

[98] These 'peace moves' are more fully discussed in Akintoye, *Revolution*, Chapter 6, pp. 152–84. A copy of the 1886 Treaty is in Johnson, *History*, pp. 527–31.

[99] Awe, 'The Rise of Ibadan', p. 327.

[100] *Ibid.*, pp. 346–7.

[101] Falola, *Political Economy*, p. 8. Falola has since published further articles and a monograph on the colonial period, *Politics and Economy in Ibadan 1893–1945* (Lagos, 1989).

[102] Falola, *Political Economy*, Chapter 5, pp. 126–58.

[103] *Ibid.*, pp. 42–86.

[104] *Ibid.*, pp. 87–125; pp. 159–91.

as 'a definite political structure'.[105] He assumed Ibadan was an expansionist 'military aristocracy' within a struggling Yoruba nation and based Ibadan's economic success on an undefined concept of peace.[106] In a later article, Falola preferred the notion of 'military republic'. He then emphasised the intense power rivalries of Ibadan politics and suggested that the battlefield was an important forum for their resolution.[107]

Unlike Yoruba urbanism, the Ibadan militarism described by Awe and Falola *is* constituted by historical facts. Simultaneously, it is also a conceptual representation. They locate Ibadan in a teleological model, one which documents the growth of a military state that saved the larger Yoruba polity from destruction. The wars were *the* central experience of the Yoruba-speaking peoples during the nineteenth century. With Ibadan as his base, Samuel Johnson, supremely, was their interpreter.[108] As we shall see, the view of the pre-colonial Ibadan past in Awe's, Falola's and, inevitably, my own work is partly the ideological heritage of *The History of the Yorubas*.

An imposed teleological pattern is evident in Awe's tendency to ascribe altruistic motives to Ibadan military campaigns. Until about the mid-1850s, she contends, the main interest of warrior chiefs was to save other Yoruba towns from Ilorin invasion.[109] She continually emphasises that a long-term political aim to protect the Yoruba country was a more important motive for war than short-term material gain. Akintoye challenges this view and she herself revises it in a later article.[110]

Both Awe and Falola argue that Ibadan pursued its own imperial policy in defiance of the *Alaafin* from the 1860s.[111] Although there is certainly evidence for expansionism, there are also indications that the imperial vision of the chiefs was by no means coherent. On several occasions, sections of the army literally refused to go into battle. For example, Johnson described their reluctance to launch a campaign against Ilesha in 1867: 'Not from any love of Ilesa or fear of its almost impregnable forts, but rather that titles should be re-arranged so that they might have promotions.'[112]

Awe rates military preparedness as the defining feature of Ibadan political culture and presents civil disorder as an outcome of the context of generalised warfare.[113] When she refers to intrigues or suicides, she describes them as isolated incidents which resulted from the misguided rule of chiefs like *Are* Latosisa.[114] Similarly, Falola does not investigate Ibadan political crises in any detail. He only draws attention to the competition for titles in his conclusion, when he proposes that chiefs sometimes went to war to further their political careers.[115] Thus, despite their

---

[105] *Ibid.*, pp. 24–5.

[106] Falola, *Political Economy*, pp. 24–5, pp. 32–4; p. 67; p. 193.

[107] Toyin Falola, 'The Political System of Ibadan in the 19th Century', in *Evolution of Political Culture in Nigeria*, ed. J.F. Ade Ajayi and Bashir Ikora (Ibadan, 1985), p. 112.

[108] Peel, 'Yoruba Ethnogenesis', p. 206.

[109] Awe, 'The Rise of Ibadan', p. 97.

[110] Akintoye, *Revolution*, p. 38; Bolanle Awe, 'Militarism and Economic Development in Nineteenth Century Yoruba Country: the Ibadan Example', *Journal of African History* 14 (1973), p. 67.

[111] Awe, 'The Rise of Ibadan', p. 132; Falola, *Political Economy*, p.146

[112] Johnson, *History*, p. 378.

[113] *Ibid.*, p. 255.

[114] *Ibid.*, p. 255.

[115] Falola, *Political Economy*, p. 194.

awareness of the centrality of warfare to the politics of chieftaincy, Awe and Falola maintain their focus on the external relations of Ibadan, which they regard as a coherent polity.

This pervasive bias relates to an assumption that the Ibadan warrior chiefs took actions within a wider constitutional framework of the Yoruba nation. As Samuel Johnson wrote, Ibadan *made* Yoruba history.[116] Through the course of the nineteenth century, it developed into the largest, most powerful polity in the region which became Yorubaland. Its militarism generated cultural homogenisation as diverse groups of people settled in the city or were conquered by it. Simultaneously, pan-Yoruba solidarity was made against Ibadan, by an alliance of states which jointly opposed it.[117] In part, the Ibadan political community was constituted through its imperial relationships and military interactions with other polities.

Johnson did not restrict Ibadan's history-making to the battlefield. His chronology of the nineteenth-century Yoruba past set out a regular pattern: Ibadan chiefs embarked on a military campaign; they returned; they intrigued; they went to war again. Awe and Falola overlooked this pattern and established a false dichotomy between external and internal Ibadan politics, treating the latter as less important. However, Johnson did not recount civil disorder as an irrelevant aberrance. Rather, he presented it as a constituent practice of Ibadan political life.

This suggests that historians require a perspective on nineteenth-century Ibadan political culture which shows why and how militarism and civil disorder were connected.

'Prowess in the field for the public benefit': militarism and civic power

In 1851, the missionary David Hinderer reported in his journal: 'the jealousy of the principal men of the place seems not at present to admit of the election of a man invested with the power to rule'.[118] Two days later, he suggested that rivalry between chiefs was, on occasion, purposely mobilised:

> 'War never done', is an awful but very true watchword in this country especially with the Mahomedans. Some weeks ago this town was called upon by the people of Ilorin & those of Ife to join them in the destruction of some towns N & E of this but the wariers here, if highway robbers & kidnappers deserve that name, thought it to be more gain to them to make an expedition of their own against some small & quiet town. For this purpose was the giving of titles to several individuals ... not indeed to asign to them different offices, but rather to inspire & incourage them for their work of destruction [sic].[119]

As far as Hinderer was concerned, the politics of the city was the politics of the battlefield. He was not a neutral observer. He explicitly acknowledged the

---

[116] Johnson, *History*, p. 293.
[117] Peel, 'Yoruba Ethnogenesis', p. 208.
[118] CMSB, CA2/049/103: Hinderer Journal, 7 June 1851.
[119] *Ibid.*, 9 June 1851.

relationship between his missionary enterprise and his pessimistic political outlook: 'Some people might take statements as the above to be disheartening but I would say: In the Name of God to such people the gospel must be preached.'[120]

A Christian destiny also directs the Rev. Samuel Johnson's telling of the Yoruba past. The arrival of missionaries in the 1840s was, as he saw it, the fulfilment of 'an old tradition in the country of a prophecy that as ruin and desolation spread from the interior to the coast so light and restoration will be from the coast interiorwards'.[121] For Peel, this was Johnson's 'ideological coup': a persuasive alignment of Christian *and* Yoruba destinies by means of a grand Romance of national redemption.[122]

Ibadan was central to this redemption. After describing the first installation of chiefs in the city, Johnson went on:

> They [Ibadan people] seemed to be now settled, yet they really lived by plunder and rapine.... Violence, oppression, robbery, man-stealing were the order of the day.... Yet they were destined by God to play a most important part in the history of the Yorubas to break the Fulani yoke and save the rest of the country from foreign domination; in short to be a protector as well as a scourge in the land.[123]

In Johnson's model of historical facts, Ibadan militarism was part of a Divine Plan for a potentially Christian nation. Over half of *The History of the Yorubas* is devoted to elaborating a dramatic tale of the expansionist development of Ibadan, its subsequent military stalemate and, finally, the peace negotiations from the 1880s onwards (in which Johnson was a participant) that culminated in the 1893 Agreement. The text is concerned mainly with the actions and passions of Ibadan chiefs, both in their city and on the battlefield.[124]

Having established a providential aspect to Ibadan militarism, Johnson, in contrast to Hinderer, presents the chiefs' warfare as a noble enterprise. For example, when he recounts how Aiyejenku was rejected for promotion to *Balogun* in 1865, Johnson regrets that the chief was not given an opportunity 'to retrieve his good name by prowess in the field for the public benefit'.[125] This 'public' was a political community that was Ibadan and Yoruba *at the same time*. As we have seen, its ideological heritage remains present in the work of Awe and Falola.

Johnson repeatedly shows how the warrior chiefs and their followers realigned their competing households into the formidable military force of the Ibadan army. For example, he describes a quarrel between *Ekerin Balogun* Orowusi and some of the *Bale* war chiefs during a march against the Ijesha during the early 1850s. The dispute was serious enough that 'the expedition nearly collapsed before they came in sight of the enemy'.[126] Neither *Balogun* Ibikunle nor *Otun Balogun* Ogunmola could take sides, otherwise, 'the strife would be general'. Johnson continues:

[120] *Ibid.*
[121] Johnson, *History*, p. 296.
[122] Peel, 'Two Pastors and their Histories'.
[123] Johnson, *History*, pp. 245–6.
[124] Peel, 'Yoruba Ethnogenesis', p. 207.
[125] Johnson, *History*, p. 367.
[126] *Ibid.*, p. 310.

Ogunmola who was distinguished for his tact and diplomacy therefore sent to the *Balogun* that he should give orders for battle as if the Ijesas were coming upon them. This was done. They marched out in order of battle ... and opened fire upon an imaginary foe. They then sent a company of men to the camp to raise an alarm 'The Ijesas are in sight.' When therefore those rival chiefs heard the sound of musketry they left off fighting among themselves. The matter was amicably adjusted the next day.[127]

This account shows explicitly that the Ibadan army was not always a unified force. Instead, it reveals how the army came together to meet political objectives. These objectives were neither 'external imperialism' nor 'internal rivalry' – they were both simultaneously. The Ibadan political community came into being through its combat with another community; in this case, the 'imaginary' Ijesha. After the dispute within the ranks had been resolved, the army defeated a large number of *real* Ijesha towns.[128]

Collective warfare was also a practical way to meet economic needs. It provided immediate material rewards – slaves and spoils. Describing a campaign against the Ekiti in 1874, Johnson wrote: 'The Ibadans made an easy conquest of the whole district. Men, women and children were captured without the slightest attempt at resistance. So many were the captives and so much the booty, that the campaign appeared more like a promenade.'[129] There were also more long-term benefits – the inhabitants of subject towns had to make tribute payments to Ibadan warrior chiefs.

The militarism which brought an Ibadan political community into being was dominantly gendered as masculine. Nonetheless, Ibadan women – as wives, followers, traders, and chiefs – were also participants. For example, at the battlefront, *Iba* Oluyole was often accompanied by his wife, Oyainu. Johnson described her as 'a lady of masculine temperament and very popular' who offended the other war chiefs by swearing she could capture Ibadan's military rival of Ijaye 'if the war was left to herself alone'.[130] A daughter of *Basorun* Ogunmola, Omosa, also led her own contingent of soldiers on the field. During the 1880s, she organized caravans to supply military chiefs at the front with rifles, ammunition and food.[131] Both *Iyalode* Subuola and *Iyalode* Efunsetan had armies responsible to them, although they did not take them into battle.

Warfare also generated an *idea* of political community. For example, Johnson described the battle strategy of *Balogun* Ogboriefon as follows:

He was a brave leader and smooth tongued, knowing well how to encourage soldiers and to inspire courage into the faint hearted.... He used to remind them of home and all its pleasures, telling them that it is the bravest who will be honoured, who can break the laws with impunity. 'Remember the bazaars, the Iba market, what pleasures you often enjoy there, pleasures bordering on crime. Now is the time to atone for them if you will enjoy yourself again with impunity.' With these words he often spurred them on to the fight.[132]

---

[127] *Ibid.*, pp. 310–11. Johnson names his source for this account – a trader who later converted to Christianity and took the name Josiah Oni. Oni was sent back to Ibadan as a 'special messenger' to report on the incident to *Bale* Olugbode.

[128] Akintoye, *Revolution*, pp. 44–5.

[129] Johnson, *History*, p. 391.

[130] *Ibid.*, p. 299.

[131] Morgan, *Akinyele's Outline History (Part Two)*, pp. 93–5.

[132] Johnson, *History*, p. 380.

In this case, the *city* of Ibadan was the imagined community. Crucially, civil disorder was at the centre of its ideological mobilisation. Ibadan soldiers must be willing to sacrifice themselves for their city so that, if they returned there, they could enjoy 'pleasures bordering on crime'. Through success in battle, they atoned for street violence – in order to engage in it once again.

When a successful military campaign was concluded, the Ibadan army carried their booty to return in triumph to their city. The contingent political community that had been mobilised on the battlefield began to fragment. So much is evident from Johnson's account of *Seriki* Iyapo's return to Ibadan in 1875:

> The joy, the excitement, and the enthusiasm attending the pageantry of this young man so moved the whole town that the like of it had scarcely ever been seen. Whilst it stirred the envy of some to its very depth, it excited the admiration of others.[133]

The contradictions of Ibadan political life are aptly captured here. Nowhere were the rivalries among the warriors and their followings more fully expressed than in the battle for political offices. But what was the point? Why were titles so passionately sought?

Honour, status and civic power

In Ibadan, those who held chieftaincy posts were usually affluent, deriving income from war booty, tribute, tolls and the sale of agricultural produce from their farms. Titles were not sought because they generated wealth – by contrast, chiefs' expenses frequently exceeded their returns. Chiefs needed a personal following before they could gain a title; even then, they had to work at maintaining it. Nonetheless, despite the costs of chieftaincy status, political office was strongly desired.

Ibadan chieftaincy titles are still much coveted, although the expenses associated with them continue to be high. Today, many residents in former military households reminisce that the nineteenth century was when offices were allocated to the 'big men' with *ola*. They contrast this state of affairs with the present, which they see as dominated by 'money politics'. *Ola*, they argue, is now bought by the acquisition of a chieftaincy title, paid for in cash. Previously, *ola* was first achieved and then recognised.[134]

Yoruba speakers translate *ola* as 'honour'.[135] The concept is not specific to Ibadan; Barber argues that *ola* informs the ethos of the *oriki* of big men in early nineteenth-century Okuku. 'What men hoped to attain', she writes:

> Was not wealth as such or power as such, but a total state of sufficiency and command over their social environment, a state called *ola*. What underlies *ola* is the notion of recognition, of being acknowledged as superior, and of attracting admirers and supporters as a result.... Because the relationship between the big man and his supporters was not institutionalised it had to be continually recreated.[136]

---

[133] *Ibid.*, p. 395.

[134] This was a recurring theme in all my interviews with former military households in Ibadan during 1995–6 and 1997 and in Gavin Williams's interviews during 1970 and 1971.

[135] Weber's notion of 'social honour' is a useful parallel concept. See 'Class, Status, Party,' in *From Max Weber: Essays in Sociology* (London, 1991 [1948]), translated and edited by H.H. Gerth and C. Wright Mills, pp. 180–95.

[136] Barber, *I Could Speak*, p. 203.

47

In pre-colonial Ibadan, it was the practice of warfare that institutionalised the relationship between an Ibadan chief and his followers. He became a big man through 'prowess in the field for the public benefit'; an act which, simultaneously, embodied a material and ideological mobilisation of political community. From this association, *ola* and chieftaincy became linked with a form of public recognition that was, above all, *civic power*.

According to Johnson's tale of Ajayi Ogboriefon, the *Balogun* inspired his warboys by telling them that it was 'the bravest who will be honoured'. This statement referred particularly to the achievement of *ola* and a chieftaincy title. Amidst heavy battle, winning public recognition through the award of Ibadan political office became the basic military objective. When the army returned to the city, they returned with a collective idea of their military power. Chiefs then sought to exert this power over their own people and those of their rivals in their contest for chieftaincy titles. Ibadan's infamous 'civil disorder' was not just a reflection of political instability. It was an endeavour to assert control over an imagined civic Ibadan.

This civic community was neither centralised nor institutionalised. It was continually recreated through warfare – both inside and outside Ibadan city. According to the historian Isaac Akinyele:

> The more powerful a warrior was and the more numerous the followers he had the higher was the title he assumed. If any man presumed to assume a title that he did not deserve, the man who had the right to the title would challenge the usurper when they got to the battle to come along with him to face the enemy. If the usurper was worsted in the fight, the rightful owner would assume the title in dispute from the very battle field and all the other chiefs would support.[137]

Alternatively, the 'whole town' conspired to hound an overly powerful chief to suicide. His submission was an individual and altruistic political choice; if he did not comply, his entire *ile* would be exterminated. Lakanle, Aiyejenku and Iyapo killed themselves to save the *ola* of their household and to prevent Ibadan city being 'spoiled'. The result of this political practice was that, throughout the nineteenth century, no Ibadan chief ever succeeded in establishing an autocracy. Each *ile* had a vested interest in gaining access to the status that chieftaincy represented. Intense competition maintained a rapid turnover of titles and continually reconstituted a civic Ibadan.

Thus paradoxically, as well as external imperialism, it was rivalry and intrigue which held Ibadan together. According to Robert Oyebode's 1877 diary, the 'town's meeting day' took place on two specific occasions. One was the day that Ibadan people planned a military campaign. The other was the day that Ibadan people planned to depose a chief.[138]

A death, a treaty and a war

On 30 April 1893, *Balogun* Osungbekun died. He was either poisoned or clubbed to death by members of his household. 'However it be,' as Johnson put it, 'he was dead

[137] Akinyele, *Outlines*, pp. 97–8.
[138] KDL, IAP: Oyebode, 1877 Diary, 26 February; 30 July; 5 November. See also 1878 Diary, 18 March.

and report was conveyed to the infuriated mob assembled at the market ready for action…. The mob dispersed.'[139]

Just over a month earlier, the Ibadan army had returned to the city after sixteen years in the field. According to Johnson, there had been no military engagements since May 1892, when a British expedition bombarded Ijebu and forced the desertion of its capital, Ijebu-Ode.[140] This attack, Carter informed the Ibadan chiefs, was intended to prevent 'further arbitrary closure of the roads'.[141] Following the incident, he wrote to them again, noting that Ijebu 'had received a lesson which it is not likely they will ever forget and they fully realize what the power of the Queen of England is able to do if it is once put into action'. The relevance of the thinly veiled threat was made clear by Carter's announcement that he would soon visit Ibadan to negotiate a cessation of 'the unhappy war' with Ilorin.[142]

Governor Carter left Lagos on 3 January 1893. A fortnight later he had signed a 'Treaty of friendship and commerce' with the Egba chiefs at Abeokuta. Apart from guaranteeing that roads would not be closed without the Governor's approval, the treaty also stipulated that no Egba territory would be annexed by the British without previous agreement from the chiefs. Rather, 'its [Egba country's] independence shall be fully recognised'.[143] On 3 February Carter signed another treaty with the *Alaafin* of Oyo. The document was similar to that signed with the Egba chiefs in respect of maintaining trade routes but, significantly, it contained no clause to guarantee Oyo independence. Instead, it offered a 'yearly present' of one hundred pounds to the *Alaafin*, which could be withdrawn or suspended at the Governor's discretion.[144] As Jenkins suggests: 'The so-called Treaty, was, in fact, a list of concessions by the Alafin.'[145]

Carter's next destination was Ilorin. No treaty was signed, but the Governor and Emir Moma 'parted with an assurance of mutual friendship'.[146] Afterwards, Carter proceeded to the battlefront and met the Ibadan and Ilorin war chiefs. Neither side would decamp first; the Ibadan said they were defending their country, the Ilorin said the Ibadan had occupied theirs and should go home. 'The Governor replied that he knew all that … but he did not come there to discuss ancient history.'[147] Carter appointed representatives to accompany the warriors back to their respective towns and both camps were broken up on the same day. The Ibadan army arrived at their city walls on 22 March 1893.[148]

The warriors planned their triumphal procession into Ibadan for the next day.

---

[139] Johnson, *History*, p. 633.

[140] *Ibid.*, p. 623.

[141] Carter to Ibadan authorities, 18 April 1892. Cited in George Jenkins, 'Politics in Ibadan', (Northwestern University Ph.D. thesis, 1965), p. 108. This letter was contained in a file of Historical Papers located in the Mapo Hall Archives. Regrettably, this entire collection has since been lost and I was not able to consult it; I have thus relied on Jenkins's references.

[142] Carter to Ibadan authorities, 8 June 1892. *Ibid.*, p. 111.

[143] A copy of the Treaty is printed in Appendix A of Johnson, *History*, pp. 651–2.

[144] See Johnson, *History*, pp. 652–4.

[145] Jenkins, 'Politics in Ibadan', p. 112.

[146] Johnson, *History*, p. 627.

[147] *Ibid.*, p. 628.

[148] *Ibid.*, p. 629.

Before they could proceed, the senior chiefs had to meet and settle their differences, 'or they might find it difficult to govern the town peaceably'. This was because the town had been looted on numerous occasions whilst they had been at the battlefield, particularly by the slaves and followers of *Balogun* Osungbekun and *Agbakin* Fajinmi. Futhermore, the Ibadan chiefs 'had long been ashamed of the *Balogun* as their commander-in-chief, because he was so given up to liquor.... At the seat of war the *Balogun* was supreme and absolute, nothing could therefore be done; but at home it was otherwise.'[149] When the chiefs went to meet *Balogun* Osungbekun (the head of *ile* Orowusi), 'they found him in his usual inebriate condition'. He insulted them and, predictably, they plotted to depose him.

The Ibadan chiefs' intention became clear at the conclusion of the procession ceremonies. When these celebrations were over, the chiefs normally accompanied their acknowledged head to his compound. On this occasion, they returned to their households independently. According to Johnson, two days after their return to the town, *Balogun* Osungbekun realised his political isolation. He entrusted *Agbakin* Fajinmi with 'large presents' for delivery to the conspirators. But the *Agbakin* was concerned for his own safety and dissociated from the *Balogun*, keeping the gifts for himself.[150]

On 26 March 1893 Governor Carter arrived in Ibadan to negotiate his third treaty. In this case, however, he was unsuccessful; partly because he tried to negotiate through *Balogun* Osungbekun 'not knowing what was going on underneath'. The chiefs refused to sign the document he had drawn up and stated that the proposal for a British Resident 'was repugnant to them':

> They objected that they had been absent from home about seventeen years; they had only just arrived, the town was as yet without a head; they were not yet settled down for civil adminis-tration and hence there was no one authorized to act in an official position. These essentials must be seen to before they could consider any treaty or agreement.[151]

Carter eventually left for Lagos, warning the Ibadan chiefs that they would soon have to sign, whatever their preferences. He later publicly accused one of his Ibadan-born interpreters of dissuading the chiefs from complying with his demands.[152]

The interpreter concerned, Andrew Hethersett, was acquainted with Samuel Johnson.[153] However, Johnson appears more offended by the Governor's implicit view of the Ibadan chiefs, than by the insult given to his former colleague in the CMS: 'His Excellency might have allowed such men as could govern a town like Ibadan and all its dependencies some credit of knowing their own minds. As soon as the Governor left Ibadan the *Balogun*'s troubles began afresh.'[154] He attributes great importance to the Ibadan chiefs' need to depose *Balogun* Osungbekun before they signed the treaty. Later scholars have analysed the incident as 'internal politics' and presented it as separate from the 'external negotiations' instigated by

[149] *Ibid.*
[150] *Ibid.*
[151] *Ibid.*
[152] *Ibid.*, p. 632.
[153] Doortmont, 'Recapturing the Past', p. 96.
[154] Johnson, *ibid*, p. 632.

Carter.[155] However, it would seem that as far as the Ibadan chiefs were concerned, these machinations were part of the treaty-making process.

A meeting was held at Oja'ba after Carter left Ibadan; the townspeople decided that Osungbekun should commit suicide. Johnson's explanation is the most explicit of his text:

> A *Balogun* who has won no victory has a small chance with the Ibadans. The *Balogun* received the message with much indignation; he was determined not to die but to fight it out. When his determination was known, the people were also determined to meet him; already his quarter of the town was being deserted, for they had began to seize people about his quarters. Private messages were quickly sent to his brothers. 'You know the consequences: will you allow your father's house to be wiped off at Ibadan?' They knew very well that when the people assailed a house, it is to level it with the ground, and make it a dunghill, and the family – such as remain alive – dispersed for ever: no member thereof ever to hold a public position in the town, for fear of his rising to power hereafter and taking revenge on the children of the perpetrators.[156]

Given this potentially dire outcome, members of Osungbekun's compound murdered him at the end of April 1893. Johnson concludes: 'He was buried with full military honours as befits a *Balogun* of Ibadan.'[157] The honour and related civic status of his household, *ile* Orowusi, was saved. The *mogaji* who succeeded Osungbekun was actually called Ola. He also rose to the post of *Balogun*. In 1917, he committed suicide, after he was informed that the people of Ibadan rejected him.[158]

By 6 June 1893, Governor Carter knew of the death of *Balogun* Osungbekun. His response was ominous:

> Let me impress upon you the very serious consequences that may ensue should you fail to keep your people in proper order. The Ibadans have now for many years been the friends of the Lagos Government and it is the sincere desire of all your well wishers that the relationship between the two places shall grow more intimate and to this end I recommend you to ponder well over the Treaty.[159]

Just over a fortnight later, twenty-three chiefs were installed at Ibadan. Among these, *Abese Balogun* Fijabi became *Bale* and *Areago Balogun* Akintola, who was from *ile* Ibikunle, took the post of *Balogun*.[160] The Ibadan chiefs then informed Governor Carter that they would reconsider the treaty. Since Carter was on leave, Acting-Governor Denton replied, stating that he would come to Ibadan on 9 August. Following his arrival, he did not meet the chiefs, but appointed Rev. Olubi and Robert Oyebode as his mediators.[161]

Oyebode presented the treaty to the chiefs on 12 August. Two days later, he wrote to Denton, detailing their several objections. They rejected the posting of a British Resident to Ibadan and opposed the establishment of an alternative Court of Appeal. They raised fears that their slaves would abscond to the Resident and that their wives

[155] Awe, 'The Rise of Ibadan', pp. 322–7; Falola, *Politics and Economy*, pp. 30–1; Jenkins, 'Politics in Ibadan', pp.113–15.

[156] Johnson, *History*, p. 632.

[157] *Ibid.*, p. 633.

[158] Jenkins, 'Politics in Ibadan', p. 235.

[159] Carter to the Mayes and Agbakin, 6 June 1893. Jenkins, 'Politics in Ibadan', p. 115.

[160] Johnson, *History*, p. 637.

[161] Jenkins, 'Politics in Ibadan', p. 116.

would be taken by the Hausa constabulary, whom the Governor intended to station in the city. Finally, they asserted: 'We consider our land as our inalienable property inherited from our forefathers, and never subject to sale.... If the Governor will see that our rights are not trespassed we make no scruple to sign all the terms of the Treaty.'[162]

To accede to the chiefs' requests, Denton would have had to redraft the document. Instead, he evaded all their protests and replied that the treaty did not 'contemplate interference with the Native Government of Ibadan in any way'. Its objectives, he asserted, were 'to preserve peace, to secure open roads and reasonable freedom of action to the inhabitants generally'.[163] With the threat of military force looming, Ibadan was left with little choice. On 15 August 1893 twenty-two chiefs affixed their marks to the Ibadan Agreement, without ever having met Denton and his party.[164] Of the chiefs installed on 23 June, only *Ekerin Balogun* Suberu did not sign; it is unclear why. By December, despite the chiefs' earlier objections, Resident Captain Bower had stationed himself on the eastern outskirts of the city, together with a force of about 100 Hausa soldiers.[165]

As far as the Ibadan war chiefs were concerned, wrote the historian Isaac Akinyele, 'they regarded all as dreams, for they did not give up hope of waging war.'[166] He suggested they viewed the Agreement as a momentary respite from the battlefield, allowing time to prepare for a more vigorous military expedition.[167] Johnson reported that a common question in Ibadan during 1894 was: '*Nje Bower k'oni si ogun Ilorin yi fun wa?* Will not Captain Bower open an Ilorin campaign for us? To be at home with nothing to do was rather irksome for those whose trade was war'.[168]

In January 1894, Governor Carter learned that some of the chiefs had led a slave-raiding expedition. This was most likely necessary to shore up their political support within Ibadan. As far as Carter was concerned, their actions were 'hostile to all good Government'.[169] Two months later, he accused the Ibadan chiefs of seeking Ilorin's assistance to expel his officers and their Hausa troops. He threatened to arrest *Bale* Fijabi and warned:

> You cannot imagine that you would be able to withstand the power of the British Government which you would be fighting against, for you have to consider not only Lagos, but the power which is behind it.... I feel sure that you will not impose upon me the necessity of using harsh measures, but the Government of Ibadan *must* be carried on in the way I wish and I shall not hesitate to apply compulsion if such a course is thrust upon me by the headstrong action of your Government.[170] [Emphasis in the original.]

[162] This letter, as well as Denton's reply, are reprinted in Johnson, *History*, pp. 638–40.

[163] *Ibid.* p. 640.

[164] When Oyebode had the treaty signed, he was accompanied by a thirteen year-old Isaac Akinyele who informed Jenkins that the Ibadan chiefs never actually met Denton. Kenneth W. Post and George D. Jenkins, *The Price of Liberty: Personality and Politics in Colonial Nigeria* (Cambridge, 1973), p. 17.

[165] Johnson, *History*, p. 641.

[166] Akinyele, *Outlines*, p. 74.

[167] Akinyele, *Iwe Itan Ibadan*, p. 122.

[168] Johnson, *History*, p. 643.

[169] Carter to *Bale* Fijabi, January 1894 (the precise date is not given). Jenkins, 'Politics in Ibadan', p. 123.

[170] Carter to *Bale* Fijabi, 7 March 1894. *Ibid.*, p. 125.

Johnson claimed that although the charge was false, 'it seemed necessary in high quarters to do something which would strike terror into the whole country'.[171]

Once it had been signed, the terms of the 1893 Agreement were to be enforced, not negotiated. The Ibadan polity's loss of sovereignty was becoming apparent. In its place, at least from the British point of view, was a staged imperial order. Thus in May 1895, Acting-Resident Dr Rice sent an invitation to the Aremo Mission for a ceremony commemorating Queen Victoria's birthday. Despite his efforts, there was minimal enthusiasm in the town:

> [Dr Rice] was expecting us all this morning but none of us went, neither the chiefs, nor the Mohammedans, only a few heathens attended it. I heard he stood under the flag but saw nobody. The soldiers paraded & fired 21 salutes.[172]

Later that year, *Bale* Fijabi died. Without warfare, the procedure for chieftaincy promotion was unclear. Nonetheless, *Balogun* Akintola and his followers 'still entertained the hope that the white men would soon go, and then he would be able to carry the Title of *Balogun* to war.'[173] Akintola's motivations were economic and ideological – as well as booty and followers, he sought to 'prove his worth to the title'.[174] As the current *mogaji* of his compound put it: 'He had no job other than war, he loved to go to war. *Oyinbo* [British] had power – he wanted to go to war.'[175]

Since Akintola was unwilling to resign his post, *Otun Bale* Osuntoki was promoted. This was the first occasion that a chief on the *Bale* line had risen to its top rank. However, Osuntoki had previously been *Maye Balogun* and, backed by Akintola, he had competed with Fijabi for the *Bale* post in 1893. It was not unusual that he succeeded on his second attempt. Following *Bale* Osuntoki's death in January 1897, *Balogun* Akintola still refused to abandon his title. Instead, 'he sold the post to Fajimi the Otun Bale'.[176] Fajinmi had been the *Agbakin* in 1893 and a subordinate chief of *Balogun* Osungbekun; he had only managed to stay alive by severing his allegiance. In the end, a month after Fajinmi's installation, *Balogun* Akintola's military ambitions were proven unattainable by events further north.

Following an insurrection against him during September 1895, Emir Moma of Ilorin committed suicide. Subsequently, his successor Emir Suleiman vigorously opposed British attempts to extend their imperial jurisdiction.[177] After Captain Bower shelled the Oyo palace in November of the same year, Ilorin intransigence increased. The attack on Oyo was provoked by the 'defiance' of the *Alaafin*, who continued to make eunuchs to run his palace affairs after 1893. Eunuchs were central to the power structure of the Oyo palace; Bower's attack aimed to undermine Oyo sovereignty and assert British supremacy.[178]

---

[171] Johnson, *History*, p. 644.

[172] KDL, IAP: Allen, 1895 Diary, 24 May.

[173] Akinyele, *Outlines*, p. 13.

[174] Johnson, *History*, p. 284.

[175] *Mogaji* Ibikunle, interviewed 24 November 1995, Ibadan.

[176] Akinyele, *Outlines*, p. 14. Akinyele uses a different spelling of Fajinmi to that of Johnson.

[177] H.O. Danmole, 'The Abortive Peace Missions: Intervention of Lagos Muslims in Anglo–Ilorin Boundary Dispute, 1894–96', *Journal of the Historical Society of Nigeria* 13 (1985–86), p. 71.

[178] J.A. Atanda, *The New Oyo Empire: Indirect Rule and Change in Western Nigeria 1894–1934* (London, 1973), pp. 56–77.

Ibadan Makes History

After Oyo's subordination, the Ilorin war chiefs established a military guard south of their city and Emir Suleiman warned Denton, who was then Acting Colonial Secretary, that any messengers he sent to Ilorin would be killed. It was also reported that Ilorin sent emissaries to neighbouring towns, requesting that they have nothing to do with white men and proposing that they all combine to expel them from the region. In March and April 1896, the Ilorin army suffered heavy casualties in two attacks on Lagos government troops stationed at Odo Otin, a military camp between Ilorin and Ibadan.[179]

The Royal Niger Company (RNC) agreed to crush Ilorin hostility to the Lagos government in April 1896. However, since he was preparing for an assault on the Nupe, George Goldie, the Governor of the RNC, was unwilling to move immediately.[180] In Lagos, Governor Carter requested Colonial Office permission to launch his own attack and stated: 'Ten thousand Ibadans could be got at a week's notice to join such an expedition, and it would be a labour of love to them.'[181] However, London refused to sanction such a scheme; thus Carter initiated a diplomatic effort and maintained an economic blockade.[182]

Ilorin held strong and refused to capitulate. In January 1897, Lagos forces inflicted a heavy defeat on Ilorin soldiers at Erinmope. RNC troops began moving southward from Jebba to Ilorin on 10 February 1897. On 16 February, they forced their way into the city after two days of heavy fighting. Goldie installed himself in the Emir's palace and hoisted the British flag in front of it. Ilorin was conquered.[183]

Later that year, F.C. Fuller, Ibadan's second British Resident, suggested that 'since the pacification of Ilorin is assured' the Hausa military force stationed at Odo Otin could be withdrawn and added to the constabulary at Ibadan. He also advised that a second Resident be appointed to 'overhaul' the eastern portion of the former Ibadan Empire.[184] Although this was not done, the British victory against Ilorin was significant for sealing the fate of Ibadan militarism. The warrior chiefs were thwarted and would never again take to the field. This political shift had far-reaching implications for the realisation of Ibadan as a civic community. In the next chapter, we begin to explore them.

---

[179] R.A. Adeleye, *Power and Diplomacy in Northern Nigeria, 1804–1906: the Sokoto Caliphate and its Enemies* (London, 1971), p. 185.

[180] John E. Flint, *Sir George Goldie and the Making of Nigeria* (London, 1960), p. 238.

[181] Carter to Chamberlain, 4 May 1896. Quoted in *ibid.*, p. 239.

[182] Danmole, 'Abortive Peace Missions', p. 72.

[183] Adeleye, *Power and Diplomacy*, p. 187.

[184] NAI, Iba. Prof. 3/6: Fuller, The Resident's Travelling Journal, 5 July 1897 (hereafter, Resident's Journal).

4

A Greater Punishment than Death
Warrior Chiefs & Early Colonial Rule

Before he went on leave in July 1905, Resident Captain Elgee wrote a list of 'General Instructions' for Major Reeve-Tucker, the officer who was to administer Ibadan in his absence. Drawing attention to the rivalries characteristic of Ibadan politics, he advised: 'To, in everything concerning the welfare of the Provinces, work through and with the Ruling Chiefs and their Councils ... for confidence begets confidence, and frequent Council meetings are the safety valves of conspiracy.'[1]

Nearly five months later, *Bale* Dada addressed a Council meeting in his compound. He directed his speech at *Otun Bale* Apanpa:

> *Otun*, you know the large number of my people whom you made a secret covenant with in order to injure me. You invited Medicine men to this Town and instructed them to poison me in order that I may die and you be made the *Bale*. Had it not been for the protection of God and the white man, you would have killed me, and all my children would have been wiped off from the face of the earth.[2]

This meeting had been arranged by a delegation of six Muslims from Lagos. On arrival in Ibadan, they had reported to Acting Resident Reeve-Tucker, claiming to be sent by senior Lagos chiefs and 'with the knowledge and sanction' of the Colonial Secretary. Their intention was 'to settle differences which they stated existed between the *Bale* and *Otun Bale* of Ibadan'. They asserted their motives were 'philanthropic'; no 'interested party' had requested their involvement.[3] However, at the meeting on 26 November, *Otun Bale* Apanpa admitted: 'The Lagos men who came did not come without my knowledge. If I cry to Lagos it is not bad. If a superior person is quarrelling with one, the one must have some person to beg the Superior person. I have cried to Lagos.'[4]

---

[1] NAI, CSO 16/7 C.176/1905: Elgee to Reeve-Tucker, 7 July 1905.
[2] NAI, Iba. Prof. 3/10; Letter Book 1904/11: Minutes of a Meeting at *Bale* Dada's house, 26 October 1905. Enclosure A, Scruby (for Acting Resident Reeve-Tucker) to Colonial Secretary Speed, 9 November 1905. Another copy of this file is in NAI, CSO 16/7 C. 205/1905.
[3] NAI, Iba. Prof. 3/10: Scruby to Speed, 9 November 1905.
[4] NAI, Iba. Prof. 3/10: Minutes, 26 October 1905.

A Greater Punishment than Death

When the Colonial Secretary, Edwin Speed, heard of the incident, he maintained that neither he nor any Lagos chiefs had consented to the delegation's visit. Rather, he suggested, the group had come to Ibadan 'on behalf of their co-religionist'. Who the members of the delegation were is unknown, but there was a precedent for their intervention. Ten years earlier, a group of Lagos Muslims had tried to end the conflict between Ibadan and Ilorin by diplomatic means.[5] In 1905, Speed acknowledged that it was difficult to prevent such interventions but insisted: 'That they should do so under the pretence of a mission from the Government is of course grossly improper.'[6]

In August 1907 Resident Elgee was once more on furlough. Rev. Daniel Williams, who was an assistant to the Ibadan Council, wrote about a growing agitation against *Bale* Dada in his diary. On 19 August, *Otun Bale* Apanpa 'displayed his police' during a meeting called at Oja'ba to settle the misunderstanding.[7] A week later, the chiefs formally lodged their complaints against Dada with Rev. Williams, leaving 'with the shout of "we don't want the *Bale*!"'[8]

Alexander Akinyele, a colleague of Rev. Williams, wrote to a friend in Lagos that same day.[9] He informed him that the chiefs were determined to depose *Bale* Dada and commented: 'I don't know whether they will be able, considering that the British Government stand at the *Bale*'s back.'[10] The charges against Dada were first, that he habitually abused his chiefs and second, that he harboured robbers to steal for him. Akinyele later claimed that although the first charge was true, the second was groundless and his accusers were 'much more guilty'.[11]

---

[5] Danmole, 'Abortive Peace Missions', pp. 67–82.

[6] NAI, Iba. Prof. 3/10: Speed to Reeve-Tucker, 9 November 1905.

[7] KDL, Diaries of Rev. D.A. Williams: 1907 Diary, 19 August (hereafter, WD: 1907/19 August). During 1904, Resident Elgee's attempt to formally appoint Rev. Williams to the Ibadan Council failed; however, it appears he maintained an advisory role. NAI, CSO 16/6 C.133/1904: Colonial Secretary Harley Moseley to Elgee, 5 October 1904. Daniel Williams was a tailor who, after completing his missionary training in Lagos, came to Ibadan during 1890 as the schoolmaster of the CMS Kudeti school. He was ordained deacon of the Ogunpa mission in 1905 and retired in 1940. See Samuel Layode, 'Rebirth of Ibadan Town History', unpublished manuscript. I am very grateful to Professor Awe for allowing me access to this unique document (hereafter Layode Mss).

[8] KDL, WD: 1907/27 August.

[9] Alexander Babatunde Akinyele (1875–1968) was a son of Josiah Akinyele and Abigail Lapemo from *ile* Bolude and *ile* Kukomi respectively, two prominent Ibadan households. After early education at Aremo mission school from his uncle, Robert Oyebode, he went to Lagos in 1888. Five years later he entered the CMS Grammar School, Lagos and afterwards taught in mission schools. During 1904–06 he attended Fourah Bay College, Sierra Leone; in 1910 he became the first Ibadan man to receive a BA. On his return to Ibadan in 1907 he became a catechist under Rev. Olubi and was ordained to the priesthood in 1910. He founded the Ibadan Grammar School in 1913 and was its principal until 1933. In 1925 Fourah Bay College admitted him to a Master of Arts degree which he was awarded in 1948. After his consecration as Bishop in 1933 he was placed in charge of the Ondo District of Lagos Diocese. In 1951 he became Bishop of the newly created Ibadan Diocese and retired three years later. He was awarded the CBE in 1949. Along with his brother Isaac, he played a pivotal role in Ibadan politics throughout his adult life. See T.A. Adebiyi, *The Beloved Bishop* (Ibadan, 1969).

[10] KDL, Bishop A.B. Akinyele Papers, Box 7, Letter Book, 1907–1908 (hereafter, BAP: 7/1907–08). A.B. Akinyele to W.H. Hewitt, 27 August 1907.

[11] KDL, BAP: 7/1907–08, A.B. Akinyele to Bishop Tugwell, 21 February 1908.

Throughout the next month, Rev. Williams attended several meetings and attempted to mediate a resolution of the dispute. Nevertheless, when Resident Elgee returned at the end of October, the agitation had reached its peak. On 4 November Elgee 'went to the Chiefs and advised reconciliation'.[12] His plea was not heeded. Five days later, Rev. Williams reported: 'The town in uproar today. People cried about they refused the *Bale*.'[13] Alexander Akinyele later described how 'sometimes for half the night townspeople would go about with drums etc., singing abusive songs of their *Bale* and those loyal to him'.[14]

On 14 November: 'Capt. Elgee went to the *Bale* & gave him two alternatives. Resign or be confiscated.'[15] The second option referred to the destruction of an *ile* by Ibadan townspeople. Elgee did not mention this potential for unrest in a letter to his superiors in Lagos. Instead, he encouraged acceptance of the first option:

> The grounds on which he is to resign are inability to further carry on the work of his office owing to the estrangement of his Council, Chiefs and People. He has lost their confidence and after the most grave and careful consideration, I can see no possibility of his ever gaining it. It is not a case of the *Bale* against one or two particular Chiefs but of, with a few unimportant exceptions, the whole body of Chiefs against the *Bale*.[16]

A month later, Governor Egerton had arranged for Dada to receive a £200 annual pension on condition that he left his office.[17] In Ibadan, however, this form of resignation was unheard of. As Isaac Akinyele[18] recalled in 1938: 'He was openly rejected, deposed and asked to die or quit the Town. Dada preferred suicide to deportation which he did on the 16th December 1907.'[19]

Commenting on the incident, Akinyele wrote:

> Dada was the first *Bale* of Ibadan to suffer this kind fate because till then, there was no *Bale* of Ibadan ever deposed or deported. It was very surprising that this innovation occurred in this age of light and so-called civilisation; the *Bale*s before advent of the British Government had all powers; but at present they had none: the British Government had all the Power; one would succeed who could only enlist their sympathy.[20]

---

[12] KDL, WD: 1907/4 November.

[13] KDL, WD: 1907/9 November.

[14] KDL, BAP: 7/1907–08, A.B. Akinyele to Tugwell, 21 February 1908.

[15] KDL, WD: 1907/14 November.

[16] NAI, Iba. Prof. 3/10: Elgee to Speed, 14 November 1907.

[17] T.N. Tamuno, *The Evolution of the Nigerian State. The Southern Phase, 1898–1914* (London, 1972), p. 220.

[18] Isaac Babalola Akinyele (1882–1964) was a younger brother of Alexander. He began schooling at the Aremo mission and then accompanied his uncle Robert Oyebode to Ilesha in 1895. Three years later he entered the CMS Grammar School in Lagos. In 1901 he briefly became a tailor's apprentice; two years later he became a tolls clerk in the Ibadan Native Government under *Bale* Mosaderin and Resident Elgee. Before resigning administrative office in 1923 to farm, he wrote and published his history text, *Iwe Itan Ibadan*. Subsequently, he became deeply embroiled in Ibadan politics and eventually became *Olubadan* in 1955. Unlike his brother, he left the Anglican Church in 1925 and was closely involved with the development of the Christ Apostolic Church. He was awarded the OBE in 1948. See A. Ogunranti, *I Know a Man, a Saint* (Ibadan, 1964) and J.A. Ayorinde, *Oba Akinyele* (Ibadan, 1974).

[19] Akinyele, *Outlines*, p. 18. Although this text was not published until 1946, there is evidence within the text that Akinyele translated it from his *Iwe Itan Ibadan* during 1938.

[20] *Ibid.*, p. 19.

A Greater Punishment than Death

This version of the past is motivated by a retrospective disappointment that British authority accepted Ibadan people's rejection of *Bale* Dada. Writing two months after the chief's suicide, the historian's brother, Alexander, remarked that the *Bale*: 'was hoping government would step in to force the people to submission'.[21] British rule had ended the regional wars and brought a new group of outsiders – colonial administrators – into Ibadan politics. As far as Isaac Akinyele was concerned, their incorporation symbolised *olaju* or 'enlightenment'.[22] However, he saw British acquiescence to Ibadan intrigue as decidedly unenlightened.

Although Dada was the first *Bale* to be deposed in Ibadan, he was by no means the first chief. Alexander Akinyele did not describe the incident as unusual. Instead, he suggested it indicated the escalation of political sacrifice in the city:

> Since the tide turned the poor man resorted to the method generally adopted by native rulers of bringing an end to his own life ... Apanpa is now ruling in his place. One chief after another had to die a similar death in this town; the number of the sacrificed chiefs (if I can do use the language) has increased much, that one feels afraid whether the blood of these men will not cry in judgement against the land.[23]

What did *Bale* Dada's suicide signify? At face value, the incident was a dramatic enactment of the power rivalries between the Ibadan chiefs themselves and their competing groups of followers. Although the colonial presence was obviously a factor in the conspiracy, resonances of the 'civil disorder' of pre-colonial Ibadan are apparent.

Surprisingly, in his influential doctoral thesis, Jenkins does not acknowledge this similarity. He attributes such unrest to the political changes caused by the end of Ibadan's external military campaigns and the often unwitting intervention of British administrative officers in chieftaincy affairs.[24] The agitation against Dada, he contends, reveals that the *raison d'être* of Ibadan government was eliminated by the peace brought by the 1893 Agreement. Consequently, he posits, 'the relevance of chieftaincy as a constitutional form began a long and undignified decline'.[25]

I will argue that such a view is misconceived. First, the suicide of a chief was a common event in Ibadan politics; it does not inevitably suggest 'constitutional decline'. Secondly, Jenkins's analysis presents the 'disarray in the chieftaincy structure' as a result of the negative impact of colonial rule, an impact which necessitates further administrative intervention.[26] This account neglects an analysis of the agency and motivations of Ibadan chiefs and people in fomenting unrest.

In my view, the *Bale* Dada episode indicates that, far from declining, 'the relevance of chieftaincy as a constitutional form' was actually *increasing*. As I have already suggested, the plot manifests the civil strife which characterised the Ibadan polity. At the same time, according to Rev. Akinyele, there was another, more specific, factor involved:

[21] KDL, BAP: 7/1907–08, A.B. Akinyele to Tugwell, 21 February 1908.

[22] J.D.Y. Peel, '*Olaju*: a Yoruba Concept of Development', *Journal of Development Studies* 14 (1978), p. 144.

[23] KDL, BAP: 7/1907–08, A.B. Akinyele to Tugwell, 21 February 1908.

[24] Jenkins, 'Politics in Ibadan', p. 82.

[25] *Ibid.*, p. 83. Jenkins repeats this contention in a published version of his account, 'Government and Politics in Ibadan', in *The City of Ibadan*, pp. 213–33.

[26] Jenkins, 'Politics in Ibadan', p. 82.

They hated him because he was stingy – he would not spend for them; but no one could bring this as an accusation.

One thing I regard as a crime is the man is avaricious; he would pervert any judgement for money; now, this is more heinous but his people did not bring this as an accusation & it is probable that they themselves are not innocent on that point.[27]

Bale Dada's suicide was not an isolated incident. It was the outcome of an ongoing and increasingly fierce contest over the material and ideological bases of political mobilisation in Ibadan city.

During the pre-colonial period, militarism and civil disorder generated a civic Ibadan. The economic rewards won by the Ibadan army were slaves, booty and tribute payments extracted from the inhabitants of conquered towns. Battle prowess was the foundation of civic power – it provided a body of followers combined with *ola*. However, after 1897, external warfare ended. Without war spoils, chiefs had to find alternative means to meet their expenses and maintain their followings. In the absence of the battlefield, the strategy for attaining promotion in the chieftaincy ranks was unclear. At the same time, British officials tried to use the warrior chiefs as their governing agents.

To investigate the practices which Ibadan chiefs adopted to manage this complex political context, this chapter will explore a murder trial and the administration of justice during the early colonial period. The first part of this account uses notes taken by a clerk in the courtroom where the trial took place. These notes are in English, but it is important to realise that the language of the trial would have been Yoruba, apart from the interventions of the British Resident and his interpreter. Thus using these records as a source of 'historical reconstruction' is inherently problematic. Furthermore, as Rathbone points out, court transcripts are 'cold documents' and they do not enable us to see the demeanour of witnesses or feel the atmosphere of the courtroom.[28] Consequently, I do not reconstruct the murder case for the purpose of determining the guilt or innocence of those accused of the crime. Rather, my interest is in a constitutional issue that, I argue, informed the way the trial played out. In this context, let us begin with the final judgment.

Murder and the political body

On 8 November 1902, *Bale* Mosaderin and ten Ibadan chiefs passed judgement against three men found guilty of murder. They considered them 'worthy of death' but recommended a fine 'be inflicted' on two of the perpetrators, and the third imprisoned. The Acting British Resident, Dr Arthur Pickels, thought the sentence too lenient. After reconsideration, the Ibadan Council raised the fines imposed on each of the convicted from £50 to £75 pounds. Pickels questioned their decision once again. *Balogun* Apanpa rose as spokesman and stated:

---

[27] KDL, BAP: 7/1907–08, A.B. Akinyele to Tugwell, 21 February 1908.

[28] Richard Rathbone, 'A Murder in the Colonial Gold Coast: Law and Politics in the 1940s', *Journal of African History* 30 (1989), p. 450. See also Rathbone, *Murder and Politics in Colonial Ghana* (New Haven, 1993).

A Greater Punishment than Death

The Council considered that a heavy fine was a greater punishment than death and would act as greater deterrent in future. If people think that they will only be killed if convicted of murder they will not think much of it.[29]

The following day, Pickels forwarded the trial notes to his superiors in Lagos. He wrote that although he felt the sentence was inadequate, 'taking into consideration that I believe they [the accused] have only been the instruments of a higher authority I think that perhaps terms of imprisonment would meet the case'.[30] The Attorney-General, Edwin Speed, gave his opinion on 12 November: 'The *Balogun*'s assertion that a heavy fine is considered a worse punishment than death is difficult to believe, though his statement that it is not the custom to execute powerful murderers is credible enough.'[31]

Speed admitted his own personal judgement was that two of the men, Salako and Aderuntan, should be liable for the death penalty. However, considering Pickels's view, he wrote that ten years' imprisonment was acceptable. For the third, Menasara, he recommended five years' imprisonment.[32] Governor MacGregor agreed that a fine was 'quite inadequate' and concurred that the sentences suggested by Speed should be imposed as the 'least punishment'.[33] Two weeks later, Acting Resident Pickels requested that a warrant be issued for the removal of the prisoners from Ibadan to Lagos.[34] The Ibadan chiefs never received payment of the £150 fine.

The trial of Salako, Aderuntan and Menasara provides a view of political culture in early colonial Ibadan. If one looks at the case closely, it becomes evident that debate about the homicide was embedded within a constitutional arena of chieftaincy. Only within this arena does *Balogun* Apanpa's claim 'that a heavy fine was a greater punishment than death' become comprehensible. However, before investigating the murder, it is necessary to set the scene.

Chiefs and organised crime

Salu came to Ibadan as a runaway slave from Abeokuta, although he was originally from Ilorin.[35] Two of the accused and two witnesses at the trial for his murder referred to him as a *Gambari*.[36] By this term he was placed in a particular category of people who were described in 1899 as 'belonging to any tribe beyond the Niger'.[37] More specifically, he was Hausa – a group who had been in Ibadan since the 1840s

[29] NAI, CSO 16/4 C.87/1902: 'Notes taken at the trial of Salako, Menasara and Aderuntan before the Ibadan Council on November 8th 1902'.

[30] NAI, CSO 16/4 C.87/1902: Pickels to Reeves, 9 November 1902.

[31] NAI, CSO 16/4 C.87/1902: Speed to Reeves, 12 November 1902.

[32] *Ibid.*

[33] NAI, CSO 16/4 C.87/1902: MacGregor to Reeves, 19 November 1902.

[34] NAI, CSO 16/4 C.87/1902: Pickels to Reeves, 1 December 1902.

[35] NAI, CSO 16/4 C.87/1902: 'Evidence taken before the Ag. Resident and *Bale*'s Messenger at the Advisory Court Ibadan in the case of the murder of a Cowherd, Salu by name, on Sunday Oct. 5th 1902.' Igana Statement, 13 October 1902.

[36] *Ibid.* Aderuntan Statement, 14 October 1902; Salako Statement, 14 October 1902; Sumanu Statement, 13 October 1902; Babalola Statement, 14 October 1902.

[37] NAI, Iba. Prof. 3/6: Fuller, Resident's Journal, 21 January 1899.

and were among its earliest non-Oyo settlers. They were first accommodated by *Basorun* Oluyole, a warrior chief who owned extensive kola-nut plantations in and around the town.[38] The Hausa rapidly established themselves as middlemen in a trading exchange of cattle and kola-nut between the northern savannah and southern forest zones.[39]

After military raids were stopped in 1894, many Ibadan soldiers suffered material deprivation and the economic success of Hausa settlers became increasingly resented. From about 1896, they were the target of hostility. Opposition to their presence in Ibadan focused on their monopoly over the kola-nut trade, their association with the Governor's constabulary and their criminal activities. A rumour enjoining Ibadan people to kill any Hausa suspected of stealing began to circulate.[40] As we shall see, it seems this rumour still had currency in 1902.

Resident Fuller intervened during July 1897. He demanded that *Gambari* deposit their weapons and proposed 'to issue permits to those Gambaris who can satisfy me that they are here for the pursuit of an honest trade.'[41] In spite of this effort, over the next few years, many Gambari became 'a great trouble' by involving themselves in 'raiding and pillaging'.[42] As Falola has noted, this was part of a general rise in the prevalence of robbery in Ibadan during the 1890s. Since the livelihood of war could no longer be depended upon, some warrior chiefs turned to brigandage in the city as an economically rewarding venture.[43] They cooperated with members of the Governor's Hausa constabulary, who assisted by sheltering the thieves in their barracks.[44]

In June 1898, a Council meeting addressed the crime problem. Acting Resident Ehrhardt noted that *Gambari* were 'the worst offenders' and suggested that chiefs 'form a sort of police for each district of the town'.[45] A month later, *Osi Balogun* Kongi, a grandson of *Basorun* Ogunmola, was accused of sponsoring the thieving gangs. Kongi was a distinguished warrior, having been appointed *Areago Balogun* as far back as 1879.[46] In 1898, Acting Resident Ehrhardt reported: 'The *Bale* is trying to hush the case up.' The chiefs met to judge Kongi early the next week:

> He was found guilty of harbouring Gambaris, in contravention of the rule of the Council & the order of the *Bale* & was fined £50–£30 to go in compensation. The chiefs were pleased that he had not been publicly disgraced. I told them that if it had been proved that he participated in the Gambaris plunder or was cognisant of their robberies he would have been deposed & sent to the

[38] Morgan, *Akinyele's Outline (Part One)*, p. 86.

[39] This trade still exists today. See Abner Cohen, *Custom and Politics in Urban Africa. A Study of Hausa Migrants in Yoruba Towns* (London, 1969); Isaac Albert, 'The Growth of an Urban Migrant Community: The Hausa Settlements in Ibadan, *c*. 1830–1979', *Ife: Annals of the Institute of Cultural Studies* 4 (1993), pp. 1–15.

[40] Falola, 'Hospitality to Hostility', p. 65

[41] NAI, Iba. Prof. 3/6: Fuller, Resident's Journal, 24 July 1897.

[42] NAI, Iba. Prof. 3/6: Ehrhardt, Resident's Journal, 1898: 13,14, 16 May; 6 June; 16 August; 23 November. Fuller, 1899: 20, 21 January.

[43] Toyin Falola, 'Brigandage and Piracy in Nineteenth Century Yorubaland', *Journal of the Historical Society of Nigeria* 13 (December 1985–June 1986), p. 86.

[44] Cohen argues that 'Hausa Thieves' have remained a 'structural factor' in Ibadan ethnic politics throughout the twentieth century. See *Custom and Politics*, pp. 103–113.

[45] NAI, Iba. Prof. 3/6: Ehrhardt, Resident's Journal, 6 June 1898.

[46] Johnson, *History*, p. 438.

prison. The *Bale* expressed his gratitude freely & stated that in future his orders would be readily obeyed.[47]

There is little doubt that Kongi was directly involved in the robbery incidents. His *oriki* refer to the raids he made, which were carried out on horseback and with a retinue of drummers singing his praises.[48] Having previously proved his battle merit, Kongi brought the practice of winning war spoils right into Ibadan city, embodying his political status through thuggery and display of the large numbers of followers supporting him. The other chiefs most likely shared in the material rewards of his city raids; this would explain their reluctance to see him 'publicly disgraced'.

Four years later, the political climate had changed. After *Basorun* Fajinmi died in April 1902, his title became vacant.[49] Kongi maintained that even though he had not led the Ibadan army into the field, he was eligible for promotion from *Balogun*: 'He said it was folly to entertain the hope that the white men would go away and war will ensue. Kongi met with the united opposition of the whole Chiefs.'[50] This was the first time since the 1897 defeat of Ilorin that the *Bale* post had become available in Ibadan. The absence of external war had already caused one military title, that of the *Sarumi*, to become redundant.[51] *Balogun* Akintola had died in 1899, without ever having consolidated his authority through battle victories.[52] *Balogun* Kongi was unwilling to risk his own status being demeaned and thus refused to forfeit the *Bale* office.

The warrior chiefs, especially *Otun Balogun* Apanpa, opposed Kongi's claim. Apanpa pointed out that no *Balogun* had ever become the *Bale* and therefore Kongi 'had no right to be one'.[53] Although the four *Bale* installed during the nineteenth century had been *Balogun* chiefs, none had reached the highest rank of their line. They were able to succeed immediately to the *Bale* post as their seniors had been killed in battle.[54] By contrast, the two most powerful chiefs of the 1860s and 1870s, Ogunmola and Latosisa, set a precedent for Apanpa's case. Before assuming the posts of *Basorun* and *Are-ona-kakanfo* respectively, they had both been *Otun Balogun*.[55]

Neither Apanpa nor Kongi were successful in their bids to become *Bale*. Promoting Apanpa over Kongi could generate a conflict liable to destroy Ibadan altogether. Installing Kongi might enable him to extend his enterprise of robbery and extortion. Instead, *Otun Bale* Mosaderin was elected. A brother of *Balogun* Ogboriefon, he had been instrumental in the intrigue against *Seriki* Iyapo in 1877.[56] However, he did not become a chief until 1893, when he was installed *Ekerin Bale*.[57]

---

[47] NAI, Iba. Prof. 3/6: Ehrhardt, Resident's Journal, 26 July 1898.
[48] Akinyele, *Iwe Itan Ibadan*, p. 133.
[49] Fajinmi was installed *Bale* in 1897 and took the title of *Basorun* in 1900. Akinyele, *Outlines*, p. 14.
[50] *Ibid.*, p. 16.
[51] No chiefs were installed to this rank after 1893.
[52] NAI, Iba. Prof. 3/6: Fuller, Resident's Journal, 6 February 1899.
[53] Akinyele, *Outlines*, p. 16.
[54] *Bale* Opeagbe succeeded from *Osi Balogun* to *Bale* in 1850. *Osi* was the second chief under the *Balogun*. Both *Bale* Olugbode (1851) and *Bale* Fijabi (1893) were promoted from *Abese Balogun*, the seventh title in the line. Orowusi was *Asipa* before becoming *Bale* in 1870.
[55] Akinyele, *Outlines*, p. 9; p. 11.
[56] Johnson, *History*, p. 418.
[57] *Ibid.*, p. 637.

According to Resident Elgee, by 1902, he was: 'an invalid owing to the ill effects produced by over ten gunshot wounds which he had received in the wars of his youth. In consequence of this he [was] never able to take a conspicuous part in public affairs.'[58] The Ibadan chiefs probably elected him *because* of his age and frailty. In this way, they ensured that their *Bale* would not become too powerful.

By contrast, Kongi remained 'the strongest and most influential chief in Ibadan'.[59] According to Isaac Akinyele, 'the whole chiefs' rose to depose him by charging him with four offences: that he was harbouring robbers; that he had been insubordinate to both *Basorun* Fajinmi and *Bale* Mosaderin; that he had poisoned *Basorun* Fajinmi; that he 'was wicked, merciless and proud'.[60] On 2 September 1902, Acting Governor Harley Moseley approved Kongi's expulsion to Fesu Iwo, the birthplace of his grandfather Ogunmola. As Resident Elgee put it: 'he never returned alive'.[61]

Subsequently, Apanpa was promoted to *Balogun*, while *Otun Bale* Bamgbegbin took his post of *Otun Balogun*.[62] The post of *Osi Balogun* was given as a first title to the *mogaji* of *ile* Awanibaku, Akintayo, who had previously been an 'untitled soldier'. Interestingly, *ile* Awanibaku was a household which had formerly paid allegiance to *Basorun* Ogunmola as their *babaogun* – it appears that Akintayo gained his post on the basis of this connection. *Osi Balogun* was an exceptionally high title for a first installation, which suggests Akintayo played a role in the political downfall of Kongi.[63]

Custom and punishment

Amid these political manoeuvres, burglaries remained frequent in Ibadan. Resident Elgee recalled that, in 1900,

> The Bashorun asked permission to continue the ancient custom of cutting off the right hand for the first theft, the left for the second, and the feet for the third, if any. The Resident unfortunately could not see his way to grant this as it might be interpreted as being against the clause of the Ibadan Treaty, which stipulated that they should do no act not in accordance with the ordinary principles of humanity.[64]

There was in fact no such 'clause' in the 1893 Ibadan Agreement. Elgee probably referred to a letter written to the Ibadan chiefs by Acting Governor Denton the day before they signed the treaty. This letter assured the chiefs that the Resident to be stationed in Ibadan 'will not as at present proposed hold any court or take any action opposed to local customs and observances so long as they do not conflict with the ordinary principles of humanity'.[65]

---

[58] Rhodes House Library, Oxford (hereafter, RH), Mss. Afr. S.1169: E.H. Elgee, 'The Evolution of Ibadan', Typescript, p. 23. This text was originally published by the Lagos Government Printer in 1914, following Elgee's departure from Ibadan the previous year.

[59] *Ibid.*, p. 16.

[60] Akinyele, *Outlines*, pp. 16–17.

[61] RH, Mss. Afr. S.1169: Elgee, 'Evolution', p. 16.

[62] Akinyele, *Outlines*, p. 20; p. 38.

[63] *Ibid.*, p. 21; pp. 63–4. See also Johnson, *History*, p. 373.

[64] RH, Mss. Afr. S.1169: Elgee, 'Evolution', p. 12.

[65] Johnson, *History*, p. 639.

As Jenkins points out, the British defined these 'principles'.[66] Consequently, it was this assurance that later enabled colonial administrators to overrule chiefs' verdicts in certain cases, especially those which involved domestic slavery or allegations of witchcraft.[67] In 1900 'some trouble was caused by the chiefs executing two supposed murderers without permission. This led to a visit from Acting Governor Denton and the Bashorun was fined £100.'[68] It was after this incident that Fajinmi referred to the 'ancient custom' of maiming criminals. Since he rejected the practice as inhumane, Acting Resident Ehrhardt set about implementing his earlier proposal for the formation of a district police.[69] The town was divided into quarters and 'gangs of night watchmen' were stationed to guard particular areas.[70]

It is questionable whether the 'ancient custom' described by *Basorun* Fajinmi had ever been enforced in Ibadan. The punishments were likely to have been more severe. Samuel Layode reports that, between 1893 and 1895, when he was a 'house-boy' for Anna Williams (neé Olubi), it was still the practice for thieves to be executed: 'His head would be cut off and nailed to a certain tree in Iba Oluyole market.'[71] Rev. Oyebode described an 1877 criminal case which involved two hunters responsible for protecting the town walls. At this time, the Egba had imposed a blockade of trade routes to Ibadan and, although goods continued to be smuggled in, there was a serious salt shortage. Whilst on duty, one of the hunters had bartered 'a load of yam flour for an equivalent in salt'. His accomplice had then exchanged 'a load of corn for the same salt with the Egbas'.[72]

This salt was intended for the Ibadan market; thus the second transaction was considered to be a theft. The *babaogun* of the hunter who had traded away the salt was held responsible; he, not the hunter, was forced to kill one of his followers. Oyebode implied the case was heard by the Ibadan chiefs at Oja'ba: 'A man was killed in the market for the master [of the] corn matter.'[73] Nevertheless, this did not resolve the problem: 'The town men are not pacified, saying he who has two slaves to give may kill a freeborn with impunity.'[74] This suggests the townspeople contested the judgment, arguing that the *babaogun* did not have the right to kill

---

[66] Jenkins, 'Politics in Ibadan', p. 162.

[67] Throughout 1898 and 1899, Residents Fuller and Ehrhardt refer to 'hearing cases' but they do not usually provide details. When they do, slaves or 'juju' are usually mentioned. See NAI, Iba. Prof. 3/6: Resident's Journal. 1898: 10 May; 9 June; 2, 5, 21–22 July; 17, 23 August; 27, 29 October, 26 November. 1899: 2, 9 February; 14 March.

[68] RH, Mss. Afr. S.1169: Elgee, 'Evolution', p. 11.

[69] NAI, Iba. Prof. 3/6: Ehrhardt, Resident's Journal, 6 June 1898.

[70] RH, Mss. Afr. S.1169: Elgee, 'Evolution', p. 12.

[71] Layode Mss. Anna Olubi, a daughter of Rev. Olubi, married Daniel Williams in 1893. Samuel Layode (*c.* 1880–1965) was a son of 'Daddy Daniel Layode', a lay-preacher in the Kudeti mission. Daniel Williams was his headmaster at Aremo mission school in 1895. During 1901, Samuel was appointed as a 'produce clerk' for the firm of Patterson Zochonis. In this position, he installed weighing machines in numerous town markets and oversaw the transport of agricultural goods such as palm kernels and cocoa on the Lagos Railway. He resigned in 1926 to work independently. His unpublished manuscript of Ibadan history, preserved by Professor Awe, is an invaluable and hitherto unused source.

[72] KDL, IAP: Oyebode Diaries, 1877/24 September.

[73] *Ibid.*

[74] *Ibid.*

his follower without surrendering two of his slaves.[75]

A similar form of punishment was the confiscation of people and material goods from an *ile*. As we have seen, this practice was always threatened and sometimes practised against chiefs who had become unpopular.[76] It also apparently applied to criminal offences:

> If anyone in a compound offended, the offence might be great or small, the principal Chiefs like the *Bale* or the *Balogun* or the Council of Chiefs would order the plundering or devastation of the offenders compound, i.e. men, women and children met in the compound would be taken as captives and sold into slavery … every thing in the house would be taken; clothes, cattle, domestic utensils &c., all would be carried away never to be restored. Hundreds of houses were thus devasted and became desolate on account of minor offences which thousands committed today with impunity.[77]

These descriptions indicate that, in pre-colonial Ibadan, convicted felons were more likely to be killed or impoverished than disabled. If their victims were to be satisfied, some form of material compensation had to be arranged. Since maimed people were of a lesser value than healthy people, discipline via disablement would appear unsatisfactory to both sides. There is no mention of such an 'ancient custom' in Johnson's text; he also describes execution, fining or plunder as the usual punishments.[78]

In early colonial Ibadan, the threat of localised crime erupting into a full-scale Ibadan uprising plagued the minds of British administrators. During May 1901, Acting Resident Rice reported that there was a 'great deal of unrest in the town and talking against the white-man'. He requested the Officer in Charge of the Hausa constabulary 'to take any steps' necessary for equipping the force and to ensure an ample supply of ammunition.[79] Ibadan no doubt remained a dangerous place to live in 1902. In this dangerous political context, let us examine a narrative of murder.

Robbery, homicide and diplomacy[80]

Early on the morning of 5 October 1902, Salu left his wife Rekia, a seller of 'knick-knacks'. He told her he was 'going in search of a cow' and had ten pounds 'tied in his apron'.[81] Shortly afterwards, Salu met Talo, another cowherd with whom he worked;

---

[75] The meaning of this phrase is confusing. In my view, the context suggests that Oyebode meant to write 'may *not* kill a freeborn'. This interpretation explains why 'the town men' were unpacified. Nonetheless, whatever the precise meaning, my point is that maiming was not used as a punishment and that 'whole people' were considered exchangeable goods.

[76] *Foko* Aiyejenku suffered this punishment before he eventually committed suicide. See Chapter 3.

[77] Akinyele, *Outlines*, p. 70.

[78] Johnson, *History*, p. 322; pp. 373–6; pp. 501–2.

[79] NAI, CSO 16/3 C.34/1901: Rice to Moseley, 8 May 1901.

[80] In my reconstruction of Salu's murder and events immediately afterwards I have relied mostly on the first set of fourteen statements collected by Resident Pickels on 13 and 14 October 1902. I refer to these statements as 'Evidence taken'. For reasons that are discussed later, Pickels was forced to give the case a second hearing on 8 November and every witness gave another statement. These statements were less detailed but contained no significant factual differences. They are referred to as 'Notes taken'. Both sets of statements are contained in NAI, CSO 16/4 C.87/1902.

[81] Rekia Statement, 13 October 1902. 'Evidence taken'.

he informed him that he had ten pounds. Talo later asserted that this was not unusual: 'Salu always carried his money with him. I warned him about it on Saturday Oct. 4.'[82]

At 6.30 a.m., Salu was arrested. Arewa, a 'sale collector' who witnessed the arrest, testified that it was carried out by two men accompanied by 'several women'.[83] Salu was taken to the compound of Akingbinle, who was a farmer:

> I was lying near the fire suffering from Guinea worm. It was quite day when I heard the cry Thief! The noise I heard got nearer and I crawled to the front piazza. In a few moments I saw Aderuntan and Salako and they brought Salu in. I asked Salako and Aderuntan if Salu was the thief and they said yes. Salu said he was a native of Ilorin & a boy under the *Otun Bale* of Ibadan. Salu said he was looking for his cow, he was not a thief.[84]

Babalola, a *babalawo* (*Ifa* priest), was present in Akingbinle's compound at the time Salu was brought in. When Salu protested, Babalola alleged he heard Salako say: 'You are a thief, a few days ago you came to steal Aderuntan's property & you thief you will not allow people to sleep at night.'[85] Akingbinle then testified that he:

> Told Salako and Aderuntan to let Salu alone because he said he was *Otun Bale*'s man. Salako & Aderuntan said they would go with him to find his cow. I said let him alone, are you a cowherd? What business is it of yours? I dispersed the crowd & ordered Aderuntan & Salako to leave my compound.[86]

Babalola confirmed that he witnessed this exchange between Akingbinle and Salako. According to his testimony, however: 'Immediately after this another *Gambari* was arrested and brought before Akingbinle.'[87]

The name of this *Gambari* was Sumanu. While Salu went 'in search of a cow', he made his way to his farm. Just outside the town walls, he was stopped:

> I don't know by whom but think one was one of Akingbinle's boys as I saw the man helping to carry Akingbinle yesterday. I was tied up and taken to Salako's house and saw Salako, Aderuntan and Menasara and others. Salako asked why had they not killed me and asked if he had not given orders that all Gambaris arrested should be killed. The people then asked if they had to kill them if they arrested them in the daytime.... The people who arrested me said 'We have killed one! We have killed one!'[88]

Sumanu's purse containing one pound, his cutlass and three penknives were taken from him; he was severely beaten and his arm was broken. Having faced Salako in his compound, he was taken to Akingbinle but he did not see Salu.[89] According to Babalola, however, Salako and Aderuntan were present when Sumanu arrived in

[82] Talo Statement, 13 October 1902. 'Evidence taken'.

[83] Arewa Statement, 13 October 1902. 'Evidence taken'. Arewa was most likely a toll collector for one of the Ibadan chiefs.

[84] Akingbinle Statement, 14 October 1902. 'Evidence taken'.

[85] Babalola Statement, 14 October 1902. 'Evidence taken'.

[86] Akingbinle Statement.

[87] Babalola Statement.

[88] Sumanu Statement, 13 October 1902. 'Evidence taken'. Falola has suggested that killing suspected Hausa thieves was 'a law which circulated as a rumour' from 1896. See 'Hospitality to Hostility', p. 65.

[89] *Ibid.*

Akingbinle's compound. They then departed, promising 'to lead Salu to where his cow was'.[90]

Curiously, Akingbinle's testimony did not mention Sumanu. He stated it was shortly after Salako and Aderuntan left that he 'heard whispering that Salu had been killed'.[91] About half an hour later, he maintained, Salako returned alone to his compound and informed him that Salu was looking for his cow. Next, Menasara, Salako's messenger, arrived: 'I heard Menasara say Salu was not quite dead. Salako and Menasara went out talking … I heard Salako tell Menasara to go and finish Salu. Aderuntan came by the back yard to my house when Salako returned, he did not talk at all.'[92]

Menasara's testimony corroborated Akingbinle's version of events. He stated he went to look for Salu with Aderuntan and two other men from Akingbinle's compound.[93] One of them was another *babalawo* called Ige who testified that Abegunde, who had been ordered by Salako to 'remove the corpse of Salu', took him (Ige) to *Igbo Igbale*.[94] When the four men found Salu, they discovered he was 'quite dead'.[95] Abegunde and Menasara 'moved the body a small distance'[96] while Aderuntan 'stood aloof'.[97] Ige declared that he 'refused to touch him [Salu] as it is against my principles to touch the dead'.[98] Menasara confirmed this, referring to Ige as 'far distant'.[99] He confessed: 'I inflicted two wounds on Salu but he was quite dead before I inflicted them.'[100]

At the time Salu's corpse was being 'removed', Babalola, the other *babalawo*, was visiting two influential Ibadan chiefs. He testified that after leaving with Sumanu he went to *Bale* Mosaderin and from there to the barracks, where the Hausa constabulary were stationed. He then returned to *Bale* Mosaderin once again and afterwards visited *Osi Balogun* Akintayo. On his return to Akingbinle's compound, he alleged: 'I was informed that Salu had been killed by Salako & Aderuntan.'[101]

Meanwhile, after he witnessed Salu's arrest, Arewa went to Salu's house.[102] He met Igana, a leather worker; the two men then went to Akingbinle's house. They were told that Salu had been taken to *Igbo Igbale*, 'a fetish place' – they went there and discovered Salu's corpse.[103] Arewa testified that he found the corpse 'by following a track of blood'.[104] Igana stated that Salu was 'quite naked' and the string

---

[90] Babalola Statement.
[91] Akingbinle Statement.
[92] *Ibid.*
[93] Menasara Statement, 13 October 1902. 'Evidence taken'.
[94] Ige Statement. *Igbo Igbale* means 'a grove where *egungun* (ancestral masquerades) appear'. Abraham, *Dictionary*, p. 286.
[95] Menasara Statement.
[96] Ige Statement.
[97] Menasara Statement.
[98] Ige Statement.
[99] Menasara Statement.
[100] *Ibid.*
[101] Babalola Statement.
[102] Arewa Statement.
[103] Igana Statement, 13 October 1902. 'Evidence taken'.
[104] Arewa Statement.

which tied his apron, where he usually kept his money, was cut.[105] Both Arewa and Igana swore that there was 'no money on the body'.[106] With the help of some other people, the two men carried Salu's corpse to Akingbinle's compound. They emphasised that none of the accused were among those who helped them carry the body.[107] Akingbinle confirmed their testimony:

> One of Salu's relatives, I think it was Igana, brought the corpse to my gate.... I pointed out Aderuntan to the Resident's messengers as one of the murderers. I was arrested and taken to the barracks but released. Salako and Aderuntan led the messengers to where the body was found.[108]

Various visitations continued. Later that afternoon, Babalola played a crucial diplomatic role:

> Akingbinle sent me to Salako to tell him that *Otun Bale* had sent a messenger to Akingbinle about Salu the man whom he (Salako) had killed and he must answer for it after being especially warned by Akingbinle. Salako said that he had been ordered that any thief who was arrested must be killed. Salako did not deny that he had killed Salu. He did not say anyone else had killed him. Salako then went to the *Bale*'s house.[109]

Osunbiri, *Bale* Mosaderin's messenger, confirmed that Salako had come to see the *Bale*: 'He said they were watching their quarter at night and in the daytime a man was arrested who said he had a cow. The man was killed.... He did not say why he was killed.'[110]

The next day, 6 October 1902, Salu's corpse was taken by Igana and Talo to the Hausa barracks.[111] Igana recalled: 'There were no more wounds than those I saw when I found the body. It was the same body I found at Igbo Igbale.'[112] Once at the barracks, Salu's corpse was given a post-mortem examination by Dr William Thomson, the British Medical Officer. He declared the body was 'apparently healthy and about 25 years of age' and established 'fracture of the skull' as the cause of death. In addition to four extremely severe head wounds, he described another which 'completely divided the femur'. He suggested an instrument like a cutlass used with 'very considerable force' would cause the injuries. With the exception of the wounds on the lower part of the head and on the thigh, he stated that all 'had the appearance of being inflicted before death'.[113] According to the trial notes, Dr Thomson was the last person to see Salu's body. It is unclear what became of the corpse.

The administration of justice

On 13 October 1902 Acting Resident Pickels charged Salako, Aderuntan and Menasara with murder. They pleaded not guilty. Over the next two days, Pickels took

---

[105] Igana Statement.
[106] Igana and Arewa Statements.
[107] *Ibid*.
[108] Akingbinle Statement.
[109] Babalola Statement
[110] Osunbiri Statement, 14 October 1902. 'Evidence taken'.
[111] Igana Statement; Talo Statement.
[112] Igana Statement.
[113] Dr William Thomson Statement, 14 October 1902. 'Evidence taken'.

statements from the accused and eleven witnesses, without the Ibadan chiefs being present. Their only representative was Osunbiri, *Bale* Mosaderin's messenger. On 17 October, he sent the statements to Henry Reeves, the Acting Colonial Secretary in Lagos. Naming the defendants, Pickels wrote: 'I have no doubt in my mind that Akingbinle has very much more to do with it than he says but there is no evidence against him. Of the three men charged Salako is I think the chief man. Menasara I look upon more as a tool.'[114] Reeves forwarded the documents to the Attorney-General, Edwin Speed, noting: 'These proceedings seem to be irregular. They should have been taken before the Native Council.'[115]

Governor MacGregor had developed the concept of a 'Native Council' in 1901, as a cost-effective strategy for administering the Lagos Protectorate. 'Government must', he insisted, 'be carried on through the instrumentality of the chiefs.'[116] Ideally, his agents would be 'the old, well established, chiefly families, to whom administration, in their own way, of certain districts is hereditary'.[117] Regretting what he saw as the diminishing influence of these families, MacGregor proposed the Native Council Ordinance as 'a modest commencement in the attempt to develop native provincial government ... under which those usages of the country that should be maintained may be codified and reduced to order'.[118]

As we have seen, 'chiefly families' in Ibadan were not old and well established; neither was administration hereditary. Resident Fuller had begun monthly Council meetings with the warrior chiefs in August 1897, a practice he described as 'very uphill work'.[119] Initially, the Council comprised the *Bale* with four of his chiefs and the *Balogun* with five of his chiefs.[120] Two years later, the *Ekarun Bale* took the place of the *Areago Balogun*. All of the *Seriki* and *Iyalode* chiefs were excluded. This institutional model – the *Bale* heading two groups of five chiefs – was 'codified'.[121] It was also alien to Ibadan practices of government.

The 1901 Ordinance recognised the Ibadan Council as 'duly constituted' with this status:

> [The Council] shall have power to deal with all matters of internal administration or business affecting the people and area over which it possesses authority; and shall be responsible for the preservation of peace, the administration of justice and the protection and encouragement of trade and industry over such area.[122]

Importantly, it was intended that the Resident would no longer preside over Council business; he would be replaced by 'the principal or ruling chief'. Nonetheless, a British officer was still to assist at the meetings.[123]

---

[114] NAI, CSO 16/5 C.87/1902: Pickels to Reeves, 17 October 1902.

[115] NAI, CSO 16/5 C.87/1902: Reeves to Speed, 22 October 1902.

[116] NAI, CSO 1/3 Vol.5.: MacGregor to Chamberlain, 11 November 1901.

[117] *Ibid.*

[118] *Ibid.*

[119] NAI, Iba Prof. 3/6: Resident's Journal. Fuller 'drew up a set of rules' for the Council on 5 August 1897 and fixed the first meeting for 9 August. He gives an account of the second meeting on 6 September.

[120] Akinyele, *Outlines*, p. 15.

[121] *Lagos Annual Report 1899*, p. 79.

[122] Native Council Ordinance, No. 11, 1901.

[123] *Ibid.*

By acknowledging the political authority of a limited group of warrior chiefs, the Native Council Ordinance made Ibadan chieftaincy a constitutional structure of colonial governing. Such recognition introduced a significant shift in the form of civic Ibadan power. During the nineteenth century, this power had contingently centred on two sites – the battlefield and the 'town's meeting day'. After 1901, it gradually became centralised into the office of the *Bale*.

The constitutional shift was actually visible. As Resident Elgee put it: 'The native authorities took an administrative step forward by building a gaol and Advisory Court.' The court was designed by Resident Fuller, 'to meet', as his successor saw it, 'a long felt want for a place in which to hold meetings and investigate the various charges brought from time to time by chiefs and people who had anything to complain of'.[124] The fear the warrior chiefs had expressed in 1893 – that British rule would mean the establishment of a separate court of appeal – was becoming a reality.[125]

It was in the Advisory Court that Acting Resident Pickels heard evidence relating to the murder of Salu on 13 and 14 October 1902. He then sent his recommendations to Lagos. However, at this time, the 'assisting powers' of the Resident did not extend to adjudicating criminal cases between Ibadan citizens. Indeed, Acting Resident Rice had been rebuked for independently judging a murder case in July 1901.[126] Fifteen months later, Attorney-General Speed similarly criticised Pickels's actions and ordered a retrial.[127] The Acting Resident duly arranged for the case to be heard before *Bale* Mosaderin and the ten other Council chiefs on 8 November 1902.[128]

At this second hearing all the defendants changed their pleas to guilty. This action appeared to surprise Pickels:

> The Resident explained to the accused persons what the plea of Guilty meant and the results and asked them if they would care to reconsider their pleas. Each one however said he quite understood the matter and would hold to the plea of Guilty.[129]

After each witness had again presented an oral statement, Pickels asked the three men who had instructed them to kill Salu. Menasara repeated that Salako had ordered him: 'to go and remove the man who was killed.... [I] did not see the wounds inflicted before death but I inflicted wounds after death.' Both Salako and Aderuntan asserted that they were 'not ordered by anyone to kill Salu'.[130]

Subsequently, Pickels asked the Council chiefs to reach a verdict. After consultation, they 'unanimously agreed that all the prisoners were Guilty'. They sentenced Salako and Aderuntan to a £50 fine and proposed that Menasara should be imprisoned. In response, Acting Resident Pickels 'laid the facts before the Council

---

[124] RH, Mss. Afr. S.1169: Elgee, 'Evolution', p. 14.
[125] Johnson, *History*, p. 638.
[126] RH, Mss. Afr. S.1169: Elgee, 'Evolution', p. 14.
[127] NAI, CSO 16/5 C.87/1902: Speed to Reeves, 24 October 1902.
[128] NAI, CSO 16/5 C.87/1902: Pickels to Reeves, 9 November 1902.
[129] NAI, CSO 16/5 C.87/1902: 'Notes taken'.
[130] NAI, CSO 16/5 C.87/1902: 'Notes taken'.

again and considered the sentence was very mild for such a crime and was of the opinion that H.E. the Governor would think so.' The chiefs reconsidered and chose to raise the fines by £25 each.[131]

In part, this decision to impose a cash sentence was based on material needs. Once the external wars ended, administering justice was one of the few means which the chiefs could use to generate income. They were not slow to exploit it. For example, in August 1898, *Bale* Fajinmi levied fines on the family of a man accused of killing his mother, before he had actually tried the case. Acting Resident Ehrhardt intervened; he judged the man innocent and ordered Fajinmi to return the sum charged.[132] The following month, Ehrhardt warned *Balogun* Akintola for trying a case 'which he should have sent to the *Bale*'. Akintola had previously been fined five pounds 'for similar conduct' by Resident Fuller. At his second 'offence' in September 1898, Ehrhardt threatened to charge him before the other chiefs.[133] The *Balogun* must have found it difficult to accept this rebuke when his predecessors had freely operated their own courts.

In October 1898, the perquisites associated with the administration of justice were exposed: 'I heard that the *Bale* & his messengers do not adhere to the fee of 5/- fixed for each case. The *Bale* first receives 10/-, the messengers demand 5/- each & then the applicant has to pay the 5/- authorised.'[134] The issue was raised at the next monthly Council meeting:

> Complaints had been made that the *Bale* exacted a private fee in addition to the one sanctioned. The *Bale* acknowledged but pleaded that these fees for deciding cases have always been the chief source of a *Bale*'s income & with the small fee he could not meet his expenses. He was told that he must adhere to the fee sanctioned but it should be considered whether it could not be increased.[135]

Ehrhardt proposed that the fees charged could vary on a scale similar to the English County Court fees. He acknowledged that the *Bale's* messengers could receive a fee 'for service of summons' but suggested it should be regulated. He did not explain how this would be done.[136]

Four years later, colonial officers had not yet managed to eradicate such 'private fees' from Ibadan administration. When the Ibadan chiefs deposed and expelled *Balogun* Kongi in September 1902, they did so for the usual reason – he was too powerful. As far as the British authorities were concerned, the city could not continue to accommodate a chief who was running his own court to rival that of the *Bale*.[137] Far from becoming an irrelevant constitutional form, Ibadan chieftaincy was fast developing into an institutionalised framework of revenue generation. Instead of going to the battlefield and collecting war spoils, the chiefs went to the courtroom to seek out their city spoils.

[131] NAI, CSO 16/5 C.87/1902: 'Notes taken'.
[132] NAI, Iba Prof. 3/6: Ehrhardt, Resident's Journal, 18 August 1898.
[133] NAI, Iba Prof. 3/6: Ehrhardt, Resident's Journal, 8 September 1898.
[134] NAI, Iba Prof. 3/6: Ehrhardt, Resident's Journal, 25 October 1898.
[135] NAI, Iba Prof. 3/6: Ehrhardt, Resident's Journal, 6 November 1898.
[136] *Ibid.*
[137] Tamuno, *Evolution of Nigerian State*, p. 220.

A Greater Punishment than Death

Cash-on-people, wealth-in-people

Court fees were not mentioned in the trial of Salako, Aderuntan and Menasara. However, apart from the fine, another 'money question' is ever present throughout the trial notes. It is clear that Acting Resident Pickels intended to prove that Salu was killed for the ten pounds it was alleged he was carrying and, further, that his murder was part of an organised robbery operation.

In this context we need to recall that, a month prior to Salu's death, *Balogun* Kongi had been expelled from Ibadan, ostensibly on the charge of 'harbouring thieves'. In 1898, these thieves had been specifically identified as *Gambari*, the group into which Salu was classified. Given that one witness states Salu *knew* all the accused, this fact appears relevant to his murder.[138] Salu might have been a *Gambari* formerly harboured by *Balogun* Kongi who had switched his allegiance to *Otun Bale* Dada, another chief associated with organised crime.[139]

All of the witnesses, with the exception of the *Bale's* messenger and Dr. Thomson, made mention of Salu's money. Associates of Salu, such as his wife Rekia, his co-worker Talo and his living companion Igana, emphasised that Salu must have had the ten pounds with him when he was arrested. Igana makes specific mention of Salu's apron being cut and states that he 'did not see any money'.[140] On the other hand, all those who interacted with Salu after his arrest routinely deny any knowledge whatsoever of the money. As Ige put it: 'They [Salako and Aderuntan] said nothing about money. I did not get any money.'[141] In the end, Pickels was forced to conclude: 'I can only consider these men are the tools of higher authorities but am unable to adduce any proof to that effect.'[142]

It is not surprising that none of the witnesses would give any clues as to the whereabouts of the ten pounds. To do so would possibly lead to their prosecution. What does seem surprising, however, is the relative lack of interest shown by most witnesses in the money. Instead, far more than Salu's money, it is *Salu's body* that captivates their attention. This points us to the ideological basis of the financial sentence.

A turning point in Salu's homicide was his assertion that he was 'a boy under the *Otun Bale*'.[143] By doing this, Salu gave his body a value. Any threat to his body implied a threat to the body of the *Otun Bale*. Responding to this information, Akingbinle maintained that he 'told Salako and Aderuntan to let Salu alone because he said he was *Otun Bale*'s man'.[144] Babalola's testimony confirmed: 'Akingbinle told Salako to let Salu alone as he was *Otun Bale*'s man.'[145] However, Salu was killed in spite of the warning. The result was a diplomatic crisis.

As the trial played out, rival witnesses competed to indemnify themselves from

[138] Talo Statement.
[139] Layode Mss.
[140] Igana Statement.
[141] Ige Statement.
[142] NAI, CSO 16/5 C.87/1902: Pickels to Reeves, 9 November 1902.
[143] Akingbinle Statement. 14 October 1902. 'Evidence taken'.
[144] Akingbinle Statement.
[145] Babalola Statement.

the cost of Salu's body and charge it in various ways to the accused. Significantly, the accused were specifically identified as 'not *Otun Bale*'s men'.[146] The attempt at self-indemnity is most explicit in Akingbinle's testimony:

> Aderuntan came in then & I called him to see to the corpse saying you are responsible. Aderuntan said How is it? I have told you I have removed the corpse to a secret place. I said you are responsible, you know the cause of his death. I warned you not to touch the man. See to the body yourself.[147]

Aderuntan himself admitted that Akingbinle had queried him: 'Did I not tell you to be careful about this man?'[148] Another account put it thus: 'Akingbinle told Salako did I not warn you that if anything happened to Salu you would be responsible?'[149]

According to Menasara: 'I was ordered by Salako ... to go and finish Salu who was then not dead.'[150] He was exonerated by Akingbinle, who enlightened Pickels on Salako and Menasara's relationship: 'Menasara is Salako's slave. If a slave was ordered by his master to go and kill someone it would be his bounden duty to do it under penalty of any punishment the master likes to inflict.'[151] Finally, it was Babalola who communicated the demand of *Otun Bale* Dada: that Salako 'must answer' for the death of his man.[152]

At the conclusion of the trial, the Council chiefs ruled that justice would be done if Salako and Aderuntan were fined and Menasara imprisoned. Acting Resident Pickels 'could not agree with them'. Asserting himself as the Ibadan chiefs' spokesman:

> The *Balogun* then said that the custom in olden times for murder cases was that the perpetrator should be put to death, his people sold and his house destroyed but that if the offender were a man of noble birth he was heavily fined and his people sold.
>
> [...] Salako's father was a man of high birth and had held a very influential position in the town & been highly respected and for this reason they pleaded for the son.[153]

Salako was obviously the *mogaji* of a prominent Ibadan *ile*. Probably, he was the third *Mogaji Otun*-Elesin. According to Akinyele: 'This was one of the minor houses; they usually held sub-titles under the House of Ogunmola.'[154] Up until September 1902, Salako's *babaogun* had been *Balogun* Kongi. At the time of Salu's murder, *Osi Balogun* Akintayo had taken Kongi's place. Akintayo was one the chiefs involved in the flurry of diplomacy that ensued immediately after Salu's arrest.[155]

Although not conclusive, the evidence of Salako's connection to *ile* Ogunmola and, more generally, to the *Balogun* chiefs is compelling. On the other side, *Otun Bale* Dada represented a rival Ibadan chieftaincy line. He was also the head of another powerful

---

[146] Akingbinle Statement.
[147] *Ibid.*
[148] Aderuntan Statement.
[149] Adeyemika Statement, 14 October 1902. 'Evidence taken'.
[150] Menasara Statement.
[151] Akingbinle Statement.
[152] Babalola Statement.
[153] *Balogun* Apanpa, 8 November 1902. 'Notes taken'.
[154] Akinyele, *Outlines*, p. 53-4.
[155] Babalola Statement.

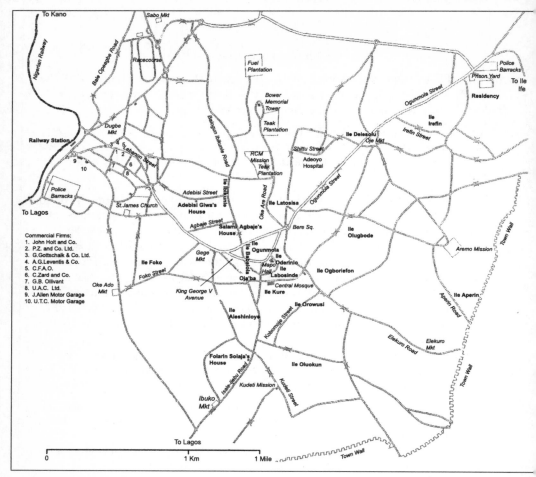

Map 3 Central Ibadan in the 1930s

warrior household, *ile* Oderinlo.[156] Significantly, these military compounds were (and are) adjacent to each other (see Map 3). In 1902, they were opposed camps in a potential civil war.

As we have seen, Ibadan chiefs had a vested interest in keeping their households and their followings together. 'Wealth-in-people' enabled a chief to embody *ola* and to express civic power in Ibadan city.[157] After 1897, however, it was unclear how chiefs would continue to maintain and build up their entourage of supporters. The conquest of Ilorin marked the end of external warfare. This removed the collective experience of battle; simultaneously, it became impossible for chiefs to augment their retinues with war captives. Curbs imposed on domestic slavery made it less feasible to exchange people in large numbers.[158] Such difficulties in recruiting followers meant that economic and political competition between chiefs was intensified.

[156] Akinyele, *Outlines*, p. 29.

[157] For discussion of the concept of 'wealth in people' see Jane I. Guyer, 'Wealth in People, Wealth in Things æ Introduction', *Journal of African History* 36 (1995), pp. 83–90.

[158] NAI, Iba Prof. 3/6: Fuller, Resident's Journal, 4–5 July 1898; 2 February 1899.

The fine which the Ibadan Council imposed for the homicide related to this unstable social context. Salu's death represented, literally, a dead material loss for *Otun Bale* Dada; it had to be compensated financially. Witnesses thus endeavoured to disown any liability for Salu's body in the first hearing of the case. The weight of blame was placed on Salako. His followers and slaves might have been involved in *Balogun* Kongi's thieving gangs. It is also possible that Salu was killed for his criminal activities. Ten pounds was a very large sum of money for a cowherd to be carrying about in 1902. One questions how he came by it and why so many witnesses knew he had it.

Equally important was *Balogun* Apanpa's description of the usual sentence imposed on men of 'noble birth' who were convicted of murder – a heavy fine and the confiscation of their followers. It appears his report was valid, at least to some degree. For example, Johnson wrote: 'A private individual would be executed at once for murder, but a chief must commit suicide by any method he may prefer, for if executed publicly his house would be demolished and his family ruined.'[159] Samuel Layode offered a different account. He maintained that during 1888, when Ibadan was enduring a trade blockade imposed by the *Awujale* of Ijebu, several influential Ijebu traders were arrested throughout the town. They were accused of being thieves and fined two hundred bags of cowries each.[160] Their leader was executed.

Layode alleges that, subsequently, this fine became the standard sentence 'for Big Offence in Ibadan town'. Significantly, the amount was equivalent to £50; *Osi Balogun* Kongi paid this exact sum for his crimes in 1898. Layode also emphasised that: 'If anyone died through action of any other man it was charged as manslaughter and the offender would be fined amount of fifty pounds.' Layode cites a 'common saying' as evidence for his assertion: *igba oke la ara emi*. He translates this to mean: 'Two hundred bags of cowries of 5/- each was a soul ransome money [*sic*].'[161]

In keeping with this practice, the Ibadan Council originally proposed to fine Salako and Aderuntan £50 each. From the chiefs' point of view, it was dangerous to execute the head of an Ibadan compound in the city. Such a public admission of guilt would be a licence for civil disorder – it would sanction the right of Ibadan citizens to confiscate the goods and people of an entire household. Even Attorney General Speed recognised this threat, perceptively noting that, 'a powerful chief might be a very inconvenient person to execute'.[162] During the early twentieth century, Ibadan warrior chiefs feared the risk of political eradication more greatly than ever.

Given the prisoners' sudden change of plea from innocent to guilty, it appears that the Council had settled the case *before* the hearing on 8 November. Salu was ultimately valued at £150; Salako and Aderuntan were each to pay £75. The 'soul ransom' had tripled. This arrangement was a pragmatic compromise conceived by

---

[159] Johnson, *History*, p. 322.
[160] Johnson explains the quantification of cowries as follows: 40 cowries=1 string; 50 strings=1 head; 10 heads = 1 bag. Therefore, 1 bag = 20,000 cowries; 200 bags = 4 million cowries! When English coins were introduced, 1 bag was made equivalent to 5 shillings. *History*, p. 118.
[161] Layode Mss.
[162] NAI, CSO 16/4 C.87/1902: Speed to Reeves, 12 November 1902.

and within the straitened circumstances of colonial rule. It allocated revenue to the chiefs and it maintained the foundation of civic Ibadan power – a body of followers. The fines also offered scope for people to be valued differentially.[163]

At the same time, because it was associated with a loss of 'social honour' or *ola*, the sentence embodied a moral deprivation akin to the act of suicide. Consequently, Menasara had to be imprisoned rather than fined – as a slave, he had minimal *ola* to lose. Finally, *Balogun* Apanpa concluded the Council's judgment by endorsing chieftaincy as a legitimate constitutional form: 'The *Bale* and Chiefs understood the native views best and all were unanimous in considering that the sentence they recommended would be felt as more severe than death.'[164]

Unfortunately for the Ibadan Council, the British neither recognised nor understood their judicial logic. As Attorney-General Speed frankly admitted: 'According to our ideas the sentence recommended is of course hopelessly inadequate.'[165] Governor MacGregor expressed himself thus: 'Cases of murder in the Ibadan District have been far too frequent of late and I look to the Native Council to maintain order. The chiefs ... must understand that they are responsible for the people's safety.'[166] In order to fulfil this different moral imperative, the chiefs' sentence was overruled and the convicted felons were removed to prison in Lagos. Without a public execution, Ibadan townspeople had no justification to loot either *ile* Ogunmola or *ile* Oderinlo. Without a cash fine, Ibadan chiefs did not receive their city spoils. The political body of Salu was an unsettled account.[167]

'Municipal life' and the jurisdiction ordinance

Six months after the conclusion of this murder trial, in May 1903, the recently appointed Resident Elgee persuaded the Ibadan Council to approve measures to tackle the crime problem. Every evening at 8 p.m. a gun would be fired to signal a night-time curfew. The gaol warders would be armed to prevent prisoners escaping. Most significantly:

> The Council resolved to substitute a civil police force for the hunters who had hitherto endeavoured to guard the town. Untrained, undisciplined and armed with Dane gunes, the hunters had proved more of a public danger than a safeguard.[168]

Initially, twenty men were enlisted. In September, the number was increased to fifty. At the end of the year, Jonathan Olubi, a son of Rev. Daniel Olubi, was appointed Police Superintendent.[169]

---

[163] Jane Guyer makes a similar argument with regard to '"Labour" and self-realization'. See her 'Wealth in People and Self-Realization in Equatorial Africa', *Man n.s.* 28, (1993), pp. 243–65.

[164] NAI, CSO 16/5 C.87/1902: 'Notes taken'.

[165] NAI, CSO 16/4 C.87/1902: Speed to Reeves, 12 November 1902.

[166] NAI, CSO 16/4 C.87/1902: MacGregor to Reeves, 19 November 1902.

[167] I borrow this phrase from Sara Berry. See 'Unsettled Accounts: Stool Debts, Chieftaincy Disputes and the Question of Asante Constitutionalism', *Journal of African History* 39 (1998), pp. 39–62.

[168] RH, Mss. Afr. S.1169: Elgee, 'Evolution', p. 19.

[169] *Ibid.*

This policing project was not the only reform encouraged by Resident Elgee; it was conceived as part of a grander plan. He explicitly stated this personal vision in the second year of his decade-long posting in Ibadan: 'I look upon it as one of my paramount duties to educate the Chiefs up to the higher standard of municipal life.'[170] Towards this end, in August 1903, he appointed three unpaid literate assistants to the Council, namely, Rev. James Okuseinde, Mr Foster and Daniel Adetoun.[171] All were associated with the CMS; Okuseinde was to maintain a mediating role in Ibadan politics until his death in 1940.[172] Three years later, Elgee appointed a Council Secretary to take minutes of the chiefs' meetings, a task previously performed by him.[173]

Another major enterprise was the introduction of 'regularised tolls' in July 1903 – an attempt to ensure a stable revenue for the Ibadan 'municipal body'.[174] However, toll stations proved impossible to supervise and the effort was abandoned in 1906.[175] An even more disastrous attempt to impose a licensing system on sales of imported liquor followed three years later. Ibadan residents responded by boycotting spirits altogether. Consequently, during the first half of 1909, expenditure exceeded revenue by £2,885. The plan was scrapped in September of the same year.[176] Further schemes of Elgee included sponsoring a proposal by the British Cotton Growing Association (BCGA) to establish a plantation near Ibadan. He also fostered the growth of the Ibadan Agricultural Society, whose members included chiefs, clergymen and farmers. The Society was more successful – it turned out that the land allocated to the BCGA was unsuitable for cotton cultivation.[177]

Elgee also invested much effort in establishing 'the *Bale*'s School'. It opened in 1906, as a secular institution to train the sons of the chiefs. Recruiting a suitable teacher proved to be an endemic problem. Attendance was so poor that, in 1911, the Council passed a law 'ordering that in future the head of every compound in Ibadan Town should be compelled to send at least one child from his compound to the *Bale*'s School'.[178] Failure to comply would initially prompt a summons; a fine of five pounds would be charged for subsequent offences.[179] The ruling was ineffective.

---

[170] Elgee to Speed, 4 November 1904. This letter was in the Mapo Hall Archives which have been lost. I have relied on Jenkins's citation: 'Politics in Ibadan', p. 140.

[171] NAI, CSO 16/5 C. 160/1903: Elgee to Speed, 25 August 1903.

[172] James Adedeji Okuseinde (1860–1940) was a son of 'Daddy Okuseinde', who came to Ibadan with the Hinderers in 1853 and headed Ogunpa mission. James schooled at Kudeti mission, Ibadan and completed further education at the CMS Training Institute in Abeokuta. He then taught in mission schools and later became an evangelist for the Abeokuta mission. After his father's death in 1891 he took over at Ogunpa; he was ordained to the priesthood four years later and transferred to Aremo. During 1903–07 he was an unpaid member of the Ibadan Council and, after the death of Rev. Olubi in 1912, he became head of the Ibadan CMS mission.

[173] Akinyele, *Outlines*, p. 19.

[174] NAI, CSO 16/5 C. 160/1903: Elgee to Speed, 25 August 1903, Enclosure I. Elgee used this phrase to describe the Ibadan Council in his address to them on 25 August 1903.

[175] Toyin Falola, 'The Yoruba Toll System: Its Operation and Abolition', *Journal of African History* 30 (1989), pp. 69–88.

[176] RH, Mss. Afr. S.1169: Elgee, 'Evolution', p. 25.

[177] Jenkins, 'Politics in Ibadan', pp.138–59.

[178] NAI, Oyo Prof. 4/5/155/1917: Council minutes, 22 April 1911.

[179] NAI, Oyo Prof. 4/5/155/1917: Council minutes, 1 June 1911.

Later that year, the Council passed control of the school to the Lagos Government.[180]

Policing was also characterised by numerous problems. In May 1904, Superintendent Olubi was sacked 'for accumulating fresh offences which make his impossible past fatally conspicuous'.[181] Two months later, Acting Resident Parsons termed these offences 'extortion'.[182] Olubi's 'impossible past' concerned an incident in 1898, when he was accused of illegally appropriating a large area of land on the Ibadan outskirts and was arrested 'on a charge of having caused death of one of his labourers'.[183] Many years later, Olubi was convicted of manslaughter and sentenced to three years' imprisonment.[184]

Acting Resident Parsons was determined that the Ibadan Police be a 'locally recruited force'. To replace Olubi, he requested his superiors to send up an Ibadan-born officer 'of tolerable character' from the Lagos Police.[185] Colonial Secretary Speed replied that he could not find any 'capable successors'.[186] Parsons compromised and appointed Horatio Johnson, 'an African and one of the old day police men of Lagos before'.[187] In an 'Interim Report' on his administration, Parsons stated that the force had been 're-clothed' and optimistically asserted that 'the Police have now taken over charge of the streets at night'. This was to be achieved by two groups of ten constables patrolling until daybreak.[188] Seven years later, Ibadan's population was estimated to be 175,000.[189] In this context, Samuel Layode's report that 'night robbers and burglary men infested the town' throughout the rule of *Bale* Dada (1904–07) is unsurprising.[190]

To make matters worse, Parsons discovered, and subsequently seized, a large stash of weapons in the compound of *Maye Balogun* Ola. After this incident, 'The Chiefs stated (what I had already learned to be the fact) that they own, and daily oil, a considerable number of rifles.' Parsons proposed that the situation should be 'regularized' by the chiefs being compelled to register all arms and ammunition.[191] His suggestion was never enforced. Instead, it was decided to make '20 spare rifles' available to staff in the 'native local government'.[192] 'In case of a local rebellion,' declared the Officer in Charge of the Hausa constabulary, 'clerks of whose loyalty one

---

[180] KDL, BAP: 49/10: Ibadan Government School – Brief History. See also Jenkins, 'Politics in Ibadan', Chapter 7, pp. 186–200.

[181] NAI, CSO 16/6 C.71/1904: Parsons to Speed, 3 May 1904.

[182] Harold Parsons, Acting Resident, 'Interim Report: First six months of 1904', *Lagos Goverment Gazette*, 29 March 1905, p. 2. Resident Elgee was not consulted about the publication of this report and, in response, he lodged a protest with Governor Egerton. See NAI, CSO 16/7 C.43/1905.

[183] NAI, Iba Prof. 3/6: Ehrhardt, Resident's Journal, 2–10 December 1898.

[184] KDL, WD: 1912/26 August.

[185] NAI, CSO 16/6 C.71/1904: Parsons to Speed, 3 May 1904.

[186] NAI, CSO 16/6 C.71/1904: Speed to Parsons, 17 May 1904.

[187] Layode Mss. This man was not a relative of Samuel Johnson, but his name suggests he might have been born in Sierra Leone.

[188] Parsons, 'Interim Report', *Gazette*, 29 March 1905, p. 2.

[189] A.L. Mabogunje, *Urbanization in Nigeria* (London, 1968), p. 199.

[190] Layode Mss.

[191] Parsons, 'Interim Report', *Gazette*, 29 March 1905, p. 8.

[192] NAI, CSO 16/6 C.86/1904: Parsons to Speed, 27 May 1904. The number was later increased to twenty-five. Parsons, 'Interim Report', *Gazette*, 29 March 1905, p. 8.

can be assured' would be supplied with arms.[193] Ironically, the Ibadan civil service in the early twentieth century shared features with a nineteenth-century Ibadan military household.

While these new policing arrangements were being devised for Ibadan city, Governor MacGregor was planning large-scale reforms for the administration of justice in the Yoruba hinterland.[194] The first step in his scheme was achieved on 13 January 1904, when the Alake and chiefs of Abeokuta signed the 'Egba Jurisdiction Ordinance'. For a period of twenty years, this agreement granted the British Government 'power and jurisdiction over all persons not being [Egba] natives' who were accused of indictable crimes and offences. In addition, it ceded 'power and jurisdiction over all persons' accused of murder and manslaughter in Egba territory to the colonial rulers.[195]

Less than two months later, Parsons encountered a debt collection case between two brothers, one of whom was resident in Lagos. In a minute to Colonial Secretary Speed, he suggested:

> I could perhaps, if so directed, use this or similar cases as a means to induce the *Bale* & Council here to adopt a treaty on the lines of the recent agreement with Abeokuta…. H.E. Sir William MacGregor indicated to me, before he left, that my work here should be directed towards the extension, in certain directions, of Supreme Court jurisdiction.[196]

The Acting Resident was warned that no 'definite proposals' should be made to the Ibadan chiefs. However, Speed encouraged 'leading the native authorities to the idea of the establishment of the S.C. in the province and familiarising them with the notion [*sic*]'.[197]

From the imperial point of view, this proposal was crucial for the further expansion of foreign trade. After the Lagos-Ibadan railway opened in March 1901, several European firms began to establish offices in the city (see Map 3). Commercial agents arrived with these businesses; other newcomers settled around the railway for trading purposes. Like a great number of Ibadan citizens, these people were born outside the city. However, since they had arrived after the 1893 Agreement, they were not absorbed into private armies. Consequently, most Ibadan *ile* had no cause to assimilate them; the group became known as 'strangers' or 'aliens'.

Initially, these strangers were under the jurisdiction of the Ibadan chiefs. On 5 June 1899, the Council ruled that 'no land should be granted to strangers within 100 yards of the Railway line'.[198] A few weeks later, regulations were passed which stated that every Ibadan resident 'will be held to be subject to the local laws, whether such a

---

[193] NAI, CSO 16/6 C. 86/1904: Lt. Hern to Parsons, 26 May 1904.
[194] Omoniyi Adewoye, 'The Judicial Agreements in Yorubaland, 1904-1908', *Journal of African History* 12 (1971), p. 614.
[195] Egba Jurisdiction Ordinance, No. 14, 1904. The agreement actually only applied for ten years. In 1914 the Egba chiefs formally surrendered their 'independence' to Governor Lugard after the Egba United Government was challenged by internal opposition. See Agneta Pallinder-Law, 'Aborted Modernization in West Africa? The Case of Abeokuta', *Journal of African History* 15 (1974), p. 79.
[196] NAI, CSO 16/6 C.32/1904: Parsons to Speed, 1 March 1904.
[197] NAI, CSO 16/6 C.32/1904: Speed to Parsons, 4 March 1904.
[198] NAI, Iba Prof. 3/6: Fuller, Resident's Journal, 5 June 1899.

person is a native of the country or not'.[199] Nonetheless, a vested interest in commercial development meant that colonial officers covertly discouraged the enforcement of these regulations. In 1903, Ibadan chiefs agreed to appoint a surveyor to demarcate legitimate land leases to six European firms that had claimed illegal titles. The Council had been resisting this decision for two years.[200] Colonial officials also sanctioned the establishment of a migrant suburb north of the railway station. It was called Ekotedo – 'the settlement of people from Lagos'.[201]

In this context of rapid growth, two specific concerns emerged. First, colonial administrators believed that the indigenous legal system was incapable of safeguarding British economic interests. For example, a case of fraudulent book-keeping in June 1903 was 'somewhat intricate and thus could not be put before Council in a sufficiently simple way'. Resident Elgee requested that 'assessors' be sent from Lagos 'to further try the case'.[202] Attorney-General Ross disagreed on the grounds that Ibadan was not under the jurisdiction of Lagos. Secondly, there was a strong view that:

> It was neither possible nor advisable for a Native Court to sit in judgement over such cases where one of the parties was an alien, nor could they be held to be competent judges in such possible cases of the murder of a native by a European or *vice-versa*.[203]

Finally, the British authorities held a generally contemptuous view of indigenous judicial practices. After a visit to Ibadan in March 1903, Governor MacGregor lamented, probably accurately, that: 'Justice, it is to be feared, is too often sold to the highest bidder in cases that come before the native tribunals.'[204]

Negotiations for a judicial agreement between the Lagos Government and the Ibadan Council began in June 1904. Jenkins has explored the episode in detail, presenting an analysis which substantially undermines his own contention that chieftaincy was a declining constitutional form in Ibadan politics.[205] Indeed, its increasing institutionalisation is further evidenced by the chiefs' success in lobbying for two more Council positions during 1904.[206] Subsequently, the *Abese Bale* and *Maye Balogun* were officially permitted to attend Council meetings. On 8 August 1904, they joined *Bale* Mosaderin and ten other warrior chiefs in affixing their marks to the 'Yoruba Jurisdiction Ordinance'.

This legislation, which followed the Abeokuta model, brought far-reaching changes to the administration of justice in Ibadan. In 1905, Ojaba Native Court opened to hear cases between Ibadan citizens; it was to be controlled by four senior

---

[199] *Lagos Annual Report*, 1899, p. 88.
[200] RH, Mss. Afr. S.1169: Elgee, 'Evolution', p. 18. Today, the district of the city where these boundaries were laid out is known as Gbagi, meaning 'to peg'.
[201] A.L. Mabogunje, 'The Morphology of Ibadan', in *The City of Ibadan*, p. 49.
[202] NAI, CSO 16/5 C.117/1903: Elgee to Reeves, 28 June 1903.
[203] RH, Mss. Afr. S.1169: Elgee, 'Evolution', p. 21.
[204] NAI, CSO 1/3 Vol. 6.: MacGregor to Chamberlain, 22 March 1903.
[205] Jenkins, 'Politics in Ibadan', Chapter 6, pp. 160–85.
[206] NAI, Iba. Prof. 3/4: 'Intelligence Report on Ibadan Town by E.N.C. Dickenson, 1938', p. 52. This report is discussed in Chapter 6. I was unable to locate the original documents approving the 1904 Council expansion and thus have relied on this source.

chiefs appointed in rotation. Appeals from this court could be lodged with the new District Court, housed in the former Advisory Court building and under the control of the recently appointed Assistant Resident, Harold Parsons. The Lagos Supreme Court was its appellate court. At the same time, Lagos assumed original jurisdiction over all cases involving strangers, 'the property and persons' of strangers and the crimes of murder and manslaughter.[207]

Colonial officialdom was delighted. As Alfred Lyttleton, the Secretary of State for the Colonies, enthused: 'The agreement with Ibadan gives to the British Govt. an even wider jurisdiction than in the case of Abeokuta and is completely satisfactory.'[208] Lyttleton referred here to the omission of the twenty-year time limit granted in the Egba agreement and the fact that the Ordinance applied not only to Ibadan city, but also to 86 subject towns. Theoretically, these towns remained under the control of warrior chiefs; in practice, the British were beginning to take over.[209]

Similar Jurisdiction Ordinances were eventually signed with Oyo, Ife, and Ijebu-Ode. An intention to protect British commercial interests does appear to have been the original impetus for the agreements. However, as Omoniyi Adewoye points out, the Lagos authorities were also motivated by a perception that the treaties signed with Egba, Oyo and Ibadan chiefs during 1893 were insufficient for the requirements of colonial rule. Each treaty recognised a different degree of independence and none gave the British direct legal powers.[210] By resolving some of these irregularities, the judicial agreements 'struck a decisive blow against the sovereignty of the Yoruba states'.[211] The Ibadan warrior chiefs would never again adjudicate a murder trial.

Suicide and the political body

Bale Dada was an '*At'apata dide*', meaning 'One who starts from a rock ... nobody built their own foundation, they became chiefs through their own individual efforts or means.'[212] He was born in Ibadan, but his father, Opadere, was not a chief. Dada began his career as a soldier in *ile* Oderinlo and, when the wars ended, he moved to his farm outside Ibadan. In 1897, a group of Ijaye people arrived to claim his land. However, 'he made them to understand that he was one of the warriors who captured Ijaye Town'. This conquest had taken place in 1862, when Dada was probably an *omo ogun*. Thirty-five years later, *Bale* Fajinmi 'felt that such a man should not be a farmer and he invited him to Town and straightaway made him a chief'.[213] By this means, Dada Opadere became *Mogaji* Oderinlo and *Ekerin Bale* at the same time.

In 1902, *Otun Bale* Dada was an influential chief. The murder of one of his followers – a cowherd called Salu – did not go unnoticed. Perhaps Salu was, or had

---

[207] The operation of the new system is explored in Lawrence Kolawole Alo, 'The Native Courts in Ibadan, 1901–1960' (Ibadan University MA thesis, 1995).

[208] NAI, CSO 16/6 C.181/1904: Lyttleton to Harley Moseley, 24 August 1904.

[209] Yoruba Jurisdiction Ordinance, Schedule I, No. 17, 1904.

[210] Adewoye, 'Judicial Agreements', p. 613.

[211] *Ibid.*, p. 623.

[212] Akinyele, *Outlines*, p. 101.

[213] *Ibid.*, p. 99.

been, involved in a gang of robbers. He was obviously in the wrong place at the wrong time on 5 October. A group of men arrested him and accused him of being a thief. Later that day, he was dead. In November, *Balogun* Apanpa had nothing to lose by supporting Dada's claim for compensation. Focused on the prospect of some material reward, Ibadan chiefs were unusually unanimous in their assertion that heavy fines should be imposed on the perpetrators.

There was no such consensus when *Bale* Mosaderin died in December 1904, at the age of over 100 years. Three chiefs – *Otun Bale* Dada, *Balogun* Apanpa and ex-*Balogun* Kongi – sought the vacant *Bale* title. Resident Elgee refused to allow Kongi to return to Ibadan from exile; thus Dada and Apanpa remained to fight it out:

> [Dada] was the senior but the second possessed the greater personality. Public opinion was divided. Each of these chiefs had an equal number of followers, and were supported by an equal number of sub-chiefs. Dada's claims consisted of his being *Otun Bale*, that is to say, the next chief in rank of the deceased, while Apampa's argument was that although *Balogun*s did not as a rule hold the *Bale*ship, yet now that fighting had ceased, war-chiefs should have the same right to election as civil chiefs.[214]

For Jenkins, 'a conflict between the two most important lines over the criteria for appointment as *Bale*' marked the beginning of a decline in the relevance of Ibadan chieftaincy as a constitutional form.[215] I suggest it indicates the reverse.

The contest between the *Bale* and *Balogun* chieftaincy lines first emerged in 1902; Jenkins correctly asserts that this particular conflict had not been a feature of nineteenth-century politics. However, competition was not novel to Ibadan political culture – civil disorder was its disease. During the early twentieth century this disease remained, but its form began to change.

After 1893 warrior chiefs continued their struggle to assert control over an imagined civic Ibadan. Since they could not amass booty or prove military valour, it became difficult for them to maintain their material base of political mobilisation, that is, a body of supporters. Crucially, this insecurity did not cause followers to be less needed. Instead, the social status of 'having people' became the main criterion for appointment to a title. As Akinyele recalled: 'When the intertribal war was stopped by the British Government and Ibadan Division became a British Protectorate, the man who had influence and many followers competed for titles.'[216]

In this situation, the need for followers increased and, consequently, rivalries to attract their political allegiance also grew. Without the battlefield, the only site for this struggle was Ibadan itself. People became a city spoil rather than a war spoil. For the chiefs, the trial for the murder of Salu was an opportunity to generate revenue and sustain their authority. The sentence they passed down was an effort to make a follower's body hold both a material and a civic value. It failed.

As far as British administrators were concerned, government was to be achieved 'through and with the Ruling Chiefs and their Councils'.[217] The *Balogun* was banned

---

[214] RH, Mss. Afr. S.1169: Elgee, 'Evolution', p. 24.
[215] Jenkins, 'Government and Politics', p. 218.
[216] Akinyele, *Outlines*, p. 98.
[217] NAI, CSO 16/7 C.176/1905: Elgee to Reeve-Tucker, 7 July 1905.

from administering justice independently in 1898; although this did not prevent him from continuing to do so, it did become more difficult. In 1901, the Native Council Ordinance recognised the *Bale* as Ibadan's 'ruling chief'. Consequently, within a relatively short time period, chiefs began to compete for the *Bale* title much more intensely. The office was sought for both political and economic reasons. First, it represented civic status. Second, as the apex of a chiefly hierarchy, the *Bale* held the prime position to manipulate and exploit the rivalries of his subordinate chiefs. In return for political favours, he could extort 'city spoils'.

By 1902 it was clear that regional warfare had ended – there were no more glories or booties to be won on the battlefield. Less than five years before, *Balogun* Akintola had refused to accept the *Bale* office for the second time. Now, the *Balogun* wanted to become *Bale*. Rather than a sign of institutional disintegration, this conflict was the result of political authority being centralised into the *Bale* title. Chieftaincy was being *made* into a constitutional form. As Berry has argued in the context of colonial Ashante:

> Chieftaincy disputes were neither symptoms of the 'breakdown' of traditional order and morality nor simple manifestations of newly emerging patterns of class conflict, but part of an ongoing struggle to define and exercise legitimate authority in a society both transformed and destabilized by the imposition of colonial rule.[218]

In the nineteenth century, battle prowess legitimated the exercise of civic power in Ibadan. In the twentieth century, Ibadan people fought to institutionalise their exercise of civic power by gaining chieftaincy titles. Those who were already chiefs strove to institutionalise chieftaincy. This explains why, in 1907, *Bale* Dada 'asked for the Council to be enlarged to include all the principal chiefs, 26 in number, including the Seriki and his *Otun* and *Osi*'.[219] His request was refused by Governor Egerton.

Dada's failure to achieve this reform was probably a cause of his political sacrifice. For, although the *Bale* was the ruling chief, his civic authority was actually highly precarious. As Post and Jenkins argue, there was now a premium on his deposition. Junior chiefs could no longer rely on death in battle to create title vacancies; opportunities for promotion were much harder to come by. To maintain political turnover, senior chiefs had to be removed. In this context, 'plotting and intrigue came to outweigh leadership and military skill as criteria for title holding'.[220] Elgee's conviction that Council meetings were 'the safety valves of conspiracy' was a delusion.[221] These meetings were a hotbed of subterfuge.

Like most Ibadan chiefs, the political authority of the *Bale* depended on a body of followers whose loyalty was contingent. To remove him from office, his rival chiefs could readily resort to the traditional method. They could incite his people to betray him. In a long speech to the Ibadan Council during November 1905, *Bale* Dada bitterly lamented this practice. He also recounted how he became *Bale*, a year earlier, when Apanpa was *Balogun*:

[218] Berry, 'Unsettled Accounts', p. 40.
[219] NAI, Iba. Prof. 3/4: 'Intelligence Report', p. 52.
[220] Post and Jenkins, *Price of Liberty*, p. 11.
[221] NAI, CSO 16/7 C.176/1905: Elgee to Reeve-Tucker, 7 July 1905.

You the *Otun* [Apanpa], there is no one you can not injure by your mischief. See how you are shaking me. The Earth and the god Ogun are hearing. The word is not as you said it. *Otun* you were my friend.

[...] Informations reached me that the *Balogun* [Apanpa] was attempting to usurp the position and rank of *Bale*. The office, rank and position of the *Bale* of Ibadan is one of immense hard work and trouble. I never cared to become the *Bale*. The *Balogun* took all my people, my own maternal and paternal relations and entered into a secret covenant with them, and the result was this, my own people as above described did no longer recognise me as their own and they would not salute me.

[...] I said if the *Balogun* wished to be made the *Bale* by all means let him be made the *Bale*. The white men called us to a Meeting. I repeated the same things I have said to the Chiefs.

[...] The day came when I was to be made the *Bale*. I never expected it.... I was told that if I did not go to the Barracks I shall offend the white man ... [when] I reached the Barracks the white man nominated me to be the *Bale* of Ibadan.

You the *Osi* [Olafa] it was your turn when I was promoted the *Bale* that should you be promoted the *Otun Bale*. But the *Balogun* usurped your title and applied to be promoted the *Otun* with a view that when I died he the *Otun* may be made the *Bale*.[222]

According to Dada, he never sought the *Bale* office. Both Akinyele and Resident Elgee claim otherwise. Akinyele writes that, following *Bale* Mosaderin's death, 'Dada the *Otun Bale* naturally prepared for installation.'[223] Resident Elgee recalled Dada and Apanpa as 'the two candidates for the vacant *Bale*ship'. He also explained how the contest was resolved: 'The case was referred to the Alafin of Oyo, who gave a decided opinion in favour of Dada, who was accordingly elected with the approval of Government.'[224] *Balogun* Apanpa then took the title of *Otun Bale*.

This was the first occasion that the British authorities brought in an external arbitrator to resolve a lack of agreement between the Ibadan chiefs. In part, it was made possible by a clause in the judicial agreement which stated that Ibadan recognised the *Alaafin* as 'King and Head of Yoruba land.'[225] In August 1904 Secretary of State Lyttleton was 'doubtful' about the inclusion of the clause, choosing to remind Acting Governor Harley Moseley that 'the overlordship of Oyo over Ibadan is at present founded only on tradition and sentiment, and is in practice non-existent.'[226] As will be revealed in the next chapter, a decade after Dada's election, colonial officials adopted a strikingly different view.

Whatever the precise political intentions of Dada Opadere in December 1904, just over three years later, Alexander Akinyele strongly regretted that 'he would pervert any judgement for money'.[227] At the same time, *Bale* Dada was 'stingy'. Herein lies an important shift in Ibadan political culture. During 1877, *Foko* Aiyejenku was opposed because it was feared he might one day 'rule with rigour'.[228] Thirty years later, *Bale* Dada was opposed because he was 'avaricious' and tight-fisted. Since

[222] NAI, Iba. Prof. 3/10: Minutes, 26 October 1905.
[223] Akinyele, *Outlines*, p. 18.
[224] RH, Mss. Afr. S.1169: Elgee, 'Evolution', p. 24.
[225] Yoruba Jurisdiction Ordinance, Schedule II, No. 17, 1904.
[226] NAI, CSO 16/6 C.181/1904: Lyttleton to Harley Moseley, 24 August 1904.
[227] KDL, BAP: 7/1907–08, A.B. Akinyele to Tugwell, 21 February 1908.
[228] Johnson, *History*, p. 408.

Ibadan chiefs could no longer further their economic and political ambitions on the battlefield, these personal characteristics were deeply resented – they required that their head chief 'spend for them'.[229]

In this situation, *Otun Bale* Apanpa appropriated 'the confidence and love of the whole Chiefs and people of Ibadan whom he stirred against *Bale* Dada.'[230] Like many before him, to prevent his successors being 'wiped off the face of the earth', *Bale* Dada committed suicide. By killing himself, he preserved the political body of his *ile*. He also enabled *Otun Bale* Apanpa to assume rule of the recently constituted 'municipal body' of the Ibadan Council. Evidently, during the early years of colonial rule, chieftaincy politics was as much the same as it was different. Continuity and change were mutually constitutive.

[229] KDL, BAP: 7/1907–08, A.B. Akinyele to Tugwell, 21 February 1908.
[230] Akinyele, *Outlines*, p. 18.

5

A Great Blot

Indirect Rule, Native Gentlemen & Renowned Capitalists

For his diary entry on 29 April 1920, Akinpelu Obisesan made a note of his dream the previous night. He wrote: 'Capt. Ross and Mr. Grier were tried with a court of native lawyers & sentenced to six months.'[1] Obisesan does not state what charges were brought against the British administrators. His subconscious probably needed no explanation, as he was all too conscious of the regime of *Si fila dobale* or 'Off with your cap! Prostrate flat!'[2]

The casualties of Ibadan chieftaincy politics during the first four decades of colonial rule were *Bale* Dada, *Bale* Irefin and *Balogun* Ola – all of them committed suicide. *Balogun* Kongi died in exile at Iwo; *Bale* Situ was banished to Shaki in 1926 and died there six years later. In the previous chapter, I argued that the deposition and death of *Bale* Dada was not an indication of the breakdown of chieftaincy as a constitutional form. Rather, I contended that this political incident signified a strengthened connection between civic status and chieftaincy.

The institutionalisation of this link had been encouraged both by British officials and by the chiefs themselves – its effect was to change the endemic competition of Ibadan politics. First, the office of *Bale* became much more sought after. Second, since there were no longer battle casualties, plotting and conspiracy intensified as strategies to achieve promotion. Nonetheless, the maintenance of a body of followers remained crucial for maintaining political authority.

This chapter focuses on Ibadan politics between 1912 and 1926. Isaac Akinyele characterised the era as:

A GREAT BLOT

We exposed here very reluctantly the great blot or stain pertaining to the Administration of these Residents. At this age of light and knowledge and the considerable civilization of the time, that a British Resident would give room to rebellion and conspiracy such that were not even usual when we were in so-called barbarous state was a great surprise.[3]

[1] KDL, Akinpelu Obisesan Papers, Box 55: 1920 Diary, 29 April. (hereafter, OP/55: 1920, 29 April.)

[2] Akinyele, *Outlines*, p. 85.

[3] *Ibid.*, pp. 80–1.

86

Ironically, the administration of Ross and Grier aspired to eradicate the culture of conspiracy in Ibadan chieftaincy. Although their project was ideologically justified as 'indirect rule', it became, as Jenkins aptly summarizes: 'largely a matter of very direct control mitigated only by intrigue'.[4] To analyse this contested politics, I will first explore the installation and deposition of *Bale* Irefin. The death of *Balogun* Ola and the removal of *Bale* Situ are examined in the latter part of the chapter. These incidents related to the introduction of direct taxation and Resident Ross's constitutional vision, which he endeavoured to symbolise through legislative action.

Ibadan's experience of indirect rule was especially deplored by Christian-educated Yoruba men. This circle had been active political brokers between British officials and indigenous chiefs since the treaty negotiations of the late nineteenth century. A decade after the signing of the Ibadan Agreement, Resident Elgee sought to raise the 'municipal life' of the city Council. To support his administrative project, he recruited men from the second generation of Yoruba Christians.

By contrast, Resident Ross and District Officer Grier aimed to empower the *Alaafin* of Oyo to extend his political jurisdiction over Ibadan and its subject towns. This enterprise pointedly excluded 'educated natives' from city government. For example, Isaac Akinyele had become a tolls clerk in 1903; he resigned from the Native Authority in 1920. For him, the memory of Ross was a bitter one: 'The Great "Oga" Master hated the educated civilized men and usually termed them "Lagido", a monkey; he caused the chiefs also to hate them; and he did practically nothing for the school during his time.'[5] It was partly in response to this perceived hostility that, in 1914, a small group of these men organised themselves into an historical Society called the *Egbe Agba O'tan*. The cultural/political identity cultivated by this association is the second focus of this chapter.

'A man in certain respects that circumstance has made to become object of worship to we his peers.'[6] The subject of this adulation was Sanusi Adebisi, an Ibadan-born merchant who worked for the firm of Miller Brothers. He belonged to a new set of contenders for chieftaincy titles – the *ile olowo*. These 'households of money' emerged during the 1920s and comprised mostly 'native' Muslims involved in the boom and bust of Ibadan commercial enterprise. In the final section of this chapter, I will introduce the two most prominent members of this group and their oscillation between fraternization and rivalry with 'educated civilized men'. My account is drawn mostly from the social commentary of an aspiring entrepreneur, Akinpelu Obisesan.[7]

---

[4] Jenkins, 'Politics in Ibadan', p. 88.

[5] Akinyele, *Outlines*, p. 85. 'The school' was the Ibadan Government School, opened as 'the *Bale*'s school' by Resident Elgee and Governor Egerton in September 1906.

[6] KDL, OP/55: 1923, 12 November.

[7] Akinpelu Obisesan (1887–1963) was the son of a slave woman and an Ibadan chief. After schooling at Aremo mission school and the CMS Training College, Oyo, he became a clerk on the Lagos Railway. He returned to Ibadan during 1913 and, through the next two decades, worked for various mercantile firms. At the same time, he managed his family's extensive cocoa farms and struggled to defend them against land claims. Following bankruptcy in 1931, he became President of the Ibadan Cocoa Cooperative Marketing Union in 1934 and, subsequently, a leading figure in the Nigerian Cooperative Movement. It was through this economic enterprise that he eventually achieved the local social and political status that he so desired. He

Unceremonious interference and profound secrets:
Bale *Irefin and the* Egbe Agba O'tan

On 13 September 1912, *Bale* Akintayo died. He had risen to Ibadan's highest title in just eight years, due to his installation as *Osi Balogun* after *Balogun* Kongi's deposition in 1902.[8] At the time of Akintayo's death, Resident Elgee was on leave. Captain William Alston Ross, the first District Commissioner of Oyo, was serving in his place.

Six years earlier, the posting of Ross to Oyo had been a matter of some concern to the Ibadan Council. When *Bale* Dada complained that they had not been consulted, Governor Egerton replied bluntly: 'The Alafin is not under Ibadan.'[9] *Otun Bale* Apanpa then joined the exchange: 'The Alafin is our paramount Chief, that is, we take this interest in him and his affairs. We do not like his being separated from us.'[10] Responding, the Governor successfully evaded the issue: 'It appears to me that the only person who should feel at all aggrieved is the Resident, Ibadan, who has had some of the territory formerly administered by him taken away.'[11] The complaint was dropped.

When he departured on furlough in April 1912, Resident Elgee informed District Commissioner Ross that *Bale* Akintayo was unwell. He noted: 'If he dies there will be much competition for his place. Irifin the *Otun Bale* is not very popular owing to his character for stinginess.'[12] He described *Osi Bale* Akinwale, *Balogun* Situ and *Ekerin Bale* Ola as the 'runners up' and proposed Irefin or Akinwale as the best candidates 'from the Government point of view'.[13] But at the time the post became available, the election did not proceed in the way Elgee had anticipated. On the *Bale* side, Akinwale declared support for Irefin and made no claim. Against him, Ola (who had recently been promoted to *Asipa Bale*) was in favour of *Balogun* Situ's nomination.[14] According to Acting Resident Ross, the result was that: 'The *Balogun* seems to be the popular man, probably more by intrigue than merit.'[15]

Of these four chiefs, two came from *ile* whose leaders had been prominent warriors during the nineteenth century. Situ was a son of *Are-ona-kakanfo* Latosisa.[16]

---

[7] [(cont.)] served as an Ibadan Councillor between 1939–42; was a member of the Nigerian Legislative Council (1943–51) and sat in the Western House of Assembly (1947–51). In 1948, he received the OBE and, three years before his death, he became an Ibadan chief. His diaries (in English) for the years 1920–60 provide fascinating insights into the personalities and politics of colonial Ibadan. I am grateful to Gavin Williams for giving me his extensive notes which proved an invaluable guide to my consultation of the diaries.

[8] Akinyele, *Outlines*, p. 21.

[9] *Ibid.*

[10] *Ibid.*

[11] *Ibid.*

[12] NAI, Iba. Prof. 3/10: Elgee, Handing Over Note, in Acting Resident Ross to Acting Colonial Secretary James, September 1912. The exact date is missing from this letter; however, it must have been written in the course of 22–25 September.

[13] *Ibid.* Elgee uses incorrect spellings of Irefin and Akinwale.

[14] KDL, WD: 1912/15 September.

[15] NAI, Iba. Prof. 3/10: Ross to James, September 1912.

[16] For details of his chieftaincy promotions see Appendix II.

Ross proposed to refer to him 'in code' as 'debtor', perhaps because he assumed Situ had borrowed money in order to pay his supporters.[17] Ola had been appointed *mogaji* of *ile* Orowusi in 1893, following the death of his brother, *Balogun* Osungbekun.[18] Since he was older than both Situ and Irefin, Ross coded Ola as 'ancient'.[19] Akinwale was from *ile* Ogunsola, a lesser-known military household, whose founder had held the title of *Ekarun Balogun* before his death in 1880.[20] In 1910, *Bale* Akintayo had raised Akinwale from *Maye Bale* to *Osi Bale*, blocking the promotions of two chiefs, one of whom was Ola. Akinwale filled the vacancy which resulted from the upgrade of *Osi Bale* Irefin to *Otun Bale*. Thus it appears that Akinwale and Irefin were allies; meanwhile, Ola and Akinwale had previously blocked each other's promotions.[21] These machinations constituted the political allegiances of 1912. Captain Ross was unaware of them. He described Akinwale as 'the most intelligent and useful member' of the Ibadan Council.[22]

In contrast to these households, *ile* Irefin was established after the 1893 Agreement.[23] Irefin's father, Ogunlade, had fled his destroyed town of Owu and joined the soldiers of Oluyole during the 1830s. His son was also an *omo ogun*. He probably established his *ile* around 1895, when he was installed *Asaju Bale* by *Bale* Osuntoki.[24] As Akinyele put it, 'he rose to Chieftaincy by his own effort. He was Mogaji to none; and his family held no title before him.' For this reason, his nomination as *Bale* 'was opposed by majority of the Principal Chiefs especially those in the *Balogun*'s line.'[25]

Furthermore, according to both Elgee and Ross, Irefin was not known for his generosity. Indeed, Ross coded him 'stingy'.[26] As was shown in the previous chapter, such a reputation was a serious accusation in colonial Ibadan chieftaincy politics, especially for an aspiring *Bale*. This title was invested with a great deal more status than it had been previously, but the incumbent still depended on the allegiance of fellow chiefs and followers. In return for their political loyalty, they expected him to be munificent. Irefin's habit was all the more resented because, as Akinyele also noted, he was rich.[27]

Campaigning for installation: custom and the rowdy element

Three days after *Bale* Akintayo's death, on 16 September 1912, an entourage of *Otun Bale* Irefin's subordinate chiefs and followers met with *Alaafin* Ladugbolu in Oyo. He reported to his District Commissioner that the party had informed him 'that the

[17] NAI, Iba. Prof. 3/10: Ross to James, September 1912.
[18] For details of his chieftaincy promotions see Appendix II.
[19] NAI, Iba. Prof. 3/10: Ross to James, September 1912.
[20] Akinyele, *Outlines*, p. 43.
[21] See Appendix II.
[22] NAI, Iba. Prof. 3/10: Ross to James, September 1912.
[23] Akinyele, *Outlines*, p. 35.
[24] *Mogaji* Irefin, interviewed 9 January 1996, Ibadan. See also Appendix II.
[25] *Ibid.*, p. 22.
[26] NAI, Iba. Prof. 3/10: Ross to James, September 1912.
[27] Akinyele, *Outlines*, p. 22.

Balogun of Ibadan is always rude to them, and directly they have got a head [meaning a *Bale*] they will fight with him'.[28] The next day, Ladugbolu received a large group of *Balogun* Situ's supporters. In addition to Situ's own followers, there were also representatives of *Iyalode* Lanlatu, *Asipa Bale* Ola and 'some petty chiefs', as well as the heads of the *Sango* and *Egungun* religious cults. Despite this widespread support for Situ, the *Alaafin* was opposed to his election on the grounds that 'he has no experience at all, and I do not think that he likes Oyo'. Ladugbolu favoured either Irefin, Ola or Akinwale.[29]

On 18 September Acting Resident Ross called a Council meeting. *Osi Bale* Akinwale spoke in support of Irefin but *Balogun* Situ dissented. Although Situ had entered the chieftaincy ranks only one year after Irefin and his promotions had been less erratic, Ross refused to support his claim. He asserted the *Balogun* 'was rather young and not of great experience as the *Otun*' and stated 'that the matter would be referred to the Alafin of Oyo and his Excellency the Governor whose decision of the matter would be final'.[30] *Balogun* Situ's followers took to the Ibadan streets. On 19 September Rev. Williams wrote: 'Today's night till Saturday morning – no sleep, plot, songs etc against Irefin's nomination.'[31] Three days later, he recorded that Situ and Ola were summoned to the Residency and 'threatened'.[32]

After this meeting, Ross wrote to his Lagos superiors. He asserted:

A *Bale* is chosen from members of Council by the majority of votes of members and the support of minor Chiefs and religious Heads subject to the approval of the Alafin.

The *Otun Bale* (the right hand) has every right to expect that by the native customs he will succeed on the death of the *Bale*.[33]

As far as the chiefs were concerned, the 'custom' for succession to Ibadan's ruling title was rivalry between candidates in both the *Bale* and *Balogun* lines. However, for Ross, 'custom' was the fact that five *Otun Bale* had ascended to higher office since the onset of colonial rule.

Ross was doubtful about Situ's loyalty to the Lagos government and the Oyo throne. Misleadingly, he wrote that *Alaafin* Ladugbolu supported only the *Otun Bale*. Anticipating that 'several of *Balogun*'s supporters will have gone to *Otun*'s side' Ross indicated he would soon call another Council meeting. He concluded:

It is possible that if *Balogun* is not elected the rowdy element will make some demonstration of dissatisfaction but I anticipate no difficulty in dealing with it and if I can detect the ringleaders exemplary punishment will have an excellent effect on Ibadan.[34]

On 26 September, Ross announced to the Ibadan Council that *Alaafin* Ladugbolu had nominated Irefin to be *Bale* and that Governor Lugard had approved. The

---

[28] NAI, Iba. Prof. 3/10: Ladugbolu to Ross, 16 September 1912.
[29] NAI, Iba. Prof. 3/10: Ladugbolu to Ross, 17 September 1912.
[30] NAI, Iba. Prof. 3/10: E.H. Oke, Secretary, Ibadan Native Government, 'Report upon the terms of the appointment of the Bale of Ibadan', n.d. (hereafter, Irefin appointment report).
[31] KDL, WD: 1912/19 September.
[32] KDL, WD: 1912/21 September.
[33] NAI, Iba. Prof. 3/10: Ross to James, September 1912.
[34] *Ibid*.

election campaign was over. The Acting Resident summarized the duties of Ibadan's *Bale* and stipulated that he 'expected obedience of, and cooperation from, the Chiefs.' He also asserted that Irefin's appointment was subject to his maintaining the approval of the *Alaafin* and the Governor.[35]

At 7.30 a.m. the next day, the Oja'ba market 'was packed with all grades of Chiefs, Heads of families, Traders, Farmers and Artizans [*sic*].' About 25,000 people were present to witness the installation of *Bale* Irefin. Two new rituals were introduced. Conferring political authority and representing 'native custom', the messengers of the *Alaafin* [*Ilari*] 'handed over the sacred leaves' to *Oluwo* Faeso.[36] Both the *Oluwo* and the *Ilari* had long been associated with Ibadan chieftaincy installations. However, the *Ilari* had previously been present only as witnesses; they had not held this powerful intermediary role.[37]

Representing municipal bureaucracy and conferring the power of the written word, Ernest Oke, the Secretary of the Ibadan Council 'handed a paper' to *Otun Bale* Irefin.[38] Its contents were then read out:

'It is my wish and I do promise to go to Oyo and salute the Alafin after my installation as soon as necessary and convenient. I do promise to obey and respect the Alafin and to obey all lawful authorities over me.'

This was signed in the presence of the vast assembly.

Irefin *Bale*   his

       X

       mark

The leaves were then placed upon the head of Irefin and pronounced 'you are the *Bale* of Ibadan from today' then followed the firing of guns.[39]

For the first time, Ibadan's ruling chief had publicly conceded his political allegiance to the *Alaafin* of Oyo. Amidst the lavish celebration of Irefin's inauguration, the practical effect of this constitutional amendment was not immediately apparent.

Corruption, crime and constitutionalism

Ten days after *Bale* Irefin's installation, *Agbakin* Akinoso, an uncle of Akinpelu Obisesan, 'cut off his throat at Residency'.[40] This junior chief had been exiled during

[35] NAI, Iba. Prof. 3/10: Irefin appointment report.

[36] *Ibid.*

[37] Morgan, *Akinyele's Outline (Part Three)*, pp. 167–9.

[38] For an interesting analysis of political interactions between the institutions of colonial chieftaincy and literacy see Isabel Hofmeyr, 'The Spoken Word and the Barbed Wire: Oral Chiefdoms Versus Literate Bureaucracies', in *We Spend Our Years as a Tale That is Told: Oral Historical Narrative in a South African Chiefdom* (London, 1993), pp. 60–8.

[39] NAI, Iba. Prof. 3/10: Irefin appointment report. Ernest Henley Oke (1847-1930) was born in Ijaye but moved to Lagos as a child where he completed his schooling and became a teacher. After a period as Head Warden of Lagos Prison, he was appointed as headmaster of the *Bale*'s School in Ibadan during 1909. Three years later he became Secretary of the Ibadan Council, a position he held until 1916 when he resigned. He was appointed as the Oyo Province representative to the Legislative Council in 1924 and was also a founder of the Ibadan branch of the United African Church. Jenkins, 'Politics in Ibadan', p. 440.

[40] KDL, WD: 1912, 8 October. See also, OP/N: 1914, 16 April. Obisesan was not living in Ibadan during 1912. In 1917–18, he sporadically used his 1914 diary as a notebook, recording specific past events of recent years.

1911; a punishment for his membership of the smallpox cult of *Sanponna*, whom Resident Elgee suspected of spreading the disease.[41] Akinoso subsequently became involved in a complex extortion racket between clerks in the Ibadan administration and senior Council chiefs. On condition that he expose the scam, just before the death of *Bale* Akintayo, Captain Ross allowed the *Agbakin* to return to Ibadan city.[42]

After several interviews with Police Superintendent Leslie, on 8 October 1912, Akinoso ceased cooperating. 'The Agbakin ... on this last occasion refused to give evidence or assist.... [Leslie] reminded him of his previous statements, and told him to go home.' Fearing retribution for his role as a double agent, the doomed chief 'committed suicide on the road leading to the town between the Residency Offices'.[43] Ibadan politics thus continued to claim its sacrifices. This was of considerable irritation to Captain Ross, whose case against the chiefs and clerks subsequently collapsed because of a lack of evidence.[44]

The Acting Resident did not fully disclose the circumstances surrounding *Agbakin* Akinoso's death until early December.[45] On 20 January 1913, Governor Lugard attended a Council meeting with Ross and the three most senior title-holders from each of the *Bale* and *Balogun* lines. Although these six chiefs made up less than half the statutory Council membership, an important administrative amendment was passed. The Ibadan police force would be significantly reduced and the town was to be divided into nineteen quarters, each under the 'management' of a chief, assisted by an *akoda*.[46] In pre-colonial times, this term had meant 'sword-bearer and executioner of chiefs'; in modern usage, it connoted 'Native Administration law-court-messenger'.[47]

According to Akinyele, the new method of policing 'fully protected the town from the infestation of Robbers'.[48] Layode writes that the head chief 'enacted Law in the town that every man must be sleeping at the gate of his House'.[49] A resultant decrease in burglary, the two historians argue, caused the rule of *Bale* Irefin to be prosperous. Neither was aware of the constitutional reform associated with this improvement in public safety. The *akoda* were subject to the rule of *Bale* Irefin but, in turn, he was accountable to the Resident:

> The Council agreed that the Resident as representing the Governor had the right to deal with any case that he thought fit to deal with regardless of the Chiefs or their decision and that his sentence shall be binding on all parties.[50]

Ironically, Captain Ross' assumption of absolute judicial power in Ibadan marked the legislative advance of a governmental system that was hailed as 'indirect'.

[41] RH, Mss.Afr. s.1169: Elgee, 'Evolution', p. 34.
[42] NAI, Iba. Prof. 3/10: Ross to James, 9 December 1912.
[43] NAI, Iba. Prof. 3/10: Ross to James, 9 November 1912.
[44] NAI, Iba. Prof. 3/10: Ross to James, 9 December 1912.
[45] *Ibid.*
[46] RH, Mss. Brit. Emp. S.76/f. 163: Lugard Papers, 'At the [Ibadan] Council Meeting held 20 January 1913'. See also, RH, Mss.Afr. S.1169: Elgee, 'Evolution', p. 35.
[47] Abraham, *Dictionary*, p. 384.
[48] Akinyele, *Outlines*, p. 22.
[49] Layode Mss.
[50] RH, Mss. Brit. Emp. S.76: f. 163.

Indirect Rule, Native Gentlemen & Renowned Capitalists

'A dash at reforming'

Almost a year after Irefin became *Bale*, another appointment was being contemplated. Selwyn Macgregor Grier had first come to Nigeria in 1906 and was posted to Zaria, which had fallen to British forces four years earlier.[51] During August 1913, after a year in the adjacent province of Bauchi, Grier learned that Governor Lugard proposed to send him to Ibadan.[52]

By 5 November, Grier had arrived. Resident Elgee was to proceed on leave in ten days. His replacement noted: 'Elgee is a pleasant little man and very hospitable but is supposed to be not very efficient.'[53] Unknown to him, after a decade in Ibadan, Elgee was being removed. He returned briefly during April 1914, at which time Grier regretted: 'I am afraid he feels leaving Ibadan dreadfully.'[54] Elgee was posted to Ijebu-Ode; in 1916, he resigned the Colonial Service. He died of a drug overdose in October 1917 – tragically ending his life in a similar manner to numerous Ibadan chiefs.[55] 'Cap. Elgee', recalled Akinyele, 'was very kind, not troublesome or fault finding, but a perfect gentleman cool as dove.'[56]

After a fortnight in Ibadan, Grier wrote to his mother, Grace. He told her: 'I should like to have a dash at "reforming" this place - I don't believe it would be nearly so difficult as most people imagine.'[57] At the end of his first month, Grier's wish came true – Lugard officially informed him of his duty to 'propound a scheme for a more effective native administration of Ibadan'.[58] This 'scheme' was intended to extend Lugard's policy of 'indirect rule' – a model of governance which he had already put into practice in the emirates of northern Nigeria.[59]

'Administration in this part of the world has been absolutely and entirely neglected', declared Grier.[60] This view, utterly dismissive of the previous twenty years of British rule and especially of the determined efforts of Resident Elgee, was a reflection of Grier's inappropriate expectations of Ibadan chieftaincy. In his words: 'The *Bale* I may say is the native ruler corresponding to the Emir in the North. I wish he was more like a Northern Emir in capacity & intellect!'[61] In practice, the *Bale* of Ibadan held neither the civil nor religious authority of an Emir. Such autocratic power was anathema to civic Ibadan politics.

By 9 December, Grier was aghast: 'Ibadan is undoubtedly in a dreadfully backward

[51] Adeleye, *Power and Diplomacy*, p. 247.
[52] RH, Mss. Afr. S.1379: Papers of Selwyn Macgregor Grier, 2/5/f. 10; S.M. Grier to Grace Grier, 28 August 1913.
[53] RH, Mss. Afr. S.1379: 2/5/f. 12; S.M. to Grace, 5 November 1913.
[54] RH, Mss. Afr. S.1379: 2/7/f. 10; S.M. to Grace, 5 April 1914.
[55] Jenkins, 'Politics in Ibadan', p. 141.
[56] Akinyele, *Outlines*, p. 78.
[57] RH, Mss. Afr. S.1379: 2/5/f.13; S.M. to Grace, 18 November 1913.
[58] RH, Mss. Afr. S.1379: 2/5/f.15; S.M. to Grace, 30 November 1913.
[59] The literature on indirect rule in Nigeria is vast. Two useful introductions are: A.H.M. Kirk-Greene, *The Principles of Native Administration in Nigeria: Selected Documents, 1900–1947* (London, 1965); Michael Crowder and Obaro Ikime (eds), *West African Chiefs: Their Changing Status Under Colonial Rule and Independence* (Ile-Ife, 1970).
[60] RH, Mss. Afr. S.1379: 2/5/f.15; S.M. to Grace, 30 November 1913.
[61] RH, Mss. Afr. S.1379: 2/5/f.14; S.M. to Grace, 26 November 1913.

state.... The whole Native System of rule seems to have degenerated into a reign of petty extortion and worse.'[62] His administrative characterisation was probably quite accurate; a tribute to the success of the Ibadan chiefs at institutionalising 'private fees'. A week later, Grier was relieved by a visit to Oyo, a place that was 'quite a treat' compared to Ibadan. He wrote of his delight at seeing 'a genuine native town clean and well ordered, while here everything is dirt and confusion with a people who have lost all respect for their natural Chiefs'.[63]

Grier attributed this lack of respect to the imperial impact. He stressed that he needed to start 'reforming' as soon as possible:

> The more I see about this place [Ibadan] the more I feel that we have done more harm than good here, & unless a very strong line can be taken, which existing Treaty rights possibly prevent, I shall ask Lugard to let me go elsewhere. I can not adapt myself to the policy of laissez faire which has been followed here year after year.'[64]

Such were the official beginnings of indirect rule in Ibadan.

Grier was no longer so glum in April 1914. Major Boyle, the Lieutenant Governor of the Southern Provinces, had agreed to allow him and Ross 'a pretty free hand'. The opportunity, he admitted, was to be relished: 'it will be very interesting seeing how things turn out'.[65] In the meantime, *Bale* Irefin had been deposed.

'A pang in our minds'

The Protectorates of Northern and Southern Nigeria were ceremoniously united on 1 January 1914. Ross was promoted to Provincial Commissioner, while Grier gained the post of Ibadan District Officer.[66] 'Amalgamation Day' in Ibadan, as Grier recalled, 'was nothing very exhilarating ... many of them ['the natives'] weren't at all delighted with the local arrangements and the *Bale* has been giving Trouble ever since'.[67] This 'Trouble' had begun in the form of a petition, dated 14 January, and addressed to Governor Lugard. It was entitled: 'The Native Chiefs' Complaints Against Commissioner Ross'. Ibadan chieftaincy was fighting back. The collective battle strategy was no longer militaristic – it was discursive.

Bale Irefin and thirteen of his chiefs detailed three major grievances in their six-page document. The first was:

> That most of the Towns tributary to your petitioners are being unceremoniously interfered with by the Alafin of Oyo, and in this connection Captain Ross the D.C. of Oyo from time to time exerts his potent official influence to aid him to deprive us of our possessions.[68]

As was shown in Chapter 3, the 'subject towns' of Ibadan's military empire helped constitute the civic status of its chiefs, both economically and socially. They made

---

[62] RH, Mss. Afr. S.1379: 2/5/f.16; S.M. to Grace, 9 December 1913.
[63] RH, Mss. Afr. S.1379: 2/5/f.17; S.M. to Grace, 15 December 1913.
[64] *Ibid.*
[65] RH, Mss. Afr. S.1379: 2/7/f.12; S.M. to Grace, 15 April 1914.
[66] RH, Mss. Afr. S.1379: 2/7/f.2; S.M. to Grace, 13 January 1914.
[67] RH, Mss. Afr. S.1379: 2/7/f.6; S.M. to Grace, 4 March 1914.
[68] KDL, Herbert Macaulay Papers (hereafter, HMP), 27/2: Native Chiefs to Governor Lugard, 14 January 1914.

tribute payments to *ajele* (agents) which found their way into chiefs' private purses. Collectively, 'subject people' added to the following claimed by a warrior chief – he asserted himself as their *babakekere*. However, from the earliest years of colonial rule, British authorities began undermining this '*ajele* system'. Concurrently, they increased the political jurisdiction of the *Alaafin* of Oyo.

This policy was adopted for pragmatic reasons. As Resident Fuller described him, *Alaafin* Adeyemi was: 'certainly the most "royal" native I have seen in Yorubaland'.[69] For colonial administrators, a personified, centralised power was a more useful agent of rule than decentralised jurisdiction. Three years after the bombardment of the Oyo palace, Governor McCallum set about resurrecting the power of the *Alaafin* on imperial terms. As part of this project, certain towns were 'transferred' from Ibadan to Oyo during March 1898.[70]

Ibadan chiefs strongly protested this usurpation of their dependencies.[71] Nonetheless, by 1914, their loss of jurisdiction had become widespread. As far as the petitioners were concerned, the developing administrative policy was contrary to the provisions of the 1893 Agreement. For example, Iseyin was specifically named in the treaty as one of the towns whose 'internal affairs' were vested in 'the general government of Ibadan'. Under Ross, it was being ruled through the Oyo throne. Explicitly drawing attention to the simultaneously material and symbolic value of their empire, *Bale* Irefin and his chiefs reminded Governor Lugard 'That these Towns were won at enormous cost to lives and property and the fact that the blood of our dear Fathers and Relations contributed to the price of these Towns create a pang in our minds.'[72]

At the same time, Ibadan itself was being made 'tributary' to *Alaafin* Ladugbolu. Appropriating the terminology of indirect rule, the aggrieved chiefs argued such a practice was based on a misconception of 'the Yoruba customs and usages'. Against it, they wrote: 'The relationship between the Alafin and the Ibadan is that of mutual friendship and courtesy but not the relationship of a Head lording it over his subjects.'[73] Significantly, 'the Ibadan' were identified as an independent polity.

This first grievance of the 'Native Chiefs' Complaints' concluded ominously. If the 'unwaranted tampering' of *Alaafin* Ladugbolu did not cease, the signatories warned, it was not possible to guarantee that peace in the Lagos hinterland was 'perfectly assured'. Rather: 'It is an innovation fraught with consequences for the Alafin to tamper with Ibadan's possessions.'[74] This allusion to the pre-colonial military past hinted that, just as it had been in 1893, peace in 'the Yoruba Country' was dependent upon Ibadan.

The second grievance related to a form of political subordination that was

---

[69] NAI, Iba. Prof. 3/6: Fuller, Resident's Journal, 7 January 1898.

[70] J.A. Atanda, *New Oyo Empire*, p. 102.

[71] See accounts of resistance from *Ekerin Balogun* Suberu and *Asipa Balogun* Apanpa. NAI, Iba. Prof. 3/6: Ehrhardt, Resident's Journal, 23 December 1898; 10 March 1899.

[72] KDL, HMP, 27/2: Native Chiefs to Governor Lugard, 14 January 1914.

[73] *Ibid*.

[74] KDL, HMP, 27/2: Native Chiefs to Governor Lugard, 14 January 1914. This sentence is an editorial addition of Herbert Macaulay. It is written in his handwriting on the copy of the petition in his private papers. Macaulay's involvement in the politics of Irefin's deposition will be discussed shortly.

physically literal – Captain Ross's command that all Ibadan chiefs, excepting only the *Bale*, 'must perforce prostrate flat on the bare ground in saluting him'.[75] Atanda suggests that this standard of greeting was an extension of the 'customary respect' which Ross believed was owed to the *Alaafin* of Oyo.[76] The 1914 petitioners were at pains to emphasise that no other British officials had demanded 'that they be thus adored'. Still today, this practice of 'enforced prostration' remains bitterly remembered and recalled in the appellations of *Ajele Pataki* and *Gba mi l'eti*.[77] The former makes a sarcastic reference to Ross's self-importance; the latter means 'the period of 'Slap-me-on-the-face'.[78]

The final grievance of the petitioners concerned *Abese Balogun* Amida. According to them, Amida had 'no respect for all the late *Bale*s and always acted in opposition to their wishes, all of which ended in his being deposed'. Having begun with Ibadan's glorious military past, the petition ended by stating 'that when a chief is deposed it is imperative for the Chief to quit the Town of Ibadan or die'. Names of chiefs who had suicided or been expelled were listed; the complainants noted that there were 'many many others too numerous to mention here'.[79] In this way, the political practices which made a civic Ibadan – militarism and civil disorder – were textually represented *together*.

Ingeniously, the text adopted colonial terminology to explain the basis of indigenous constitutionalism:

> No other motive underlies your Petitioners' most earnest desire to see that Amida, the Ex-*Abese*, quit the Town of Ibadan other than the Native Customs most sacred to them be respected thereby maintaining peace and order in the Town and avoid wanton violation of customary laws and usages.[80]

Again, the petitioners concluded with a warning. To maintain stable government, it was vital that Governor Lugard approve the expulsion of Amida. With this action, he would maintain customary political practices, as his predecessors had done in the cases of *Balogun* Kongi and *Bale* Dada.[81]

Unlike the hapless Dada, however, *Abese Balogun* Amida was supported by the local British authorities. As well as staying alive and resident in Ibadan, he also kept his title. Five years later, Amida was *Osi Bale* and a judge in the Ojaba Native Court.[82] According to Captain Ross, he was 'a very wise and loyal old man'.[83] Akinpelu Obisesan held an opposed view. When *Otun Bale* Amida died in 1929, he recalled 'a sinister figure ... the man who sold political liberty of Ibadan to the Alafin'.[84]

Throughout the nineteenth century, deposition and consequent death or deporta-

[75] *Ibid.*
[76] Atanda, *New Oyo Empire*, p. 175.
[77] Chief Ayorinde, *Asipa Olubadan*, interviewed 16 September 1995, Ibadan.
[78] Akinyele, *Outlines*, p. 79.
[79] KDL, HMP, 27/2: Native Chiefs to Governor Lugard, 14 January 1914.
[80] *Ibid.*
[81] *Ibid.*
[82] NAI, Iba. Prof. 3/1: Criminal Record Book, 1917/18.
[83] NAI, CSO 26/14935: Ross to Secretary, Southern Provinces, 2 May 1925.
[84] KDL, OP/47: 1929, 18 July.

tion had been a pragmatic, short-term strategy to curb the influence of an overly powerful Ibadan warrior chief. During the early colonial period it also became a means to ascend the political ranks. By 1914, it was being presented as a 'sacred Native Custom'. Chieftaincy politics in this city was impressively adaptive.

'Elders still exist'

On 30 January 1914, a fortnight after *Bale* Irefin and his chiefs submitted their petition to Governor Lugard, a group of Christian-educated Yoruba men established a cultural society in Ibadan. They called themselves the *Egbe Agba O'tan*, a name meaning 'Elders still exist'.[85] In spite of this title, most members were barely middle-aged. They included Rev. Williams, Rev. Akinyele and his younger brother Isaac; as well as Moses Adeyemi, a tutor at the CMS Training College, Oyo. Samuel Layode was appointed Treasurer. Daniel Obasa, who became Secretary, had come from Lagos to Ibadan in 1901 as a sales clerk for Paterson Zochonis, where he worked with Layode. The 'President' and 'Acting Chairman' were Ernest Oke and Rev. Okuseinde respectively, men who had direct links to Ibadan government.[86]

In later years, the *Egbe Agba O'tan* claimed members in other Yoruba towns. For example, with the society's support, Adesoji Aderemi was installed *Ooni* of Ife in 1930.[87] During the same year, the group raised £37 11/6d for a London student hostel planned by Ladipo Solanke, the Abeokuta citizen who founded the West African Students Union (WASU).[88] It is in this pan-Yoruba context that the appellation of 'Elders' becomes comprehensible. As Olufunke Adeboye has argued, the group's claim to this status derived from their self-confident membership of the second generation of an indigenous Christian-educated elite.[89]

For example, the Akinyele brothers were nephews of Rev. Oyebode, a key broker in the 1893 treaty negotiations.[90] Rev. Okuseinde had been a pupil of Rev. Johnson at Kudeti mission school and, during 1875, Samuel had married Lydia, Okuseinde's sister.[91] It was perhaps this family connection which helped the *Egbe* Agba *O'tan* to secure Dr Obadiah Johnson as their 'Patron'.[92] Dr Johnson might have been rewriting his brother's monumental history book at the time the society was founded; this project could have stimulated his interest.

During the third decade of colonial rule, this literate Christian status group self-

---

[85] KDL, BAP/44: *Constitution, Rules and Regulations of* Egbe Agba-O-Tan (Ibadan, 1914).

[86] Layode Mss.

[87] Aderemi had formerly worked as a clerk (with Obisesan) on the Lagos Railway. KDL, OP/47: 1930, 27 June; 7, 11, 12 July; 22 August; 25, 27 October.

[88] KDL, OP/P: *Egbe Agba O'tan* Letter Book, 1928–31, Obisesan to Solanke, 10 March 1930. Solanke was initiated into the Society on 10 July 1930. See OP/47: 1930, 10 July. On WASU see James S. Coleman, *Nigeria: Background to Nationalism* (Berkeley, 1963), pp. 204–7.

[89] Olufunke Adeboye, 'The *Egbe Agba O'tan* of Yorubaland: an Educated Elite Organisation, 1914-1944', paper presented to Department of History, University of Ibadan, 14 December 1995. See also, J.F.A. Ajayi, *Christian Missions in Nigeria 1841–1891: the Making of a New Elite* (Ibadan, 1965) and E.A. Ayandele, *The Missionary Impact on Modern Nigeria, 1842–1914* (London, 1966).

[90] Akinyele, *Outlines*, p. 55.

[91] Doortmont, 'Recapturing the Past', p. 22.

[92] Layode Mss.

consciously embarked on a new phase of making their cultural heritage. 'Yorubaness' linked into local political activism – these educated men sought to use their writing skills to act in an advisory capacity to indigenous rulers. As Layode wrote, the purpose of the *Egbe Agba O'tan* was 'to be approaching Resident and the chiefs about Ibadan town affairs [and] to promote and preserve Yoruba culture'. Members pursued these interests by presenting themselves as the custodians of a past that they shared with their chiefly Elders and which they were obligated to uphold. In this vein, the constitution stated:

> That this Society's aim and object shall be to institute researches into all Yoruba Religions, Customs, Philosophy, Medical Knowledge, Arts, Sciences, Manufactures, Poetical Cultures, Political and National Histories & c.[93]

A publication committee was established with Isaac Akinyele as general editor. The preface of his *Iwe Itan Ibadan* is dated 1911 – he writes that the work originated with an invitation to give a lecture on 'Ancient and Modern Ibadan'.[94] However, it appears the text was published during 1916, along with *Iwe Itan Oyo*, completed in 1914 by M.C. Adeyemi.[95] These were the only history books which the Society managed to issue.[96]

'Only Native Gentlemen of Yorubaland are eligible for membership', proclaimed the *Egbe Agba O'tan* constitution. The ceremony of initiation was explicitly Christian, featuring a specially composed hymn and prayer. Regular meetings were opened and closed with hymns; five prayers were recited during the course of business. This aura of respectability was further enhanced by a code of practice and hierarchical structure adopted from Freemasonry. Members referred to each other as 'Brothers' and named Ibadan as 'No. 1 Lodge'. The top rank in the society, open to 'active and hard-working members', was 'Knights of the First Degree'. Those in the second rank were men 'found zealous and deeply interested'; newly admitted members joined the 'Knights of the Third Degree'.[97]

This appropriation was not unusual – Freemasons had been in West Africa since the eighteenth century.[98] From the 1850s onwards, prominent African men in the Gold Coast and Lagos Colony had sought to augment their social standing by jointly founding Lodges with British officials and European merchants. For example, Lagos Lodge No. 1171 opened in 1868; it was multi-racial from its earliest meetings.[99] By

---

[93] KDL, BAP/44: *Constitution*.

[94] Falola, 'Kemi Morgan and the Second Reconstruction', p. 93.

[95] Law, 'Early Yoruba Historiography', p. 90. Law cites a review of the two books in the *Lagos Standard*, 18 October 1916.

[96] Toyin Falola and Michel Doortmont, '*Iwe Itan Oyo*: a Traditional Yoruba History and its Author', *Journal of African History* 30 (1989), p. 302.

[97] KDL, BAP/44: *Constitution*.

[98] Augustus Casely-Hayford and Richard Rathbone, 'Politics, Families and Freemasonry in the Colonial Gold Coast', in *People and Empires*, ed. Ajayi and Peel, pp. 143–60. Casely-Hayford and Rathbone (p. 146) name Richard Hull as the first Mason in West Africa; he was appointed provincial Grand Master for the 'Gambay' in 1735.

[99] W. Bro. W.R.D. Matches, *Ibadan Lodge 5316, 1931–1966* (Ibadan, 1967), p. 8. In contrast to Lagos, Ibadan Lodge No. 5316 was not established until 1931 and, even then, its membership was predominantly European. The 1940s and 1950s saw the foundation of several African Lodges, in which an *Egbe Agba O'tan*

1906, there were seven active Lodges in the city and many had African clergymen as members. In 1914, T.A.J. Ogunbiyi founded the 'Christian Ogboni Society', a Freemasonry organisation whose name reflects its merging of indigenous and imported religious/cultural rituals. Two decades later, opposition to the perceived 'paganism' of the group forced it to change its title to the 'Reformed Ogboni Fraternity' (ROF).[100]

The Masonic qualities of the *Egbe Agba O'tan* were also evident in its promotion of a cult of secrecy: 'To avoid leakage of the Society's movements, the proceedings of every meeting are to be kept a profound secret and must not be divulged to outsiders.' A member who was absent from a meeting would not be informed about its business or discussions. 'Proved cases of Leakage' would result in instant dismissal.[101]

Ignoring the Freemasonry connection, Jenkins argues that the society was clandestine because the 'community leaders' who comprised it feared that Captain Ross would perceive their activities as subversive.[102] This view neglects an analysis of the cultural identity which Native Gentlemen aimed to project. These men understood their audience to be others like them – 'secrecy' was a strategic practice, not a form of submission. It enabled this status group to assure themselves of their allegiance to a set of social values which they saw as shared by other 'respectable native' and 'official' circles. These values espoused elitism, but on educational rather than racial grounds. Surprisingly, Jenkins also claims that *Egbe* members 'made no open intervention in politics.'[103] His later work with Post revised this contention, suggesting that the association became politically involved 'in reaction to the excesses of the Alafin and Captain Ross and their disgust with the Ibadan chiefs'.[104]

After a violent disturbance in the city during 1919, the Society eschewed secrecy and petitioned the Resident. 'The tumultuous noise of the night' on 29 May was the sound of a riot led by *Balogun* Oyewole; it revealed yet another intrigue between Ibadan chiefs. 'On behalf of the community of Ibadan in general', the gentlemen pleaded, 'help us remove a deeprooted and accursed custom.'[105] A month later, the Resident met the *Egbe Agba O'tan* and discussed their petition with them.[106]

Further consultations were held during 1920. On 24 June, a delegation met Resident Ross and spent an hour 'discussing matters [of] politics with him ... he laid strong emphasis on the system of Native Administration, what he has done and [is] still doing to preserve the Rights of Native Authority'. Spokesman Obasa questioned the administrator about corruption amongst the chiefs; whilst Ross admitted the problem, he declared it was 'not opportune to stop same'.[107]

---

[99] (cont.) member, Rev. Akinyele, was an active participant. However, his involvement with Lagos Masons earlier in the century remains uncomfirmed. See KDL, BAP/41/2: Lodge Activities of A.B. Akinyele.

[100] E.A. Ayandele, *The Educated Elite in the Nigerian Society* (Ibadan, 1974), p. 20. The involvement of R.O.F. members in Ilesha politics caused great animosity from rival associations and led, in part, to a riot during 1941. See Peel, *Ijeshas and Nigerians*, pp. 186–96.

[101] KDL, BAP/44: *Constitution*.

[102] Jenkins, 'Politics in Ibadan', p. 86.

[103] *Ibid*.

[104] Post and Jenkins, *Price of Liberty*, p. 16.

[105] KDL, BAP/49/9: *Egbe Agba O'tan* to Ross, 7 June 1919.

[106] KDL, WD: 1919, 1 July.

[107] KDL, OP/55: 1920, 24 June.

Four days later, this discussion was reviewed at the 'Lodge meeting'. Rev. Akinyele reported that he had once requested Captain Ross to appoint an Advisory Board to assist the Council chiefs. However, the Resident 'objected & Entirely force against it'.[108] Herein lay the gentlemen's frustration – Ross deigned to meet them, but he refused to grant them any official recognition. His governing project opposed their political participation – an explicit element of indirect rule ideology.[109] As far as Obisesan was concerned, the practice showed 'the plan of the present day political officers to keep educated and enlightened youngsters in subjection, repress and set chiefs against them'.[110]

In 1925, Resident Ross dismissed the *Egbe Agba O'tan* as 'locally of no importance'.[111] Readers of *The Yoruba News*, launched in January 1924 as a local paper and the Society's mouthpiece, would doubtless have disagreed. Daniel Obasa became its editor; his first enterprise was to publish a number of articles entitled 'Our Needs'. These were, in order of precedence, roads, electricity, piped water and cemeteries.[112] A series on the theme of 'True Patriotism' followed:

> The educated people are the connecting link between the Government and our rulers. Our patriotism should always direct us how to move between the Authorities and our rulers so as to avoid all sources of disagreement.[113]

As we shall see, this form of political brokerage was fully played out during the 1930s. When Resident Ross left Ibadan in 1931, Rev. Okuseinde could only lament that, 'he dealt most unfairly with our honourable Egbe and shelved us as "nobodies"'.[114]

Post and Jenkins imply that the political activism of the *Egbe Agba O'tan* was initially precluded by its cultural focus.[115] Yet, as Peel has argued, the historical context of pan-Yoruba consciousness conceived politics and culture as mutually constitutive, not mutually exclusive.[116] Furthermore, it seems hardly coincidental that the society was formed only a fortnight after *Bale* Irefin and his chiefs submitted their 'Complaints' to Governor Lugard. These chiefs were illiterate – they could not have written the petition. It has not been possible to determine conclusively who did. However, there is some evidence to suggest that the *Bale* employed the literary skills of Herbert Macaulay, a Freemason who belonged to St John's Lodge No. 2668, Lagos.[117] As the furore stimulated by the critical document deepened, two more Native Gentlemen, Rev. Okuseinde and Dr Obadiah Johnson, became involved.

Exploring this layered fraternity returns us to the political career of *Bale* Irefin.

---

[108] KDL, OP/55: 1920, 28 June. This political body was finally introduced in April 1941. See NAI, Oyo Prof. 1/1696: Government of the City of Ibadan; NAI, Oyo Prof. 2/1/Oy. 3131: Ibadan Advisory Board.

[109] Lord Lugard, *Political Memoranda*, 1918: Memo 9, Para. 45.

[110] KDL, OP/55: 1923, 4 December.

[111] NAI, CSO 26/14935: Ross to Chief Secretary Tomlinson, 17 June 1925. This file concerns the deposition of *Bale* Situ, to which the *Egbe Agba O'tan* was vigorously opposed.

[112] NAI, *The Yoruba News*, 1924: 22, 29 January, 5, 12 February.

[113] NAI, *The Yoruba News*, 1924: 22 April.

[114] KDL, BAP/53B/011: Rev. Okuseinde to Rev. Akinyele, 25 August 1931.

[115] Post and Jenkins, *Price of Liberty*, p. 16.

[116] Peel, 'Yoruba Ethnogenesis', p. 201.

[117] Ayandele, *Educated Elite*, p. 20.

Indirect Rule, Native Gentlemen & Renowned Capitalists

'Fanned into flame'

He was a Bold Minded chief and An Industrious fellow. He was the first *Bale* to own Money on Hand quite well Before He Became *Bale*. Through Farm Work Managing. His words were Law. He Reported Captain Ross the Resident to Lagos governor of the time Because Ibadan chiefs and the people did not want to be under Alafin Authority and Domination.[118]

Samuel Layode, the first treasurer of the *Egbe Agba O'tan*, was an admirer of *Bale* Irefin. Selwyn MacGregor Grier was not. On 9 February 1914 he wrote: 'The ruling chief of Ibadan is to my mind a most hopeless individual … it is quite time that Lugard made a definite move.'[119] At that time, the 'Native Chiefs' Complaints' would have been circulating Lagos bureaucracy for about three weeks.

According to Isaac Akinyele, this petition was not initiated by *Bale* Irefin. He suggests that its production represented a new conspiratorial strategy: 'Amidst prosperity, sudden and unexpected intrigue arose; the *Bale* was urged by the Chiefs to prepare a Petition for the Governor.'[120] Irefin complied; the document was written and delivered. From the perspective of 'educated civilized men', what happened next was a surprise: 'We fully expected that the Senior Resident would put a stop to this evil at the very start, but instead it was apparently fanned into flame by the source.'[121]

For District Officer Grier, the view was rather different. A Lagos political activist was in league with *Bale* Irefin; the British official was confronted by an alliance that, to his eyes, was repugnant.[122] Grier had expressed unease about the potential of such affinities in his very first letter from Ibadan. He wrote to his mother: 'The station itself is very pretty … hampered by the educated nigger of Lagos who interferes in every way he can & is not above preaching sedition.'[123] Grier does not mention the name of the Lagosian associated with Irefin; neither does Akinyele or Layode. However, today, the 'Native Chief's Complaints' are found in the private papers of Herbert Macaulay – 'the bête noire of the Nigerian government for nearly forty years'.[124] This 'native agitator' had initially come to official notice during 1908, through his involvement in protests against the Colony's decision to levy a water rate on Lagos residents.[125]

The evidence of Macaulay's authorship of 'The Native Chiefs' Complaints' is circumstantial; no correspondence soliciting the petition could be found. Nonetheless, the document *was* amended in Macaulay's handwriting and his editorial changes were incorporated into later reprints of the petition. Furthermore, *Bale*

---

[118] Layode Mss.

[119] RH, Mss. Afr. S.1379: 2/7/f. 3; S.M. to Grace, 9 February 1914.

[120] Akinyele, *Outlines*, p. 22.

[121] *Ibid.*, p. 81.

[122] RH, Mss. Afr. S.1379: 2/7/f. 7; S.M. to Grace, 17 March 1914.

[123] RH, Mss. Afr. S.1379: 2/5/f. 12; S.M. to Grace, 5 November 1913.

[124] Coleman, *Background to Nationalism*, p. 197. Herbert Macaulay (1864–1946) was a grandson of Rev. Samuel Crowther, the first African Bishop of the Niger Mission. After qualifying as a licensed surveyor in England, he returned to Lagos in 1893 and subsequently became a leading political figure. Today, he is represented as the 'father' of Nigerian nationalism on the one naira coin.

[125] *Ibid.*, pp. 179–80.

Irefin's wealth would have enabled him to employ the services of an experienced lobbyist, a fact which Grier complained of the following year.[126]

Notwithstanding the petition, it is clear that colonial officialdom was a key agent in Irefin's downfall. As Grier put it:

> He [Irefin] is a nasty old man and we are quietly arranging for his deposition, for as long as he is where he is it will be quite impossible to get things straight here....
> The chiefs seem to have at last realized that both Ross and myself mean business.[127]

Governor Lugard had agreed to Irefin's removal; however, 'he wished to avoid the appearance of acting arbitrarily'.[128] Consequently, Grier held 'an independent enquiry ... all the Ibadan Chiefs, except two, recommended the deposition of the *Bale*.'[129] By Akinyele's account, at this enquiry, the chiefs 'were frightened into denying they had authorized the petition'. They accused *Bale* Irefin of initiating an 'unjustifiable complaint' and claimed that he had forged their marks on the document.[130]

On 14 March 1914, Ibadan's head chief was removed from office; two days later, Rev. Williams led a delegation 'to sympathise' with him.[131] By contrast, the District Officer was positively gleeful:

> We 'outed' the *Bale* here on Saturday last.... His successor was publicly announced the same day to prevent the usual outbreak of intriguing & bribery which goes on when the result is doubtful. Never was a coup d'etat so sudden and so quiet. The Lagos agitator who had got hold of the late *Bale* (hence his downfall) will be <u>mad</u> & the gutter press will probably be screamingly funny.[132]

Balogun Situ, a chief once characterised as 'the rowdy element', became *Bale* of Ibadan. On 3 April, he invited Rev. Williams to his compound and 'asked for advice re government'.[133] Ex-*Bale* Irefin was deported to live in exile on his farm.

The 'exceedingly wealthy man' did not give up. In 1915, he went to Lagos. As Grier later recounted, 'Ibadan was kept in a state of unrest by continual intrigues and messages engineered by certain people.'[134] At the time, he angrily corresponded that

---

[126] RH, Mss. Afr. S.1379: 2/8/f. 3; S.M. to Grace, 10 February 1915. According to Ross, Macaulay did not offer his support cheaply – when *Bale* Situ was in a similar political predicament to Irefin in 1925, Macaulay rejected £25 as an insufficient payment. NAI, CSO 26/14935: Ross to Tomlinson, 2 May 1925. However, Macaulay did ultimately become involved on Situ's behalf, sending telegrams to the Acting Governor and Lieutenant Governor during June and July 1925. See KDL, HMP, 20/5; 24/6.

[127] RH, Mss. Afr. S.1379: 2/7/f. 6; S.M. to Grace, 4 March 1914.

[128] NAI, CSO 26/14935: Minute by Tomlinson, 14 July 1925. No official Government correspondence on the Irefin deposition could be found. However, the incident was referred to during the removal of Situ eleven years later.

[129] NAI, CSO 26/14935: Minute by Tomlinson, 14 July 1925.

[130] Akinyele, *Outlines*, p. 22.

[131] KDL, WD: 1914, 16 March.

[132] RH, Mss. Afr. S.1379: 2/7/f. 7; S.M. to Grace, 17 March 1914.

[133] KDL, WD: 1914, 3 April.

[134] NAI, CSO 26/11122 Vol. I: Minute by Grier, 19 August 1924. This file concerns the Deposed Chiefs Removal Ordinance, No. 59, 1917. In 1924, Governor Clifford proposed to strengthen this law and prevent deposed chiefs from living in Lagos. Grier was then Secretary for Native Affairs and he strongly supported the amendment, using Irefin's case as evidence. He maintained that Irefin was wealthy until 'bled white' by Lagos activists; in his view, this impoverishment caused his suicide.

there would be 'a very serious disturbance' if Irefin returned. 'The truth is,' Grier wrote, 'that Lugard has overdone things and is not the man he was. He is far too easily influenced by his immediate surroundings.'[135] According to Layode, among those 'influencing' the Governor were two members of the *Egbe Agba O'tan*, Rev. Okuseinde and Dr. Obadiah Johnson. They met Lugard and secured permission for Irefin's return to Ibadan.[136]

Despite Grier's fear, there was no 'disturbance'. Shortly after arriving in his compound, Irefin 'died an unnatural death'.[137] The episode ended in the customary way – suicide. In 1920, the Secretary of the *Egbe Agba O'tan* recalled the chief as a martyr: 'The late *Bale* Irefin fought and sacrificed his life for his country ... the intelligent class really appreciate what [he] did.'[138]

Unlike the case of *Bale* Dada, this deposition was a consequence of direct imperial intervention. In this sense, it was not customary. Never before had an Ibadan chief's removal centred on a written text and a contingent connivance between plotting chiefs and British officials. The new *Bale* did not neglect to reward his former ally – *Osi Bale* Ola was promoted to *Balogun*. As Akinyele put it: 'The *Balogun*'s line was again restored.'[139] For over thirty years, no *Otun Bale* was promoted.[140]

A very big show? A mere mayor and the Ile Olowo

A month after Irefin's deposal, Resident Ross requested permission to shift his headquarters to Oyo.[141] The largest administrative unit in Southern Nigeria – later known as Oyo Province – came into being. Moving the government base made no practical sense; even Grier acknowledged that the newly demarcated 'Ibadan Division' constituted 'the most populous and important part' in the region.[142] In 1921, Ibadan's population was estimated to be 238,075; more than twice that of municipal Lagos (99,690), Nigeria's second largest city.[143]

Such practicalities were ignored. More important was an ideological conviction that the constitutional position of Ibadan's *Bale* could only be legitimated by his subordination to the *Alaafin*. According to Grier's misconceived historical view, 'Ibadan was once under Oyo, but declared itself independent about 100 years ago.'[144] The task for indirect rule, as he and Captain Ross saw it, was to 're-establish' Oyo suzerainty. There was ample evidence that the Ibadan chiefs and people opposed this policy and were likely to continue resisting it. Grier, however, had little patience for

---

[135] RH, Mss. Afr. S.1379: 2/8/f. 3; S.M. to Grace, 10 December 1915.

[136] Layode Mss.

[137] Akinyele, *Outlines*, p. 81.

[138] KDL, OP/55: 1920, 3 November.

[139] Akinyele, *Outlines*, p. 23.

[140] See Appendix II.

[141] NAI, Oyo Prof 2/3 C.17: Ross to Secretary, Southern Provinces, 17 April 1914. This file is currently missing in the Nigerian National Archives. I rely on Atanda, *New Oyo Empire*, p. 133.

[142] RH, Mss. Afr. S.1379: 2/8/f. 8; S.M. to Grace, 1 June 1915.

[143] Mabogunje, *Urbanization in Nigeria*, p. 199; p. 257.

[144] RH, Mss. Afr. S.1379: 2/8/f. 8; S.M. to Grace, 1 June 1915.

what he perceived as political dysfunction: 'It [Ibadan] is a difficult place for there is no hereditary chief as in Oyo where they believe in the divine right of Kings & the result is continual intrigue & want of proper authority; consequently chaos.'[145]

Shortly after the commencement of the Great War in August 1914, Governor Lugard decreed that all chiefs in the Southern Provinces should be 'graded'. Lists of the chiefs to be recognised were requested from each Provincial Commissioner.[146] Since Captain Ross was engaged against German forces in Cameroon, his reply was not received until December. When it came, the chief with the largest constituency was absent from the list. Justifying his exclusion, the Resident declared that: 'The *Bale* of Ibadan is not a crowned head but is the Alafin's *Bale* of Ibadan and is appointed by him and is not entitled to any royal insignia … he is merely a mayor.'[147]

Over the next 15 years, the 'New Oyo Empire' was built by Captain Ross and his Ibadan District Officers.[148] To Grier's irritation, administrative reorganisation was initially delayed by European hostilities. 'But for the war stopping much of what had been intended,' he complained in 1915, 'this might have been a very big show.'[149] After the promulgation of the Native Authority Ordinance in 1916, 'the show' finally began.[150]

Treasuries, tax and a shrewd man

For District Officer Grier, the most important element in Governor Lugard's project of colonial governing was 'a systematised form of taxation'.[151] In his eyes, to establish 'Native Treasuries' in the Southern Provinces, colonial administrators simply needed to make tribute equivalent to tax. Levies previously paid in agricultural goods could be converted to cash sums. Chiefs could serve as tax collectors and be compensated with fixed salaries.[152]

As part of this scheme, the Ibadan Council consented, in January 1917, to provide an annual sum of £200 to recognise the *Alaafin* 'as our dear father and head'.[153] This financial contribution 'systematised' the nominal tribute of kola–nuts which Ibadan had previously given to Oyo. Eight months later, Resident Ross significantly raised the amount. On 5 September, he coerced the Ibadan chiefs to agree that, if required, half of the Oyo monarch's salary of £4,500 would be paid by the Ibadan Treasury.[154] *Balogun* Ola steadfastly opposed the plan; when the other Council chiefs failed to

---

[145] RH, Mss. Afr. S.1379: 2/8/f. 5; S.M. to Grace, 2 July 1915.

[146] NAI, Oyo Prof. 6/1 C.924/1914: Secretary, Southern Provinces to Ross, 19 August 1914.

[147] NAI, Oyo Prof. 6/1 C.924/1914: Grier, Acting Commissioner to Secretary, Southern Provinces, 11 December 1914. Grier quotes 'notes' sent by Ross.

[148] See Atanda, *New Oyo Empire* for a detailed historical study of Indirect Rule in Oyo Province between 1894 and 1934.

[149] RH, Mss. Afr. S.1379: 2/8/f. 10; S.M. to Grace, 4 December 1915.

[150] Margery Perham, *Native Administration in Nigeria* (Oxford, 1937), p. 70.

[151] RH, Mss. Afr. S.1379: 2/8/f. 10; S.M. to Grace, 4 December 1915.

[152] Lugard, *Political Memoranda*: Memo 5, Para. 28. Lugard quotes Grier in reference to Ibadan.

[153] NAI, Oyo Prof 1/1511: Bale and Chiefs to Ross, 3 January 1917.

[154] Council Minutes: 5 September 1917. These minutes were in the Mapo Hall Archive which is now lost. Quoted in Jenkins, 'Politics in Ibadan,' p. 236.

support him, he killed himself. For this 'honourable act', Ola is remembered as *Balogun* Kobomoje ('he who does not spoil his name').[155]

On 29 September 1918, 'soldiers armed with their guns' stood by while Captain Ross announced to the assembled Ibadan crowd that every adult male in the town would henceforth be charged a tax of seven shillings.[156] The city chiefs were expected to exact this sum from their followers. Since the Ibadan chief-follower relationship was neither permanent nor territorial, the institutional framework for tax collection was, from its origins, inherently unstable. As Jenkins explains, instead of choosing a *babaogun*, modern Ibadan citizens chose a tax collector.[157] The chiefs with the largest retinues produced the most tax receipts. 'Having people' was now directly linked to generating civic revenue.

It thus became even more vital for aspirants to Ibadan titles to have a substantial following and, relatedly, a secure income base. During the early twentieth century, a man with both these attributes was Okunola Abasi. An affluent Muslim trader, Abasi professed to be a grandson of Bankole Aleshinloye.[158] Family sources claim that Bankole was the first *Balogun* of Ibadan; Johnson names him as a 'lieutenant' of *Are-ona-kakanfo* Lakanle, who was killed by soldiers loyal to the politically ambitious Oluyole.[159] Abasi himself made a fortune by monopolising the trade in yam flour. When the Lagos Railway reached Jebba in 1908, he was the first to start transport of the food staple from there to Ibadan, purchasing it at seven shillings a bag and selling it for twice the price.[160]

As a result of his wealth, Abasi had a large group of hangers-on who, according to his son, would come to his house 'for their daily bread'.[161] From *Bale* Situ's point of view, Abasi was an attractive candidate for a title – theoretically, he would be able to levy a substantial tax revenue from his following and make a significant contribution to the Ibadan Treasury. For Abasi, a title was a necessary credential for establishing civic status.

'He was the first man to become chief in Ibadan through good luck', writes Samuel Layode.[162] About 1910, *Basorun* Apanpa requested *Ekarun Bale* Bola to cease attending Council meetings on account of his frailty. Bola, then head of *ile* Aleshinloye, complied and sent his nephew Abasi as a representative. When the elderly chief died in 1918, *Bale* Situ installed Abasi straight to the rank of *Ekerin Bale*.[163] For most of the next three decades, this 'shrewd ... unlettered man of business' was a key figure in Ibadan politics.[164] Or, as one observer put it, he was 'the green snake under the green grass'.[165]

[155] *Mogaji* Kobomoje interview, Ibadan, 13 April 1997.

[156] KDL, OP/N: 1914, 6 November. Entry dated 26/9/18.

[157] Jenkins, 'Politics in Ibadan,' p. 345.

[158] *Alhaji* Akande, interviewed 12 April 1997. *Alhaji* Akande became Abasi's private driver in 1925.

[159] Akande interview, 12 April 1997; Johnson, *History*, p. 257.

[160] Layode Mss.

[161] Bello Abasi (deceased), interviewed by Gavin Williams, Ibadan, 14 November 1971.

[162] Layode Mss.

[163] Akande interview, 12 April 1997.

[164] NAI, Oyo Prof. 1/1696: Comments by Chief Commissioner on Report on Local Government of Ibadan Town by I.W.E. Dods, District Officer, 29 June 1937. Commissioner Hunt gave this characterisation of Abasi at a time when other Ibadan chiefs were seeking to depose him. See Chapter 7.

[165] NAI, Iba. Div., 1/1/18 vol. VIII: Joseph Ogunseyi to Resident H.F.M.White, 3 May 1941.

In the eyes of colonial officers, Ibadan tax collection was not a resounding success. During the second assessment, Tax Officer Hodge was highly critical of the chiefs, particularly *Bale* Situ '[who] personifies incompetence, idleness and vulgarity'.[166] Of concern was the town ruler's familiar practice of greeting – 'jauntily throwing out a hand which I can only describe as representing the "Hallo! Old Son!" of a coster, rather than the salutation of a paramount Chief'. Mr Hodge was perhaps unaware that Ibadan's *Bale* was 'merely a mayor'. As far as he was concerned, the amassing of £15,000 in 12 working days had been achieved 'in spite of' the head-chief.[167]

With this revenue, the Ibadan Treasury began subsidising the Oyo Palace. In 1919, the salary of the *Alaafin* was fixed at £4,800 and, every year from then until 1934, Ibadan taxpayers supplied him with a payment of £2,400. The amount was reduced in 1934; however, a sum of £2,100 continued to be collected annually throughout the next decade.[168] The *Bale* was paid £2,400, more than three times the amount given to his next in rank, the *Balogun*.[169] Although the Ibadan ruler's salary was substantially less than that of the Oyo monarch, it was still the second highest sum drawn by any chief in the Southern Provinces. As one senior Lagos official pointed out, 'the *Bale* of Ibadan is not a small boy.'[170]

A second-class city

On 13 September 1917, a fortnight after *Balogun* Ola's suicide, Ibadan's *Bale* was appointed as a 'sole Native Authority made subordinate to the Alafin'.[171] In the parlance of indirect rule, the *Alaafin* was '1st class' while the *Bale* was '2nd class'.[172]

To recognise this fabricated hierarchy, Governor Lugard designed specific material objects. Chiefs who had been designated first-class were to be presented with a letter of appointment on a parchment scroll and a staff topped by a silver finial in the shape of the St Edward Crown, the standard symbol of British royal authority. Those who ranked second-class were to receive a staff with a brass finial. It was planned that the chief involved would recite an oath of allegiance to King George V when the appropriate items were presented to him.[173]

Captain Ross was requested to make arrangements for this imperial ritual as early as April 1917. He strongly disapproved. If the *Alaafin* was asked to make a formal oath of his allegiance, he warned, the Yoruba monarch might become wary. It was certainly not appropriate to confer such privileges on the *Bale* of Ibadan, 'whose loyalty to the Government has not been above suspicion.' In the Resident's view, the ceremony would jeopardise, not encourage, the implementation of direct taxation.[174]

---

[166] NAI, Oyo Prof. 4/7/324/19: Hodge to Ross, 20 February 1920.
[167] *Ibid.*
[168] NAI, Oyo Prof. 1/1768: Outram to Findlay, 3 March 1937. See also NAI, Oyo. Prof. 1/1511: Alafin's Salary-Contribution to by Ibadan Native Administration.
[169] NAI, Oyo Prof. 2/3 C.101: Chiefs' Salaries.
[170] NAI, CSO 26/14935: Minute by Tomlinson, 14 July 1925.
[171] *Nigeria Gazette*, 13 September 1917, Govt. Notice No. 104.
[172] Lugard, *Political Memoranda*: Memo 9; Para 26.
[173] *Ibid.*
[174] NAI, Oyo Prof. 2/3 C. 189, Vol. I.: Ross to Secretary, Southern Provinces, 20 May 1917.

Ross' superiors accepted his opinion.[175]

Over two years later, Governor Clifford ceremoniously handed over the hierarchical staves. 'A very good day by', remarked Rev. Williams, 'the *Bale* of Ibadan & others presented with a staff each.' Significantly, *Alaafin* Ladugbolu was simultaneously decorated with the Companion of the Most Distinguished Order of Saint Michael and Saint George. His title was afterwards *Alaafin*, C.M.G.[176]

This event took place in the midst of the 1919–20 trade boom, a prosperity largely stimulated by high cocoa prices. In this context, another set of political players – the *ile olowo* – enter the chieftaincy stage.

Cash, commerce and collusion

On 2 February 1922 the Secretary of the *Egbe Agba O'tan* visited *Balogun* Oyewole and *Otun Balogun* Aminu. He went in company of Ibadan's wealthiest African men, Salami Agbaje and Sanusi Adebisi. Commenting that the merchants were 'revered', he noted in his diary that 'certainly money is worth having.'[177] The following day, he continued to reflect upon the meeting and remarked that, financially, he was 'in hell fire'. Questioning whether he was a 'nonentity', he continued:

> Nobody in this town will revere anyone of no means, he would be counted as no-man – the great presents made to us forced me to recognise that Messrs Agbaje and Adebisi are being held in a very high esteem – after all what is our intelligence, our school going and reading of books without getting money to back these three things.[178]

In the third decade of colonial rule, self-assured respectability was obviously not enough for Akinpelu Obisesan – a middle-aged, Ibadan Christian gentleman.

Nine years earlier, Obisesan had resigned from the Lagos Railway and left his post of Station Master at Ikirun. After he returned to Ibadan, he worked erratically for several different European mercantile firms, seeking to establish himself as a trader.[179] Towards this end, he ordered a book entitled *600 ways to Get Rich* from a distributor in the United States.[180] However, the aspiring entrepreneur was not particularly successful – in 1922, he remained on the outer reaches of Ibadan's commercial sphere. Obisesan sought to gain a footing by seeking help from the Muslim merchants at its centre. Thus, when engaged as a cocoa buyer later that year, he saw himself as 'under the protecting mantle of Mr Agbaje as on the threshold to a new life'.[181]

Salami Agbaje was born in Lagos about 1880; by the early 1920s, he was Ibadan's richest 'native'. During the turbulent pre-colonial war years, his father, an Arabic teacher, had migrated from Iseyin. His mother was an Ibadan woman. Agbaje began his career as a tailor and then became apprenticed as a driver. Around the turn of the

[175] NAI, Oyo Prof. 2/3 C. 189, Vol. I.: Secretary, Southern Provinces to Ross, 4 July 1917.
[176] KDL, WD: 1919, 15 December.
[177] KDL, OP/53: 1922, 2 February.
[178] KDL, OP/53: 1922, 3 February.
[179] NAI, *The Yoruba News*, 1943: 4 May.
[180] KDL, OP/N: 1914, 10 September.
[181] KDL, OP/53: 1922, 16 August.

century, he came to Ibadan with his maternal uncle and involved himself in the timber industry, supplying logs to Mr Moody, who sold sleepers to the Lagos Railway.[182] Layode writes that Moody was swindled by his paymaster about 1905, who absconded with cash intended for employees working on the Iwo line.[183] Moody died shortly after going bankrupt and his business was taken over by 'Ibadan men' – almost certainly, one of them was Salami Agbaje.[184] Obisesan claimed (on the basis of hearsay) that Agbaje first made money by defrauding some sawyers who had sold him planks on £2000 credit.[185]

Once he had gained a position in the timber trade, Agbaje expanded into the burgeoning cocoa market. The cultivation of this cash crop had begun in farms around Ibadan shortly after the cessation of regional warfare. Its introduction was a result of local initiative, not British enterprise. Berry has explained the rapidity of its adoption as a consequence of the demobilization of large numbers of soldiers who sought new economic opportunities.[186] Using material on Ijesha, Peel challenges this generalization, pointing out that a decade elapsed between the end of the wars and the planting of cocoa trees on any significant scale.[187]

It was more immediately relevant, Peel argues, that cocoa offered a cash income, which was 'becoming a universal necessity'. He emphasises that a cash economy already existed in Ilesha at the end of the nineteenth century. What grew, he contends, was the cultural influence of money in the negotiation of social and political relationships.[188] A similar trend can be identified in Ibadan – the trial of Salu's alleged murderers and the chieftaincy careers of *Bale* Dada, *Bale* Irefin and Okunola Abasi attest to it. In addition, Peel suggests, a crucial prerequisite for cocoa production was the ability to command adequate labour resources. Thus pioneers were more likely to be older, established household heads than young, unemployed soldiers.[189]

This contention also seems applicable to Ibadan. For example, from 1892 onwards, the Aperin family gradually transformed an extensive tract of forest south-east of the city into a cocoa-growing area. Obisesan Aperin, who was an elephant hunter, had claimed authority over this land whilst protecting Ibadan from Ijebu invaders during the late 1880s. He gained the title of *Agbakin* in 1893 and was a signatory to the Ibadan Agreement.[190] Akinpelu was Aperin's son; in 1914, he took on the task of managing his family land and protecting their rights to allocate it.

As was shown in Chapter 2, rights over land in and around Ibadan were asserted by 'settling people'. Subsequently, these 'tenants' were liable to pay *isakole* (tribute) to the family who had granted them land. From around the turn of the century, these

[182] Olufunke Asake Ojo, 'The Life and Times of Chief Salami Agbaje' (Ibadan University B.A. Long Essay, 1988), p. 22.
[183] Layode Mss.
[184] Layode Mss.
[185] KDL, OP/55: 1923, 12 January.
[186] Sara Berry, *Cocoa, Custom and Socio-economic Change in Rural Western Nigeria* (Oxford, 1975), p. 52.
[187] Peel, *Ijeshas and Nigerians*, p. 118.
[188] *Ibid.*
[189] *Ibid.*, p. 119.
[190] Johnson, *History*, p. 637.

Photo 5.1 A view of Ibadan from Oke Are Road. Salami Agbaje's house, built in the 1920s, stands out in the central foreground
(*Photograph by the author*)

Photo 5.2 A contemporary photograph of Adebisi Giwa's house in Idikan, Ibadan
(*Photograph by the author*)

practices became increasingly contested in two related arenas. The first was a series of disputes between rival familes of hunters and their respective tenants. The second was the claim by Ibadan chiefs that they, and not the descendants of hunters, were entitled to preside over land disputes.[191] However, it was not until the 1930s that the colonial authorities actively intervened in the matter.[192] By contrast, negotiating land cases was Obisesan's main concern throughout most of his life. As he wrote in 1920, this preoccupation was partly the reason why 'all around … young men are dazzling in riches whilst I remain poor'.[193]

During the Great War, Salami Agbaje accumulated a large stock of cocoa to ship to England. According to one report, the produce amounted to 'some thousands of tons, which he sold to great advantage' when freight restrictions were lifted after the Armistice.[194] The capital gained from this success enabled him to set up a motor transport business and a mechanical workshop. Continuing to purchase cocoa, palm produce and maize for direct export, the entrepreneur began importing manu-factured European goods, such as trade spirits, textiles and building materials.[195]

In 1921, Resident Ross wrote in the Oyo Province Annual Report of Agbaje's 'motor service on three important trade routes', his 'substantial concrete houses and shops' and reported that he had started a printing press.[196] This latter enterprise related to the anticipated launch of a newspaper – the *Ibadan Weekly Review*. A new association was established to manage the publishing venture; it was called the Ibadan Native Aboriginal Society (INAS) and involved several members of the *Egbe Agba O'tan*.[197]

During this year, several Yoruba gentlemen, among them Obisesan, expressed an interest in the political ideas of Marcus Garvey.[198] Obisesan envisioned himself as the *Review* editor and planned to ask advice from Ernest Ikoli, the editor of the Lagos-based *Daily Times of Nigeria*.[199] At the end of 1921, however, internal divisions between the interested parties caused the entire operation to collapse.[200] The press was ultimately purchased by Daniel Obasa and used to print *The Yoruba News*.[201]

Early in 1922, the INAS re-emerged as the *Ilupeju* Society ('The Community Together') with Salami Agbaje as President. To a greater degree than the INAS, this association avidly courted affiliations with Ibadan chiefs – its first outing was to visit *Bale* Situ who 'recounted his indignities under Ross'.[202] The meeting of 2 February,

---

[191] Gavin Williams, 'Social Conflict in Rural Ibadan Division', unpublished paper, University of Durham, 1972, p. 5.
[192] See Chapter 7.
[193] KDL, OP/55: 1920, 10 May.
[194] NAI, *The Yoruba News*, 1926: 9 March.
[195] Ojo, 'Salami Agbaje', p. 29.
[196] NAI, CSO 26/06027: Oyo Province Annual Report 1921, para. 23.
[197] KDL, OP/55: 1921, 7 October.
[198] For more discussion see Gavin Williams, 'Garveyism, Akinpelu Obisesan and his Contemporaries: Ibadan, 1920–22', in *Legitimacy and the State in Twentieth-Century Africa: Essays in Honour of A.H.M. Kirk-Greene*, eds Terence Ranger and Olufemi Vaughan (London, 1993), pp. 112–32.
[199] KDL, OP/55: 1921, 29 August.
[200] Jenkins, 'Government and Politics', p. 222.
[201] Layode Mss.
[202] KDL, OP/53: 1922, 22 January.

which gave Obisesan such cause for reflection, was under the auspices of this group. As we have seen, the gathering also included Sanusi Adebisi, Ibadan's second-richest African merchant. Unlike Agbaje, he was born in Ibadan; his mother was a cloth-dyer and his father had been a soldier. In 1913, Adebisi became *Mogaji* Lanipekun.[203] By the 1920s, he was the main agent for Miller Brothers' textile stores. He also operated as a produce buyer, but on a smaller scale than Agbaje.

Although Adebisi had attended one meeting in connection with the publishing venture, his interest was ephemeral.[204] To him, gaining a chieftaincy title was of greater importance. Obisesan observed this at a dinner he attended with the two moneyed men in October 1921: 'Adebisi was singled out amongst us by the *Bale* [Situ]. Certainly the star of the young renowned capitalist has risen and is shining most brightly.'[205] Four months later, Adebisi, Obisesan and others discussed how the *Ilupeju* Society might gain official recognition from the Ibadan Native Authority.[206] Captain Ross's suspicions were aroused – in June 1922, he summoned members to the Residency. Agbaje assured him that 'there was nothing political in the Society's plan'. As Obisesan remarked, this was to call '[a] hoe – a spade'.[207]

A week later, delegates of the *Ilupeju* Society were summoned to explain themselves before several Christian gentlemen, including Rev. Okuseinde and Rev. Akinyele. Ross had requested these 'elders' to investigate. To Agbaje's displeasure, Obisesan and the society's secretary, J.A. Adelagun, disclosed its 'real purposes' and were criticised for seeking government recognition.[208] It appears the Resident's intervention caused the group to collapse; the *Ilupeju* Society does not feature in Obisesan's diary again. The experiences of 1921 had shown that liaisons between Christian gentlemen and Muslim merchants were a competitive business. To meet his repressive objectives, Captain Ross only needed to exacerbate their rivalries.[209]

There was now a more pressing concern. On 15 July, Isaac Akinyele told Obisesan that *Alaafin* Ladugbolu proposed to tax every Ibadan male an additional four shillings to assist in rebuilding his *Afin* (palace), which had recently been damaged by fire. *Bale* Situ and most of his chiefs had refused to sanction the proposal. However, 'Oyewole *Balogun* is said to have taken £150 to the Alaafin secretly'.[210] Early in 1923, the 'diabolical plans to shatter to pieces Ibadan independence' were becoming ever more evident.[211] When Adebisi and Obisesan visited *Bale* Situ in August, he 'quoted many instances to convince us that he is at present a mere puppet at the hands of the D.O. and Alafin and that politically Ibadan is doomed at present'. Nevertheless, the very same day, Adebisi affirmed his intention 'to become a political chief'.[212]

The *Alaafin* became sole Native Authority for both Ibadan and Oyo Divisions in

---

[203] Akinyele, *Outlines*, p. 47.
[204] KDL, OP/55: 1921, 29 August.
[205] KDL, OP/55: 1921, 12 October.
[206] KDL, OP/53: 1922, 13 February.
[207] KDL, OP/53: 1922, 24 June.
[208] KDL, OP/53: 1922, 30 June.
[209] Williams, 'Garveyism, Obisesan', pp. 120–3.
[210] KDL, OP/53: 1922, 15 July.
[211] KDL, OP/55: 1923, 4 February.
[212] KDL, OP/55: 1923, 6 August.

A Great Blot

June 1924.[213] To appoint rulers in the towns of their former military empire, Ibadan chiefs had to obtain approval from Oyo. Permission to install chiefs in Ibadan city had been required since 1914. During August 1924 Captain Ross announced that only the *Bale*, *Balogun*, *Otun Bale* and *Otun Balogun* were legitimate members of the 'Native Executive Council'; all lower ranks should cease attending meetings.[214] On a visit to Adebisi's house in November, Obisesan heard that 'Ross'[s] plan to overthrow Situ [was] now complete'.[215] Three weeks later, Adebisi visited *Alaafin* Ladugbolu, apparently on behalf of the *Bale*. He returned only with talk of the Oyo monarch's boast to 'kill' Ibadan chiefs who get 'too big for him to control'.[216]

Ross did not report his drastic reduction of the Ibadan Council until 3 February 1925.[217] Later that month, *Otun Bale* Amida and *Balogun* Oyewole openly accused *Bale* Situ of 'making them small boys'.[218] A complex conspiracy was well under way. However, it was a British Prince who ultimately brought the plot to fruition.

A royal pageant

On 25 March 1925, *The Nigeria Gazette* published an itinerary for the forthcoming visit of H.R.H., The Prince of Wales. The programme included a 'Durbar of Yoruba Chiefs' at Oyo.[219] However, an outbreak of bubonic plague meant that the event was relocated to Ibadan, three days before it was to take place. A 'reception committee' was hastily convened to decorate main roads in the city 'with flags, patriotic mottoes and bunting'.[220]

At 9 a.m. on 20 April, the royal coach arrived at the Ibadan railway station, en route from Kano to Lagos. After Prince Edward and Governor Clifford had alighted, Captain Ross introduced them, successively, to the *Alaafin* of Oyo, the *Alake* of Abeokuta, the *Ooni* of Ife and the *Owa* of Ilesha.[221] *Bale* Situ and the Ibadan chiefs were absent. As the Resident wrote in his especially produced *Brochure of Yoruba History*, Ibadan's ruler, 'is not an OBA but is chosen like a Mayor'.[222] To Ross's mind, it was no doubt appropriate for such a chief to wait for his imperial monarch at his Council Hall – never mind that, in April 1925, this Hall was no more than a building site on a 'recently cleared and levelled' *Oke* Mapo (Mapo hill).[223]

Ceremonies at the railway station commenced. Prince Edward 'gave a touching address' which the Honourable Ernest Oke M.L.C. then translated into Yoruba for the assembled paramount chiefs. Next, Major Ruxton, the Acting Lieutenant

[213] *Nigeria Gazette*, 26 June 1924, Govt. Notice No. 58.
[214] NAI, Iba. Prof. 3/4: Intelligence Report, p. 53.
[215] KDL, OP/55: 1924, 17 November.
[216] KDL, OP/55: 1924, 8 December.
[217] NAI, Oyo Prof. 1/1329: Ross to Secretary, Southern Provinces, 3 February 1925.
[218] NAI, CSO 26/14935: Council Minutes, 27 February 1925.
[219] *Nigeria Gazette*, 25 March 1925.
[220] NAI, *The Yoruba News*, 1925: 21 April.
[221] *Ibid.*
[222] NAI, Oyo Prof. 4/12/178/1924: *Brochure of Yoruba History*. This *Brochure* is missing in the National Archives, Ibadan. I rely on Atanda, *New Oyo Empire*, p. 158.
[223] NAI, *The Yoruba News*, 1925: 21 April.

Governor of the Southern Provinces, was invested with the C.M.G. When these proceedings came to an end, the Prince entered his car.[224] On 17 April, he had informed *Alaafin* Ladugbolu that: 'I hope to drive through this the largest town in West Africa which I know is situated in the country over which you rule so wisely and so well.' He acknowledged that it was 'immemorial custom' that the *Alaafin* never leave his Oyo palace, but he requested the Oba to make an exception 'in the very special circumstances'.[225]

Whilst the welcoming reception was under way, the Council Hall site filled with people. *The Yoruba News* described a scene of 'the *Bale* and his chiefs in gorgeous robes together with the elite of Ibadan in their best garments'. Numerous children, representing all of the Anglican, Methodist, Baptist and Catholic mission schools, as well as the Government School, were also present. In addition, it was reported:

> The different Societies in Ibadan with all available drummers were concentrated at this point. There were about 80 richly caprisoned horses ridden by the Chiefs, Giwas and prominent gentlemen in the community: there were also 200 well-dressed cyclists intended to act as a Guard in honour of His Royal Highness.[226]

Among this throng were the 'renowned capitalists' – Agbaje and Adebisi. The Giwas were members of a Muslim convivial society, the *Egbe Kila*. Adebisi had become President of this group in 1919; afterwards, he added the title of Giwa, meaning 'Manager', to his name.[227]

The *Egbe Kila* were particularly known for their conspicuous consumption and lavish displays of wealth. Layode writes that, soon after they appointed Adebisi as President, he arranged a sumptuous party, where 'even paper currency … was used to make fire to roast fry yams [*sic*]'.[228] This remembrance is almost certainly a translated epithet of Adebisi's *oriki*; recent interviewees have also referred to it.[229] Contemporary observations of the entrepreneur's extravagance abound in Obisesan's diary. For example, he described the funeral of the merchant's father as 'the greatest event I have ever seen in my life'.[230] In August 1924, he reported on Adebisi's visiting style – the *gbajumo* ('glad hander') arrived by car, with three followers on horseback and several others on bicycles.[231]

The '200 well-dressed cyclists' prepared to revere Prince Edward were most likely attired by the munificent capitalist. However, they never acted out their royal role. After laying a wreath at the Great War memorial near the solid commercial warehouses of the foreign-owned firms, the Prince returned to the railway station. Following a brief meeting with 'all the Europeans in the community', he re-entered his train and departed the city at 10.15 a.m., barely an hour after he had arrived.[232]

[224] *Ibid.*

[225] NAI, Oyo Prof. 2/3 C.200: Prince Edward to *Alaafin* Ladugbolu, 17 April 1925.

[226] NAI, *The Yoruba News*, 1925: 21 April.

[227] Layode Mss. See also KDL, OP/28/1/f.5.

[228] Layode Mss.

[229] Ogunniran interview, 19 October 1995; *Mogaji* Agbaje, interviewed 12 April 1997, Ibadan.

[230] KDL, OP/53: 1922, 22 March.

[231] KDL, OP/55: 1924, 20 August.

[232] NAI, *The Yoruba News*, 1925: 21 April.

The Ibadan multitudes had assembled in vain. Led by Adebisi Giwa, they protested. In the future, they sang, the *Alaafin* of Oyo would no more appoint the *Bale* of Ibadan. Instead, Ibadan people would select the *Alaafin*.[233]

That evening, a five-hour parley was held at Salami Agbaje's house. 'The object of the meeting', wrote Obisesan, 'is to organise a body of youngmen to petition the Resident for constitutional reform of Ibadan council.'[234]

Predictably, neither objective was achieved.

A 'wickedly deposed' *Bale*

On 2 May 1925, Resident Ross officially charged *Bale* Situ with having an 'unsatisfactory attitude'. He made his wider intentions clear:

> In my opinion the whole constitution of the Ibadan Division and control is utterly wrong. The mistake was made when the Egba Missionary influence, and our ignorance of conditions, led to the signing of the Agreement of 1893 ... I have always maintained that ... [it] should never have been made.[235]

The Resident recommended that the Ibadan chiefs be prevented from exercising any political jurisdiction whatsoever; that the Oyo and Ibadan Treasuries be amalgamated; and that the *Bale* title be filled by hereditary succession, 'along the lines of all Yoruba towns'.[236] He possibly had in mind his suggestion of 1914, that 'some popular branch of the Oyo family connected with the Ibadans' should take over the post. 'Nothing will really be satisfactory in Ibadan,' he predicted, 'whilst the position is sought for and filled as at present by men who have no claims to dignities.'[237] Eleven years later, Ross's radical constitutional vision remained unfulfilled. In Acting Governor Baddeley's view, 'A treaty is a treaty and [is] not to be lightly tampered with.'[238]

The more immediate political objective of deposition was achieved.[239] On 21 May, all the Ibadan chiefs assembled for a meeting; sixteen more than the four who constituted the Executive Council. They had come to hear the Resident speak. His primary charge, addressed to *Bale* Situ, was as follows:

> The other day when the Prince of Wales came to the Town of Ibadan, there was some impertinent singing close to the *Bale*, (about the Alafin) and that shows that there is a bad spirit. If anybody dares to sing these offensive songs and they are not arrested there is something wrong. The mere fact that everyone in the Town heard and knew that they were sung shows there is a good deal of 'munafiki' [mischief] in the Town.[240]

Captain Ross imperiously ordered Situ to go to Oyo and face charges of

[233] Jenkins, 'Politics in Ibadan', p. 247.

[234] KDL, OP/55: 1925, 20 April.

[235] NAI, CSO 26/14935: Ross to Tomlinson, 2 May 1925.

[236] *Ibid*.

[237] NAI, Oyo Prof. 6/1 C.924/1914: Grier, Acting Commissioner to Secretary, Southern Provinces, 11 December 1914. Grier quotes 'notes' sent by Ross.

[238] NAI, CSO 26/14935: Minute by Baddeley, 13 May 1925.

[239] For detailed investigation of this episode see Jenkins, 'Politics in Ibadan', pp. 240–69.

[240] NAI, CSO 26/14935: Council Minutes, 21 May 1925.

'disloyalty' from the *Alaafin*. The *Bale* protested strongly but went three days later. He never returned to Ibadan alive. As Obisesan saw the matter, he was 'wrongfully and wickedly deposed'.[241]

Ross's arbitrary intervention drew strong criticism from Acting Chief Secretary Tomlinson, who feared that the Lagos Government was exposed to a legal challenge. 'We should be on firmer ground', he wrote, 'the Resident's denunciation of the *Bale* does not amount to "proof" of the charges.'[242] In response, on 13 June, Ross organised for Situ to be called before *Alaafin* Ladugbolu 'to explain his conduct and hear accusations'.[243] Two days later, the Resident obtained a petition signed by the majority of Ibadan chiefs; they stated they would henceforth 'disregard' Situ as their *Bale*.[244] 'This evil device & stratagem are highly characteristic of Capt. Ross', remarked Obisesan.[245] Acting Governor Baddeley sanctioned the deposition on 27 June.[246] The ex-*Bale* remained in Oyo for a year and was then deported further north, to Shaki.[247] In 1932, his corpse was returned to Ibadan to be buried in his compound, *ile* Latosisa.[248]

Balogun Oyewole, a son of *Foko* Aiyejenku, was subsequently installed to Ibadan's ruling title.[249] On 7 August, *Asipa Bale* Abasi became *Balogun*. Within seven years, the wealthy trader of foodstuffs had risen from no title to Ibadan's second-highest political rank. 'Fate has wrought a marvel for this man', declared Obisesan, 'in fact his case is the most unprecedented one in the annals of Ibadan history.'[250]

Having put Ibadan political affairs in order, Resident Ross went on leave. When he returned, he cancelled the status of the *Bale* office as a sole Native Authority (N.A.). In October, the *Alaafin* reappointed the Ibadan N.A., this time as a joint body of the *Bale* and his three most senior chiefs.[251] The assumption of Governor MacGregor's Native Council Ordinance, that the *Bale* was Ibadan's 'principal chief', was thereby undermined. However, Ross's legislative revision did not restrict the individual autonomy of the *Bale* in order to recognise a collective civic Ibadan. As Atanda points out, his procedure of reinstatement was itself an assertion of Oyo overlordship.[252]

'Surely money is the God of the world'

On 28 June 1925, the day after Acting Governor Baddeley authorised *Bale* Situ's removal, Obisesan reported: 'It is stated that Messrs Agbaje and Adebisi at Alafin's invitation visited Oyo yesterday & that the former sold off the *Bale* to the wicked

---

[241] KDL, OP/55: 1926, 16 January.
[242] NAI, CSO 26/14935: Minute by Tomlinson, 31 May 1925.
[243] NAI, CSO 26/14935: Buchanan-Smith to Tomlinson, 23 June 1925.
[244] NAI, CSO 26/14935: Balogun and Chiefs to Ross, 15 June 1925.
[245] KDL, OP/55: 1925, 17 June.
[246] NAI, CSO 26/14935: Baddeley to Tomlinson, 27 June 1925.
[247] NAI, CSO 26/14935: Ross to Chief Secretary, Lagos, 28 May 1926.
[248] NAI, Iba. Div. 1/3/0920: District Office Lapage to Resident Ward Price, 20 October 1932.
[249] KDL, WD: 1925, 10 July.
[250] KDL, OP/55: 1925, 7 August.
[251] NAI, Oyo Prof. 1/1329: Ross to *Alaafin* Ladugbolu, 3 October 1925.
[252] Atanda, *New Oyo Empire*, p. 166.

potentate – whether this is correct or not God will prove.'[253] A month later, Obisesan had a lengthy discussion with Adebisi, ambiguously noting that, 'he [Adebisi] now sees clearly that water can never ally itself with water in relation between him & chiefs'.[254] The next day, Abasi was appointed *Balogun*. For his commercial rival, the chieftaincy prize was more elusive.

During April 1926, Obisesan welcomed rumours of Adebisi's impending installation: 'If this can be done', he wrote, 'the new age is come.'[255] Five months later, the Christian gentleman was much less complimentary: 'Wasting his money for vain, empty & inglorious & humbled political title of Ibadan. Adebisi is a fool.'[256] This scorn related to Obisesan's disgust that Adebisi was playing politics according to Resident Ross's rules – the next week, the Muslim merchant and his retinue left for Oyo to salute *Alaafin* Ladugbolu.[257]

Towards the end of the year, District Officer Ward Price gained his second posting to Ibadan. He was warned:

> Adebisi Giwa is striving to become a chief and the Ibadan Chiefs and Alafin want to make him Ashaju *Bale* – a quite junior title. If this is done, it will be, I think a new departure in Ibadan, and whether the time is ripe for members of the intelligentsia to be made chiefs is debatable. Owing to his wealth he has much influence.[258]

The replacement officer did not interfere; Adebisi was installed on 26 November. 'Warmest congrat', rhapsodised Obisesan, 'he rose from the rank of political servants to that of political masters. Surely money is the God of the world: in this way he fulfilled one of his life's greatest ambitions.'[259]

[253] KDL, OP/55: 1925, 28 June.
[254] KDL, OP/55: 1925, 3 August.
[255] KDL, OP/55: 1926, 9 April.
[256] KDL, OP/55: 1926, 20 September.
[257] KDL, OP/55: 1926, 26 September.
[258] NAI, Oyo Prof. 4/11/59/23: Dew to Ward Price, 14 November 1926.
[259] KDL, OP/55: 1926, 26 November.

6

Breeding Civic Pride
Progressive Politics & Pageantry

Four days into his tenure as Ibadan's head-chief, *Bale* Oyewole 'prostrated three times for the Resident to the great surprise of many'.[1] Afterwards, Captain Ross 'spread the cement-mortar with a small Ebony-handled Silver Trowel presented him and placed the Stone in position saying: I declare the Foundation Stone of the Ibadan Council Hall well and truly laid'. The Honourable Ernest Oke M.L.C. then gave a speech. 'We are aware and thank you', he said, 'for the great building put up for our Oba, the Alafin of Oyo.' In reply, Resident Ross acknowledged that the Hall was originally 'Capt. Elgee's plan before he left'.[2]

Preparations for construction had begun two years earlier. District Officer Ward Price recommended the location of *Oke* Mapo (Mapo Hill) as 'an excellent place for such a building which would be seen from almost every quarter of Ibadan. There is no other site to compare with it.'[3] According to Ross, at a meeting on 23 November 1923, 'the chiefs and representatives of the educated community unanimously pressed' for £10,000 of the 1924/25 Treasury Estimates to be given over to the scheme.[4] Obisesan, who attended the meeting, remarks only: 'Mapo Hall plans shown.'[5]

Robert Jones, the Ibadan Native Administration Engineer, designed and drew up an architectural blueprint during his 1924 furlough. In November, his drawings and a detailed estimate of costs were forwarded to the Lagos authorities.[6] Four months later, approval to start work had not been received. Frustrated, Captain Ross informed his superiors:

A Council Hall is a real necessity. At present Judicial and all other Council Meetings are held

---

[1] KDL, OP/55: 1925, 14 July.
[2] NAI, *The Yoruba News*, 1924: 21 July.
[3] NAI, Oyo Prof. 1/790 Vol. I.: Ward Price to Ross, 16 August 1923.
[4] NAI, Oyo Prof. 1/790 Vol. I.: Ross to Secretary, Southern Provinces, 18 December 1923.
[5] KDL, OP/55: 1923, 23 November.
[6] NAI, Oyo Prof. 1/790 Vol. I: Ross to Secretary, Southern Provinces, 11 November 1924.

117

in the verandah of the Bale's house, and there are strong objections to this. The Chiefs have recently refused to meet there and now hold meetings in a grass shed.[7]

At that time, intrigues against *Bale* Situ were well under way. A month before the visit of the Prince of Wales, construction was authorised.[8]

Originally, a Committee involving Rev. Williams and Rev. Akinyele had intended Prince Edward to lay the foundation stone. They planned to order a golden trowel engraved with a picture of *Okebadan* for the purpose, which would afterwards be given to him.[9] It is doubtful that Resident Ross would have sanctioned this ceremony; in any case, the delay in official authorisation for the Hall prevented it. During May 1925, Resident Ross requested District Officer Williams-Thomas to organise the occasion before his departure on leave, anticipated as 3 June.[10] However, since the *Bale* had to be deposed first, the event was delayed six weeks.

The Hall took over four years to build and cost £23,914, well above the original estimate of £18,000.[11] In Isaac Akinyele's view, it 'was simply built to perpetuate his [Ross's] own name: there was a selfish motive at the back of it'.[12] There is scarcely any contemporary evidence that the Ibadan chiefs were in favour of the project, apart from Ross's claim that they were 'most anxious for the Hall'.[13] A failure to provide labour represents their sole presence in the building records. Ten months before completion, Ross threatened that:

> When the time comes for any of them to be recommended for promotion I shall not approve any chief who obviously has so small a following that he cannot supply the small demands made on him.[14]

The Resident requested his District Officer to check labour lists and establish that chiefs had supplied adequate workers before putting them forward for political elevation. Interestingly, Ross also intended an 'official residence' for the *Bale* to be built adjacent to the Hall.[15] Two decades later, the Council was still deliberating on the scheme.[16]

Arrangements for the formal opening of Mapo Hall commenced during June 1929. Three 'presentation keys', none of which actually fitted the Council Hall lock, were ordered for Resident Ross, District Officer Lawton and Engineer Jones.[17] In September, Captain Ross stipulated that invitations to the event 'should be issued in the name of the Alafin and the Bale and Council'.[18] In contrast to the visit of Prince Edward, the Resident did not require the *Alaafin* to leave his palace. Ross requested

---

[7] NAI, Oyo Prof. 1/790 Vol. I: Ross to Secretary, Southern Provinces, 10 March 1925.

[8] NAI, Oyo Prof. 1/790 Vol. I: Secretary, Southern Provinces to Ross, 19 March 1925.

[9] KDL, WD: 1925, 24 January.

[10] NAI, Oyo Prof. 1/790 Vol. I: Ross to Williams-Thomas, 18 May 1925.

[11] NAI, Oyo Prof. 1/790 Vol. I: Ross to Secretary, Southern Provinces, 24 January 1930.

[12] Akinyele, *Outlines*, p. 81.

[13] NAI, Oyo Prof. 1/790 Vol. I: Ross to Secretary, Southern Provinces, 10 March 1925.

[14] NAI, Oyo Prof. 1/790 Vol. I: Ross to Kirk, 13 December 1928.

[15] NAI, Oyo Prof 1/1058: Ross to District Officer, Ibadan, 30 March 1927.

[16] NAI, Oyo Prof 1/1058: Council Minutes, 14 April 1947.

[17] NAI, Oyo Prof. 1/790 Vol. I: Ross to Assistant Engineer, 16 June 1929.

[18] NAI, Oyo Prof. 1/790 Vol. II: Ross to Lawton, 11 September 1929.

Photo 6.1 The opening of Mapo Hall, 5 October 1929. Governor Thomson stands on the far right and next to him, with hands clasped and facing the camera, is Captain Ross. An interpreter (his back to the camera) faces the *Aremo*, seated under an umbrella. The Ibadan chiefs are on the far-left of the photograph
(*Reproduced with kind permission of Professor J.D.Y. Peel*)

that the Yoruba monarch send his son, *Aremo* Adeyemi, 'in State with such people that you consider necessary should accompany him on such a big occassion'.[19]

'A red letter day in Ibadan', gushed Obisesan.[20] On 5 October 1929, Mapo Hall was declared open by Governor Thomson and Resident Ross. As well as the *Aremo*, his entourage, and the Ibadan chiefs, the ceremony was attended by representatives of the *Eleko* of Lagos, the *Alake* of Abeokuta, the *Awujale* of Ijebu-Ode, the *Ooni* of Ife, and the *Owa* of Ilesa. Today, a bronze plaque remains next to the main door, commemorating the building's completion 'in the time of Shiyanbola Ladugbolu Alafin, C.M.G. and Oyewole Bale Ibadan'. According to the civic Ibadan of Captain Ross, the *Alaafin* always came first.

Rev. Akinyele chose to ignore these allusions to Oyo supremacy. On 8 October, he wrote to Captain Ross on behalf of the staff and pupils of Ibadan Grammar School. The principal wished to congratulate the Resident 'for living & for being among us to see the Beginning & End of the Great & Imposing Hall on Mapo Hill, Ibadan'. He concluded with suitably purple prose:

> As Citizens of the Province, we cannot but feel proud that to *our Province* belongs, for the present at any rate, the *Grandest Building in the whole of Nigeria*.

[19] NAI, Oyo Prof. 1/790 Vol. II: Ross to *Alaafin* Ladugbolu, 25 September 1929.
[20] KDL, OP/47: 1929, 5 October.

119

The lift and good Name given us and our Province … are stored up and implanted in our youthful breasts. We hope we may be spared to press them out at some future date.[21]

Nearly two decades later, the *Southern Nigeria Defender* described 'the scene of a brilliant dinner party in honour of Mr H.L. Ward Price'. A Deputy Director of the 'Empire Division' of the British Council, Ward Price was visiting Nigeria for the first time since his departure from Ibadan in December 1936. The Chairman of proceedings was Bishop Akinyele. Proposing a toast to the former Resident, he extolled 'the name of Ibadan' and proclaimed that: 'wherever mentioned, the Mapo Town Hall stands as a symbol of her power and her greatness. The guest of honour was the architect of that symbol'.[22]

Contemporary Ibadan citizens concur. They associate Ibadan's Council Hall with Resident Ward Price.[23] The objective of this chapter is to explain why. It will investigate the success of a new association, the Ibadan Progressive Union, at mobilising constitutional change and securing Ibadan's political independence from Oyo. After this achievement, Resident Ward Price explicitly reinvented an imperial civic Ibadan, a task that was enthusiastically taken up by 'progressive citizens'. I will consider this symbolic shift in political culture against significant continuities in practices of promoting chiefs in the context of a growing impetus for administrative reform.

Prosperity and enlightenment, 1930–36

Bale Oyewole died on 9 May 1930. He was, in Obisesan's estimation, 'the most unpopular ruler that ever ruled'.[24] Akinyele wrote that Oyewole's tenure was characterised by such a degree of political interference from the Oyo palace that, 'the agreement of 1893 … was practically reduced to a mere scrap of papers'.[25] On 21 May, *Alaafin* Ladugbolu informed the Acting Resident that he wished his messengers to install *Balogun* Abasi as *Bale* in two days' time.[26] Ward Price replied that he would not agree 'until I know that the Ibadan chiefs have been consulted'.[27] He took the unusual step of travelling to Ibadan himself, in order to discuss the matter. The installation took place on 30 May. Obisesan was none too pleased, noting that Abasi's first appointment as *Ekerin Bale* was 'an innovation which all at Ibadan had gone against unsuccessfully'.[28] Ross wrote from his home in Hertfordshire to grant the new *Bale* success 'under the wise guidance of the Alafin'.[29] Ward Price wished him 'long life

[21] KDL, BAP/11: 1926–32, 8 October 1929.
[22] NAI, *Southern Nigeria Defender*, 1945: 22 December. See also RH, Mss. Afr. S.656, Papers of Ward Price.
[23] On most occasions interviewees were initially unsure about who opened Mapo Hall; after thinking over the question they asserted that it was Ward Price. Two respondents were particularly emphatic that it was Ward Price, 'correcting' my notion that it was Captain Ross. Chief Ayorinde, *Asipa Olubadan*, interviewed 16 September 1995, Ibadan; Chief Omiyale, *Ekerin Balogun*, interviewed 14 October 1995, Ibadan.
[24] KDL, OP/47: 1930, 9 May.
[25] Akinyele, *Outlines*, p. 24.
[26] NAI, Iba. Div. 1/1/2263: Ladugbolu to Ward Price, 21 May 1930.
[27] NAI, Iba. Div. 1/1/2263: Ward Price to Ladugbolu, 21 May 1930.
[28] KDL, OP/47: 1930, 30 May.
[29] NAI, Iba. Div. 1/1/2263: Ross to *Bale* Ibadan, 12 May 1930.

Photo 6.2 Folarin Solaja posing next to his Rolls Royce motor car *c.* 1930
(*Reproduced with kind permission of the Solaja family*)

and a very prosperous and happy time'.[30] *Bale* Abasi took the latter option. He remained in office for sixteen years, longer than any other Ibadan head chief, before or since. During the first fifteen months of his tenure, he asked for a £200 bonus for installation expenses, a salary increase and a new car.[31] Only the latter request was refused.[32]

Social life and patriotism

Two months after taking office, *Bale* Abasi conferred the title of *Ikoloba Balogun* on Folarin Solaja, a wealthy Muslim trader.[33] Folarin was a son of Solaja Sodeinde, a warrior chief in the 1880s, whose father had joined Ibadan forces after the Ijaye war. The family came from Ijebu Remo and played an important mediating role in conflicts between Ijebu and Ibadan during the late nineteenth century.[34] By the time Folarin was of working age, the wars were over. In 1901, he was employed by the British firm John Holt and, subsequently, became their main African buyer and agent in Ibadan. For Obisesan, his retirement following twenty-six years' service was 'a rare achievement'.[35] After 1927, the successful entrepreneur continued to run his mercantile business, but he did so independently.

[30] NAI, Iba. Div. 1/1/2263: Ward Price to Abasi, 30 May 1930.
[31] NAI, Iba. Div. 1/1/2263: Abasi to Wann, 1 July 1930; Abasi to Wann, 6 December 1930; Abasi to Wann, 13 August 1931.
[32] NAI, Iba. Div. 1/1/2263: Ward Price to Wann, 27 August 1931.
[33] KDL, OP/47: 1930, 3 August.
[34] On Solaja see KDL, IAP: Olubi, 1884 Diary, 15–17 November; Johnson, *History*, p. 451; pp. 613–18. On Sodeinde see Johnson, *History*, p. 359–60; p. 366; p. 441; Akinyele, *Outlines*, pp. 46–7.
[35] KDL, OP/47: 1927, 1 January.

Although he had an established military pedigree, Folarin was viewed as part of the *ile olowo*. In addition to Agbaje and Adebisi, he was one of Obisesan's main sources of financial assistance during the 1920s – his regular claims for repayment were a common cause of complaint in the Christian gentleman's diary.[36] In contrast to Agbaje and Adebisi, however, Folarin was relatively inactive in local politics until 1930. On 26 August, *The Yoruba News* welcomed his 'pleasing' entry into the chieftaincy ranks.[37] Nine days earlier, the chief had been among a group of men who attended the first General Meeting of the Ibadan Progressive Union.[38]

This meeting had its origins in a letter drafted by Victor Esan, a 24-year-old clerk in the Public Works Department. Shortly after *Bale* Oyewole's death, he wrote to his friend Sammy Oloko, who worked in the Agriculture Department:

> I can see that social function in this our town of Ibadan have here-to-for been organised and carried out by mostly strangers – I mean those who are 'no sons of the soil.'
>
> [...] It seems to me that it is our lot, we present generation to endeavour to raise the status of social life in this town.... Social life does a great deal in the advancement of a people, a town, or a race; in this I hope you will agree with me.
>
> [...]You shall get yourself in readiness for a speech, to rouse the spirits of your dormant spleened fellow-country-men to make their town 'lively' and worth living in by occasional social functions.[39]

Oloko was keenly in favour of the proposal and he discussed it with another Christian 'youngman', Daniel Akinbiyi.

Esan's letter served to remind Akinbiyi, a trader, of his disgust at a public insult given to Okunola Abasi during his 1925 installation as *Balogun*. Standing outside his shop amid the dancing and singing crowd making its way to *ile* Aleshinloye, Akinbiyi heard Janta, an *Ilari*, mock the new *Balogun* as *Alaafin* Ladugbolu's slave.[40] At the time, the *Egbe Agba O'tan* member was disappointed that his society had been unable to prevent the recent deposition of *Bale* Situ. He recalled: 'They were old people, not sufficiently progressive for my mind.... I was a passionately patriotic son of Ibadan.'[41] In July 1930, Oloko and Akinbiyi met up with Esan and J.L. Ogunsola, a schoolteacher at the Aremo mission. These four men were the founding members of the Ibadan Progressive Union (IPU).[42]

On 17 August, the Union held their first General Meeting and adopted a set of 'Rules and Regulations' in which they named their two objectives. These were, first, 'Social, Moral and Intellectual improvements of its members' and secondly, 'promotion of the spirit of Unity and Patriotism'. They did not adopt a secret code, but they did profess to restrict membership to 'natives of Ibadan'.[43] Nonetheless, this

[36] KDL, OP/55: 1921, 15 December. On this occasion Folarin bought cocoa from Obisesan, retaining £2 as payment for a loan taken on 11 June 1920. Similar incidents occurred through the decade.

[37] NAI, *The Yoruba News*: 1930, 26 August.

[38] Folarin Solaja is named as a 'foundation member' in Ibadan Progressive Union, *Fifty Years of its Founding 1930–1989 Exhibition Programme*, p. 13.

[39] Esan to Oloko, May 1930. Quoted in *ibid*. p. 15.

[40] *Ibid.*, p. 16.

[41] Chief Akinbiyi (now deceased), *Otun Olubadan*, interviewed by Gavin Williams, 25 April 1971.

[42] IPU, *Exhibition Programme*, p. 17. See also Post and Jenkins, *Price of Liberty*, pp. 19–20.

[43] NAI, Iba. Div. 1/1/839: *Rules and Regulations of the Ibadan Progressive Union* (Ibadan, 1930).

definition of citizenship was not so strict as to exclude Salami Agbaje. The merchant had recently been nominated by Captain Ross as an Unofficial Member (representing Oyo Province) of the Legislative Council. With this rank, he became the IPU Patron. Rev. Canon Akinyele was chosen as Vice-Patron.[44]

The Union's early activities centred around their interest in an 'Ibadan Reading Room'. Departing from previous policy, Captain Ross proposed a social club for clerks in the Ibadan Native Administration. He had seen such an operation in Kaduna and suggested that a room in the former Treasury building be converted into a recreational centre for 'reliable Africans' where books, draughts, billiards and possibly a gramophone would be available.[45] District Officer Wann solicited interest and recieved enthusiastic yet serious replies. Most respondents expressed concern at the intention to provide amusements; they considered reading books and periodicals more important. 'Games', as one Mr. Adelagun put it, 'should be very few in kind and of such nature as will not be very much fascinating.'[46]

On 18 March 1931, the Ibadan Reading and Social Club held their first meeting. The illiterate *Bale* Abasi was appointed President; he recommended that the Native Administration grant £100 to renovate and furnish the room as well as a yearly sum of £40 to supply reading materials. Ogunsola, Akinbiyi and Rev. Akinyele, all IPU members, joined the managing committee, whose chairman was District Officer Wann.[47] By July, the premises were organised and Wann requested permission to purchase books and encyclopedias.[48] Three months later, Secretary Akinbiyi was warned that the club would be closed down if members continued to ignore the closing hour of 10 p.m.[49] He later recollected that the most popular books were texts by John Stuart Mill and Tom Paine.[50]

Within this period, Captain Ross permanently left his post as Resident of Oyo Province. On 18 September, the *Egbe Agba O'tan*, the IPU and the Reading Club were among eight societies that held a soirée at Mapo Hall in honour of his successor, Henry Lewis Ward Price.[51] *The Yoruba News* reported that, in addition to the 600 invited guests, the building was surrounded by a crowd of over 10,000 people 'with various drums and dances'.[52]

Revision, activism and independence

According to Akinbiyi, shortly before Resident Ross departed, the IPU established a political committee with the sole intention of securing Ibadan's independence from Oyo.[53] Also in 1931, Sir Donald Cameron, previously Chief Secretary, became

[44] NAI, Iba. Div. 1/1/839: Akinbiyi to Wann, 22 February 1931.
[45] NAI, Iba. Div. 1/1/839: Ross to Wann, 19 January 1931.
[46] NAI, Iba. Div. 1/1/839: Adelagun to Wann, 23 February 1931.
[47] NAI, Iba. Div. 1/1/839: Ibadan Reading and Social Club Minutes, 18 March 1931.
[48] NAI, Iba. Div. 1/1/839: Wann to Ross, 2 July 1931.
[49] NAI, Iba. Div. 1/1/839: Wann to Akinbiyi, 19 October 1931.
[50] Akinbiyi interview.
[51] KDL, BAP/43: 'A soiree in honour of H.L. Ward Price'.
[52] NAI, *The Yoruba News*: 1931, 13 October.
[53] Akinbiyi interview.

Governor of Nigeria. Having reorganised Native Administration in Tanganyinka, he brought to the fore a significant shift in the official interpretation of indirect rule.[54]

If the authority of a chief had to be forced on a community, wrote Cameron, 'of course, the administration is not indirect and the Native Authority set up on such a basis is a sham and a snare'.[55] In this changed imperial context, the power of the *Alaafin* over Ibadan was in jeopardy. An early sign of revision was the reinstitution of meetings of the 'Full Council', previously discouraged by Captain Ross. All chiefs and *mogaji* were permitted to attend these gatherings, which were held every Monday at Mapo Hall. The smaller Executive Council, comprising the *Bale, Balogun, Otun Bale* and *Otun Balogun*, met every Tuesday.[56]

Nonetheless, the shift was not immediately in Ibadan's favour. Between 1919 and 1923, Ward Price had been District Officer in Ile-Ife. During this time, he developed a view that the *Ooni*, not the *Alaafin*, was the rightful paramount chief of Oyo Province.[57] Thus, when he took up his promotion in 1931, he initially supported an attempt by *Ooni* Aderemi to extend his political jurisdiction.[58] The campaign was at the expense of Ibadan; Aderemi sought to reclaim towns such as Ikire and Apomu which had previously been incorporated into the Ibadan military empire.[59] As it turned out, by the time Ward Price submitted his final report on the matter in December 1932, he was strongly in favour of maintaining the status quo.[60] In Akinbiyi's view, it was intense lobbying from the IPU which caused him to become 'convinced of Ibadan case'. Subsequently, the new Resident 'befriended Ibadans'.[61]

Before publicly announcing their intention to secure Ibadan autonomy, the IPU pressed for constitutional reform of the Ibadan Council. In April 1932, Obisesan attended a large meeting which discussed 'matters concerning the welfare of Ibadan' and members decided upon the political programme.[62] The IPU thus mirrored the activism of earlier associations, such as the *Egbe Agba O'tan* and the *Ilupeju* Society – unlike their predecessors, however, they obtained a sympathetic hearing.

When Ward Price returned from his first furlough in November that year, the Union presented him with an address of welcome. They requested three 'gifts'. First, members recalled that Resident Elgee had appointed educated members to the Council and they wished this practice to be reinstated on a larger scale, with the inauguration of an Advisory Board. Second, they asked that 'serious attention' be given to the supply of pipe-borne water and electricity in the city. Finally, they pleaded for: 'support, advice and guidance in any measures relative to ways and

[54] For a laudatory review of Cameron's administrative policy see Perham, *Native Administration*, pp. 325–44.
[55] Sir Donald Cameron, 'The Principles of Native Administration and their Application,' Memo dated 13 July 1934, quoted in A.H.M. Kirk-Greene, *The Principles of Native Administration in Nigeria*, p. 198.
[56] NAI, Iba. Prof. 3/4: 'Intelligence Report on Ibadan Town by E.N.C. Dickenson, 1938', p. 61.
[57] H.L.Ward Price, *Dark Subjects* (London, 1939), pp. 128–37.
[58] Atanda, *New Oyo Empire*, p. 258.
[59] NAI, CSO 26/28121 Vol. I: *Ooni* Aderemi and Principal Chiefs of Ife to Governor Cameron, 22 February 1932.
[60] NAI, CSO 26/28121 Vol. I: Ward Price to Secretary, Southern Provinces, 20 December 1932.
[61] Akinbiyi interview.
[62] KDL, OP/47: 1930, 3 April.

means of making the natives of this town, particularly our future rulers, really educated in the true sense of the word'.[63]

The Resident took up all these suggestions, including a long-term commitment to the third proposal. The provision of piped water and electricity in Ibadan city was already being discussed at the time of the IPU's request.[64] Nonetheless, it does appear that the Union's interest gave Ward Price further impetus. He suggested a 'combined scheme for light and water' and argued that residents would be willing to pay a levy for it.[65] In November 1933, the Council sanctioned a water rate of four shillings to take effect at the completion of the venture which was estimated to cost £197,000.[66] However, government concern at the high capital expenditure caused the scheme to be considerably delayed. Finally, on 3 November 1940, Governor Bourdillon attended a ceremony which concluded with the current being switched on.[67]

The first request of the IPU was the most rapidly instituted. Although Ward Price refused an Advisory Board, he did approve the appointment of Councillors. As he later reminisced:

> Nearly all the chiefs in charge of affairs were illiterate, which caused a certain amount of discontent among their more advanced subjects. It was my endeavour to get some of these men inside the administrative machine.[68]

The Ibadan chiefs were initially resistant, stating that: 'We do not agree that educated men should have titles, as this is not customary from time immemorial.'[69] District Officer Wann declared this stance 'very short sighted', noting that he doubted whether *Ekerin Bale* Adebisi was entitled to his rank 'in accordance with Native Law and Custom.'[70]

On 16 February 1933, after Ward Price had given assurances that the Councillors were not required to gain chieftaincy titles, the appointments were agreed upon. Two IPU members, Isaac Akinyele and J.O. Aboderin, were given seats on the Council.[71] Both men had past careers as clerks in colonial administration but they had resigned during the Ross regime to seek their fortunes in mercantile trade. Neither was successful; Aboderin suffered particularly heavy losses in the 1921 trade slump.[72]

Resident Ward Price reported the Councillor appointments to his superiors on 1 April.[73] Whilst Elgee had employed Okuseinde and Adetoun as unpaid assistants, Ward Price proposed that Akinyele and Aboderin should be recognised officially as members of the Executive Council and each receive an annual salary of £120. He raised the sum from savings accrued through the reduction of *Otun Bale* Ayodabo's monthly

[63] NAI, Oyo Prof. 2/1/939 Vol. I: An Address of Welcome Presented to the Hon. Ward Price, Resident Oyo Province by the Officers and Members of the Ibadan Progressive Union, 12 November 1932.
[64] NAI, Oyo Prof. 1/772 Vol. IV: Director of Public Works, Nigeria to Ward Price, 11 April 1932.
[65] NAI, Oyo Prof. 1/772 Vol. IV: Ward Price to Secretary, Southern Provinces, 9 January 1933.
[66] NAI, Oyo Prof. 1/772 Vol. IV: *Bale* and Council to Ward Price, 27 November 1933.
[67] NAI, *The Yoruba News*: 1940, 3 December.
[68] Ward Price, *Dark Subjects*, p. 277.
[69] NAI, Oyo Prof. 2/1/ 939 Vol. I: *Bale* and Council to Wann, 19 January 1933.
[70] NAI, Oyo Prof. 2/1/ 939 Vol. I: Wann to Ward Price, 23 January 1933.
[71] NAI, Oyo Prof. 2/1/ 939 Vol. I: *Bale* and Council to Wann, 16 February 1933.
[72] NAI, Oyo Prof. 2/1/ 939 Vol. I: *Bale* and Council to Wann, 20 March 1933.
[73] NAI, Oyo Prof. 2/1/ 939 Vol. I: Ward Price to Secretary, Southern Provinces, 1 April 1933.

payment.[74] Ayodabo was an elderly veteran of the nineteenth-century wars and, due to infirmity, he ceased attending Council meetings in June 1931.[75] Although the chief vehemently protested his loss of salary, *Bale* Abasi enforced it.[76] This alliance between Abasi and Ward Price marked the initiation of a series of reforms to chieftaincy which were to reverberate through Ibadan politics for the next two decades.

The Enugu authorities approved the Councillors' appointments on two conditions. First, it was suggested that the men should retain their seats for a limited period of three years. During this time, 'the general question of representation', should be reviewed, 'to evolve proposals which will have the support of public opinion, educated and uneducated'. Secondly, the salaries were challenged as too high and a reduction to £60 was recommended.[77] However, Ward Price refused to concede this point, arguing that the Councillors were effectively full-time administrators.[78] In August 1933, the full payment was authorised.[79]

That same month, *Otun Bale* Ayodabo died. Seizing the opportunity of a rare vacancy in the senior chieftaincy ranks, the Resident made a highly 'uncustomary' suggestion. He advised Salami Agbaje to seek election to the vacant title and thus become President of Oja'ba Native Court.[80] At that time, the wealthy Ibadan resident was still the Oyo Province Member of the Lagos Legislative Council.

Even self-consciously 'progressive' Ibadan citizens found this political scheme too radical. Agbaje was a most influential figure on the city's commercial scene and had already been granted official recognition by the colonial authorities. If he became a chief as well, he would become very powerful. Consequently, on 13 August, five IPU members – Aboderin, Akinbiyi, Ogunsola, Oloko and Obisesan – wrote a petition which 'corrected the wrong notion of Mr. Agbaje' that he could 'jump at once to become *Otun Bale*'.[81] A few days later, Obisesan was charged, financially, for his competing allegiances. Agbaje demanded immediate repayment of an £11 loan that had been written off in 1927, as well as the return of a recent gift of twenty shillings.[82]

At the end of the month, J.L. Ogunsola wrote to Alexander Akinyele, his fellow IPU member and recently appointed Bishop of Ondo. He summed up the political scene:

> The peace of the town is disturbed a little [by] the activities of Hon. Agbaje to become Otun Bale, there first appeared to be some official backing, but when the feeling of the chiefs was tested there seemed to be a total withdrawal of same … we thank God that the whole thing is cooling down now though the Hon. gentleman is still vigorous in prosecuting his plans.[83]

Ogunsola was mistaken, however, to assume that the entrepreneur had sought the

---

[74] NAI, Oyo Prof. 2/1/ 939 Vol. I: Ward Price to Wann, 17 June 1933.
[75] NAI, Oyo Prof 1/999 Vol. II: Wann to Ward Price, 15 December 1932.
[76] NAI, Oyo Prof 1/999 Vol. II: Ayodabo to Ward Price, 20 March 1933; *Bale* and Council to Ward Price, 30 March 1933.
[77] NAI, Oyo Prof. 2/1/ 939 Vol. I: Hawkesworth, Acting Secretary, Southern Provinces to Ward Price, 8 July 1933.
[78] NAI, Oyo Prof. 2/1/ 939 Vol. I: Ward Price to Hawkesworth, 5 August 1933.
[79] NAI, Oyo Prof. 2/1/ 939 Vol. I: Hawkesworth to Ward Price, 15 August 1933.
[80] KDL, Rev. Akingbehin Papers, File 3: Akingbehin to Ade, 9 October 1933.
[81] KDL, OP/47: 1933, 13 August.
[82] KDL, OP/47: 1933, 17 August.
[83] KDL, BAP/53B/011: J.L. Ogunsola to A.B. Akinyele, 31 August 1933.

chieftaincy title solely on his own initiative. Resident Ward Price personally admitted to Rev. Akingbehin that he had suggested Agbaje seek the appointment of *Otun Bale* because the title vacancy coincided with changes in the Native Courts Ordinance of 1933. These changes, introduced by Governor Cameron, brought the 'non-natives of Ibadan under the jurisdiction of the Native Courts' and Ward Price had intended that Agbaje would offer assistance to the aged warrior chiefs in the execution of the their increased judicial duties.[84]

This intention backfired badly. From Obisesan's daily observations of the controversy, it is clear that it was generally seen as an expression of the businessman's assertive political ambitions. In spite of his attempts to gain a title during the 1920s, by 1933, Salami Agbaje was not yet a chief. Meanwhile, his prominent *ile olowo* associates, Adebisi Giwa and Folarin Solaja, had been installed in 1926 and 1930 respectively. As we have seen, Chief Adebisi was particularly aspiring. He was no less so during the 1930s, confiding in Obisesan that he expected to rise to 'position of honour and dignity politically.'[85] Status competition between all these merchants is still enthusiastically recalled. For example, *Alhaji* Akande, who became *Balogun* Abasi's driver in 1925, reminisced that:

> One time, Adebisi took his followers for a big feast at Oluokun compound [see Map 3]. His family were weavers and some weavers lived in that compound. The people didn't know what Adebisi was going to do with them there – but what he did was to walk right through the city, past Abasi's house, past Solaja's house, Oja'ba, Mapo and down to Ayeye. They walked up and down past Agbaje's house many times singing songs that he might be a rich man but he was not a chief.[86]

In 1851, David Hinderer described how warrior chiefs' soliders 'spend their time in feasting & parading about.'[87] Eighty years on, displaying people and demonstrating rivalries remained basic to the expression of civic Ibadan power.

In September 1933, Resident Ward Price spoke publicly in support of Agbaje at an Ibadan Council meeting.[88] By that time, it was evident that his scheme to have the entrepreneur elected to a chieftaincy title had failed, at least for the immediate future. Instead, on 7 October, the descendants of military chiefs reasserted their political prerogative. *Osi Bale* Oyekola was installed *Otun Bale*, while *Ekerin Bale* Oyetunde became *Osi Bale*.[89] These promotions blocked the elevation of *Asipa Bale* Adebisi; for the short-term, 'the peace of the town' was restored. Agbaje finally gained the title of *Ikoloba Balogun* in February 1936, when the death of *Balogun* Aminu created a vacancy in the ranks.[90]

After this contest, local attention turned to re-establishing Ibadan independence from Oyo. Coincidentally, less than three weeks after Akinyele and Aboderin joined the Ibadan Council, Governor Cameron made an important policy speech to the Legislative Council. He outlined his intention to revise 'a system of medieval polity

---

[84] KDL, Rev. Akingbehin Papers, File 3: Akingbehin to Ade, 9 October 1933.
[85] KDL, OP/47: 1932, 22 August.
[86] *Alhaji* Akande, interviewed 7 May 1997, Ibadan.
[87] CMSB, CA2/049/104: Hinderer Journal, 23 October 1851.
[88] NAI, Iba. Prof. 3/4: Dickenson, Intelligence Report on Ibadan Town (1938), p. 58.
[89] KDL, OP/47: 1933, 7 October.
[90] KDL, WD: 1936, 21 February.

dependent on the relation of vassal and superior'; which, he admitted, had largely been created by British rule through the past two decades.[91] Although this statement referred specifically to the Northern Provinces, Chief Commissioner Hunt later applied it to Oyo Province. He frankly described Resident Ross's administration as a 'policy of leaving everything to the Alafin and blindly backing up a mediaeval obscurantist system.'[92]

There was consequently a significant convergence between the claims of Ibadan chiefs, the constitutional objectives of the IPU and British administrative opinion. The difficulty was to persuade the *Alaafin* to relinquish his jurisdiction. William Hunt, the Acting Lieutenant Governor of the Southern Provinces, took up the task. On 13 November, he met *Alaafin* Ladugbolu in company of Resident Ward Price and, it was later disclosed, secured the monarch's verbal consent to Ibadan autonomy.[93]

The IPU and the Council chiefs also sought to discontinue the annual Ibadan contribution of £2,400 to the *Alaafin*. However, Hunt recalled, 'I said to the Ibadans I would not consider reducing the contribution if I supported their claim to be an independent N.A. and nothing more was to be said about it.'[94] On 16 November, the Council chiefs thanked Hunt for his support, noting that 'we still expect more assistance.' They agreed to continue contributing to *Alaafin* Ladugbolu's expenses but stated that payment would cease after his death.[95] Subsequently, the Yoruba monarch's salary was reduced to £4,200, while the grant from Ibadan was cut by £300.[96]

Finally, on 6 April 1934, the Ibadan Native Authority gained official recognition of its independence from Oyo.[97] In an Extraordinary Edition of the *Nigeria Gazette*, the *Bale* and Council was listed separately from other N.A.s in Oyo Province, with the N.A.s of Ejigbo, Oshogbo, Ogbomosho, Iwo and Ede subordinate to it.[98] Hunt later expressed regret that the announcement was presented 'rather surreptitiously', commenting that 'it all ought to have been made public what Govt. was going to do before it was done'. In Ibadan city, however, there were no doubts. As Obisesan reported: 'This independence has been gained purely through the efforts of Mr H.L. Ward Price, the Resident.'[99]

Seven months later, Ward Price transferred the headquarters of Oyo Province back to Ibadan, asserting it had 'always been inconvenient' to have the Resident's office at Oyo.[100] He referred here to the established economic importance of Ibadan as

[91] Sir Donald Cameron, *Supplement to Gazette Extraordinary*, 6 March 1933. Quoted in Perham, *Native Administration*, p. 331.
[92] NAI, Oyo Prof. 1/1997: Chief Commissioner Hunt Inspection Notes, 6 October 1936.
[93] There is no record of this meeting. It was referred to in a letter dated 6 April 1938, at a time when *Alaafin* Ladugbolu was challenging Ibadan independence. See NAI, CSO 26/28775 Vol. III.
[94] NAI, CSO 26/28775 Vol. III: Minute by William Hunt, 25 May 1938.
[95] NAI, Oyo Prof. 1/1511: *Bale* and Council to Wann, 16 November 1933.
[96] NAI, Oyo Prof. 1/1768: Outram to Findlay, 3 March 1937.
[97] For more detail of this administrative process see Atanda, *New Oyo Empire*, pp. 249-82. Perham also gives an account in her *Native Administration*, pp. 189-94. However, she attributes the reform solely to policy changes introduced by Cameron and seems unaware of the IPU. This leads her to assert, incorrectly, that educated members were appointed to the Ibadan Council after independence.
[98] *Nigeria Gazette Extraordinary*, 3 April 1934.
[99] KDL, OP/48: 1934, 12 April.
[100] NAI Oyo Prof. 2/3 C. 189 Vol. I: Ward Price, quoted in Ramage to Chief Secretary, 23 November 1934.

a centre of agricultural and commercial trade, as well as its huge population. In 1914, it was illogical to attempt to run colonial administration outside of Ibadan; twenty years on, it was practically impossible.

Ward Price did not consult *Alaafin* Ladugbolu about his move, prompting criticism from the Acting Governor, Captain Buchanan Smith. However, rather than being forced to return to Oyo, the Resident was told to 'discourage any attempt by educated Ibadans and others to make capital out of the move to the disparagment of the Alafin. There have been signs of late that some of the Ibadans have not been able to resist the temptation to advertise their success.'[101] Yet, throughout the next two years, this 'advertising' continued.

Illuminating civic progress

The return of the Residency to Ibadan during November 1934 inaugurated the city's reclaimed sovereignty in both practical and ideological terms. It was further enhanced by the simultaneous publication of the *Ibadan Native Administration Chronicle*. The new monthly newspaper was funded and distributed by the Ibadan Council; it intended to report on 'the work and progress of the Native Administration'. The first issue requested designs for an Ibadan Native Administration Badge to be used on uniforms and on notepaper.[102] A small prize would be given for the winning entry. As far as Hunt was concerned, such projects made 'public parade of their [Ibadan] "independence"', a precociousness of which he disapproved.[103] The newspaper was later renamed *Ijoba Ibile Marun* and Akinbiyi, the IPU Secretary, was appointed as editor.[104] It was issued until September 1938.[105]

Another enterprise was developing the Ibadan Native Authority Band. When he heard of the expansion of the Abeokuta Police Band, Ward Price was 'anxious that Ibadan should have as good a band as they have; and have at least 21 players.'[106] Recruitment and a coaching program were organised by Mr. Ogunmefun, a Lagos bandmaster.[107] By January 1935, the Resident was optimistic that the Band would eventually earn a 'considerable sum' through being hired for private engagements.[108] During May, he proposed to employ Mr. Ogunmefun as a full-time music instructor for the Native Administration; however, his scheme was rejected by the Enugu authorities as 'an extravagance'.[109] Instead, the Council agreed to pay the music tutor on a casual basis.[110]

Robert Jones constructed a 'Jubilee Bandstand' in the Adeoyo Garden, adjacent to

[101] NAI Oyo Prof. 2/3 C. 189 Vol. I: Buchanan Smith, quoted in Ramage to Ward Price, 6 December 1934.
[102] NAI, CSO 26/29792: *Ibadan Native Administration Chronicle*, 1 November 1934.
[103] NAI, CSO 26/29792, Ramage to Maybin, 14 January 1935.
[104] D.T. Akinbiyi, General Secretary, IPU to District Officer, Ibadan, 20 March 1936. Oyo Prof 2/O.D.213.
[105] NAI, Iba. Div. 1/1/1257: Sumner to Olubadan-in-Council, 10 September 1938.
[106] NAI, Oyo Prof 1/850: Ward Price to Sumner, 20 October 1934.
[107] NAI, Oyo Prof 1/850: Ogunmefun to Sumner, 7 January 1935.
[108] NAI, Oyo Prof 1/850: Ward Price to Sumner, 29 January 1935.
[109] NAI, Oyo Prof 1/850: Ward Price to Secretary, Southern Provinces, 2 May 1935; Reply, 13 June 1935. The timing of his proposal indicates that it was related to the Jubilee. This civic pageant is discussed below.
[110] NAI, Oyo Prof 1/850: Council Minutes, 8 October 1935.

the Native Administration Hospital (see Map 3), during May 1935.[111] The Band had begun regular Saturday evening practices at Adeoyo six months previously.[112] Early the following year, hiring rates were set at 10/6 per hour and Ward Price requested that *Bale* Abasi advertise the performers' availability for funerals, weddings and parties.[113] The Band also led the chiefs to and from their meetings in Mapo Hall every Monday and accompanied *Bale* Abasi on his tours within Ibadan Division.[114]

Chieftaincy installations also came to be characterised by a more openly lavish pageantry. When Rukayat Ajisomo became *Iyalode* in 1935, 16,000 people assembled to witness the event. Lademeji Akande, a grandson of *Iyalode* Lanlatu, staged a display of horsemanship, recalling 'the glorious war days of Ibadans'. *Bale* Abasi arrived in a 'large silk damask gown' while the Iyalode–elect was resplendent in velvet and a silk *gele* (head–dress).[115] Obisesan describes the promotions of Adebisi to *Asipa Bale* in 1933 and Folarin to *Abese Balogun* in 1936 in similar terms.[116]

It was during this period that Mapo Hall was first used to represent a colonial Ibadan citizenship. As far as Ward Price was concerned, the role of the building was to 'breed civic pride'.[117] Just three months after he took office, he reconstituted its symbolism, remarking that it 'has had, as it was intended to do, a good effect politically in Ibadan'.[118] The Resident promoted this ideological shift by urging that 'the fullest use should be made of the building, providing no misbehaviour is allowed'.[119]

The Council Hall was thus no longer solely a domain of the Ibadan chiefs as subordinates of the *Alaafin*. It became used for weekly meetings of the Full Council shortly after Ward Price became Resident. In December 1932, a committee was set up to supervise its hire for public functions. It comprised six chiefs and six IPU members.[120] Ward Price also sought to establish a public library in a section of the building; however, a grant for books was refused by the Lagos authorities.[121] He later carried out the plan on a smaller scale, converting part of a police station and providing chairs and reading materials himself.[122]

In May 1935, Mapo Hall's new symbolic function was lit up. The month marked the 25th anniversary of King George V's coronation and festivities centred on 'the illumination, by means of some 280 small lights, of the Ibadan Council Hall'.[123] A

---

[111] NAI, Oyo Prof 1/850: Ward Price to Jones, 25 May 1935.

[112] NAI, CSO 26/29792: *Native Administration Chronicle*, 1 November 1934. This 'municipal innovation' was praised by Perham, *Native Administration*, p. 179.

[113] NAI, Oyo Prof 1/850: Ward Price to District Officer, Ibadan, 13 January 1936.

[114] NAI, Oyo Prof 1/850: District Officer, Ibadan to Ward Price, 19 February 1936; NAI, Iba. Div. 1/1/2263: *Bale* Abasi to Sumner, 4 October 1934; NAI, CSO 26/29792: *Native Administration Chronicle*, 1 December 1934.

[115] NAI, *Daily Times of Nigeria*: 1935, 30 January. Thanks to LaRay Denzer for this reference.

[116] KDL, OP/47: 1933, 14 July; OP/48: 1936, 7 February.

[117] In his Colonial Service memoirs, Ward Price included a photograph of Mapo Hall, noting that: 'it helped to breed civic pride in the 350,000 inhabitants of this city'. H. L. Ward Price, *Dark Subjects* (London, 1939).

[118] NAI, Oyo Prof 2/3 C.31: Ward Price to Secretary, Southern Provinces, 6 October 1931.

[119] NAI, Oyo Prof. 1/790 Vol. IV: Ward Price to Wann, 23 November 1932.

[120] NAI, Oyo Prof. 1/790 Vol. IV: Wann to Ward Price, 14 December 1932.

[121] NAI, CSO 26/28825: G.C. Whiteley to Secretary, Southern Provinces, 3 October 1933.

[122] NAI, CSO 26/29792: *Native Administration Chronicle*, 1 December 1934.

[123] NAI, Oyo Prof. 1/1463: Ward Price to Director, Public Works, 14 February 1935.

decade before, the imperial pageantry of Prince Edward's visit had centred on the paramountcy of the *Alaafin* of Oyo. Resident Ross explicitly prevented the Ibadan chiefs and people from participating in 'the royal visit', despite its reclocation to their city. By contrast, for Resident Ward Price, King George's Jubilee was an opportunity to lavishly inaugurate a reconstituted civic Ibadan. This political body was being built, quite literally, over the bones of nineteenth-century militarism. Ward Price's project, however, did not silence the pre-colonial past – it incorporated it.

His entanglement is most visible in his own account of negotiations over the construction of a 'fine boulevard' which was to terminate at 'the imposing front of the Council Hall'.[124] The 'awkward question', as he recalled, was that 'the route lay across the grave of one of the head chiefs of Ibadan'. If the street was to go ahead, the problem presented by the tomb had to be resolved. 'The townspeople', Ward Price admitted, '[were] alleging that to disturb it would certainly bring disaster in its train.' His view was equally fervent: 'To curve the street and thus avoid the grave would have ruined the vista up to the Hall, so it was necessary to overcome this opposition at all costs.'

Ward Price suggested a compromise – he promised to erect a monument on the site of the house that accommodated the buried war chief. His proposal 'was received coldly and a deadlock followed'. The Resident persisted. He instructed Jones to clear the route 'right up to this house on both sides to show the objectors how much the grave stood in the way of a big improvement'. At this point, 'a large crowd of agitated people', encamped themselves next to the house. Ward Price then gave a speech and informed the people that:

> Their children would, in the years to come, bless them for allowing such a fine roadway to be made and so add to the glory of their beloved city. This idea turned the scale. The Yoruba has a soft spot for his children and is always willing to do anything within reason to benefit them. The people assented exclusively for the sake of their descendants, and a ceremony was held to inform the spirit of the dead chief of their decision, expressing their confidence that he would also agree on such grounds.
>
> The grave was thereafter opened, amid much excitement. It was a deep hole. The surprise came when it revealed no sign of any human remains. It was thought that the dead man's spirit had removed his skeleton when he was told of the agreement to allow the street to be made. So all was well, and 'King George the Fifth Avenue' started on its career with the good will of everyone.[125]

In the modernizing era of 1930s Nigeria, Ibadan chieftaincy was recast.[126] Two decades earlier, Selwyn Grier had dismissed the institution as 'degenerated'. Under Ward Price, it became envisaged as 'traditionally modern'. This Resident would have us believe that the path of civic Ibadan progress compelled dead military chiefs to remove their skeletons from its chosen route!

Ward Price does not name the chief who was supposedly buried in this grave. Oral accounts claim the body as that of *Bale* Fijabi, a principal signatory of the 1893 Ibadan Agreement.[127] The material evidence remains in the city fabric – King

---

[124] All quotes are extracted from an account in Ward Price, *Dark Subjects*, pp. 278–79.

[125] *Ibid.*

[126] Perham argues that Cameron's reformist zeal was driven by an objective to modernize 'the principles laid down by Lord Lugard.' *Native Administration*, pp. 335–6.

[127] Chief Ayorinde, *Asipa Olubadan*, interviewed 16 September 1995, Ibadan.

Breeding Civic Pride

George V Avenue cuts through the middle of *ile* Babalola, Fijabi's compound (see Map 3). His grandson, the current *Otun Olubadan*, told me:

> Everybody wanted street in front of their house, King George V Avenue was precedent and they weren't so worried afterwards. Ward Price told us: 'That main street will bring civilization.' He knew how to talk to the chiefs.... Because of the street the compound was divided in two. Because of that, more light was brought into the compound, that is what they told us would happen.[128]

The reference to 'light' is both literal and symbolic. Light entered the compound because a section of it was demolished, thus reducing the physical congestion of houses. At the same time, light was equivalent to 'civilization' or *olaju*.

This Yoruba concept of development is closely associated with the social incorporation of European missionaries and officials – a project that *Bale* Fijabi was directly involved in. Improved roads were (and are) another common signifier of *olaju*.[129] Recall that Isaac Akinyele regretted the suicide of *Bale* Dada and the subsequent 'great blot' of political conspiracies between 1912 and 1925 as surprising features of an 'age of light'. For him, 'enlightenment' in Ibadan came to its ultimate fruition after 1931. He specifically connects this process with a form of social negotiation:

> Another period crept in, the successor of last Resident was quite different to him [Ross] as the day was to the night.... It was natural to him [Ward Price] to be cool, calm and to listen to everyone whether he be a chief or a poor man; in this way he was different to all his predecessors.[130]

Akinyele was a direct beneficiary of Ward Price's civic Ibadan project. Two years after his appointment as a Councillor in 1933, he was installed *Lagunna Balogun*. His colleague, J.O. Aboderin, became *Lagunna Bale*.[131] The claim that it was 'not customary from time immemorial' for educated Ibadan men to attain political office was thus revoked.[132] Contemporary oral histories suggest that the titles were a reward for the Councillors' successful campaign to secure Ibadan independence.[133] Importantly, the timing of the installations indicates that Ward Price approved them to coincide with the grandeur of the Jubilee.

In August 1934, a Colonial Office memorandum on the forthcoming Royal commemoration made suggestions for festivities throughout the Empire. Prominent among them was the proposal that 'all public buildings should be illuminated, and the people should be invited to illuminate generally'.[134] Conveniently, imperial ritual was using the same cultural metaphor as Yoruba *olaju*. Ward Price enthusiastically took up the concept. Enhanced by King George V Avenue, Mapo Hall would 'breed' both civic and colonial pride.

Accession day was 6 May 1935, three days after the installation of Akinyele and Aboderin. Morning and afternoon events were located at the racecourse – a

---

[128] Chief Fijabi, *Otun Olubadan*, interviewed 4 November 1995, Ibadan.
[129] Peel, '*Olaju*', pp. 142–43.
[130] Akinyele, *Outlines*, p. 85.
[131] KDL, OP/48: 1935, 3 May.
[132] NAI, Oyo Prof. 2/1/ 939 Vol. I: *Bale* and Council to Wann, 19 January 1933.
[133] Chief Ayorinde, *Asipa Olubadan*, interviewed 16 September 1995.
[134] NAI, Oyo Prof. 1/1463: H.A. Blake, Enclosure 2 in Colonial Office despatch, 31 August 1934.

recreational site opened for European merchants and officials during 1902.[135] After a 'parade of chiefs on horseback', a choir of 150 voices sang 'patriotic songs' as well as hymns from a collection prepared especially for the Jubilee.[136] Among them was a song composed by Ward Price himself. The Resident was known for his piano compositions; Margery Perham described him as 'a man of charm and talent'.[137] The first verse of his 'Marching Song' was as follows:

> Can you not hear? There's an army marching?
> Hark to the flutes and roll of drums.
> Whom are they seeking, over hill and dale?
> Plund'ring farms and homesteads on the trail
> Is it the army of vast Ibadan?
> Is it the horsemen out from old Oyo?[138]

This singing was followed up with 'a pageant by 400 warriors depicting an old time slave raid.'[139] In a splendid irony, the Ibadan militarism of the past was re-performed as civic entertainment.

At 10 p.m., after a radio broadcast from King George V and the poet Rudyard Kipling, the illumination of Mapo Hall was 'opened' with fireworks. In February, Ward Price had asked District Officer Sumner to purchase those 'which explode on the ground, shoot up high into the air and scatter into hundreds of coloured stars'.[140] The spectacular sight was achieved. A fortnight afterwards, the Resident informed Jones 'how glad we all are that your indefatigable efforts were such a success'.[141] Finally, on Empire Day, the Jubilee concluded: 'The Bale of Ibadan held a grand Banquet for the elites of Ibadan, including Europeans & Chiefs.'[142] It was held at Mapo Hall and 'went off very well', recalled District Officer Schofield.[143]

By 1936, this civic recontextualisation had reached the higher echelons of colonial bureaucracy. On 11 March, the Acting Chief Commissioner of the Southern Provinces, G.H. Findlay, attended a large meeting in the Council Hall 'of all the Bales of all the towns in the Ibadan Native Administration Confederation'. He remarked:

> The Mapo Hall I am assured has a great influence in the lives of the citizens of Ibadan whose particular pride it is, and I can well believe that as well as the pleasure derived from the use of it by the people, it must have an inspiring influence towards higher ideals, as did the cathedrals in middle ages set in the middle of squalid market towns. This was borne out by a spontaneous remark by Miss Watson of the Kudeti Girls Training College to my wife who was visiting the school, that their Hall was a great influence in the lives of the Ibadan children. It had broadened their outlook and given them a taste for finer things.[144]

---

[135] Elgee, 'Evolution', p. 21.

[136] NAI, Oyo Prof. 1/1463: Minutes of Jubilee Committee, 11 April 1935.

[137] Margery Perham, *West African Passage: a Journey Through Nigeria, Chad and the Cameroons*, ed. A.H.M. Kirk-Greene, (London, 1983), p. 36.

[138] KDL, BAP/47: Hymns for the Silver Jubilee of His Most Excellent Majesty King George V, 1910–1935, No. 9.

[139] NAI, Oyo Prof. 1/1463: Minutes of Jubilee Committee, 11 April 1935.

[140] NAI, Oyo Prof. 1/1463: Ward Price to Sumner, 18 February 1935.

[141] NAI, Oyo Prof. 1/1463: Ward Price to Jones, 18 May 1935.

[142] KDL, WD: 1935, 27 May.

[143] RH, Mss. Afr. S.1863: Papers of I.F.W. Schofield, 4/1, Memoirs, p. 114.

[144] NAI, Oyo Prof. 1/1997: G.H. Findlay, Inspection Notes, Oyo Province, 11 March 1936.

Photo 6.3 The 'warrior pageant', Ibadan Racecourse, 6 May 1935
(*RH, Mss. Afr. S.656/10: papers of H.L. Ward Price. Reproduced by permission of the Bodleian Library, University of Oxford*)

Photo 6.4 *Bale* Abasi's Jubilee Dinner in Mapo Hall, Empire Day, 1935
(*RH, Mss. Afr. S.1863/6 Vol. II/2: Papers of I.F.W. Schofield. Reproduced by permission of the Bodleian Library, University of Oxford*)

Photo 6.5a & b In 1932, postcards titled 'Ibadan Council Hall' were produced, enabling citizens of Ibadan to purchase their own images of Mapo Hall and thus contribute to Ward Price's reification of civic pride. In a sense, these postcards were commodities of a reconstituted civic Ibadan

(*RH, Mss. Afr. S.1863/6 Vol. I/32: Papers of I.F.W. Schofield. Reproduced by permission of the Bodleian Library, University of Oxford*)

That same month, Mapo Hall ceased being used for gatherings of the Full Council 'in order to leave the Hall free for other purposes'.[145] The meetings were convened instead at *ile* Aleshinloye. The 'real necessity' for the Council building – to prevent chiefs holding meetings in the compound of the *Bale* – was forgotten.

A few days after his visit to Mapo Hall, Findlay met with *Bale* Abasi and Chiefs Aboderin and Akinyele in the 'mayors parlour'. He wished to discuss 'their adminstrative system, but did not find them very forthcoming on the subject'. They were more interested in discussing a proposal to change the title given to Ibadan's head chief from *Bale* to *Olu*. Abasi stated that his current rank was 'too common-place'. Findlay replied that he did not consider it any more common than 'Lord Mayor of London' and he reckoned the change unnecessary. Nevertheless, he acknowledged, 'the Bale seems to be set upon it and it is really a matter, after all, for himself and not for us'.[146] Six months on, British officials were forced to realise that this view was mistaken.

'A new spirit'

By the mid-1930s, the civic independence of Ibadan had been ideologically re-created. But the realities of administrative practice were less satisfactory. A month after Findlay's visit, the recently appointed Governor Bourdillon made his first tour of Oyo Province. Significantly, on 1 April 1936, the previously autonomous Ibadan Township was incorporated in the jurisdiction of the Ibadan Native Authority. Located around the railway station, this zone had been demarcated by the Townships Ordinance of 1917 as an area of 'municipal responsibility' where only Europeans were supposed to live.[147] However, in actual spatial practice, the Town-ships Ordinance was inherently unrealistic and, after 1931, its obvious inconsis-tencies were seen to be undermining the policy of indirect rule.[148] In June 1934 Governor Cameron approved that townships should be abolished wherever possible and put under the control of Native Authorities. 'It would be convenient', remarked Acting Chief Secretary Burns, 'to treat Ibadan as a test case.'[149]

Cameron's successor Bourdillon agreed to the abolition of the Ibadan Township on the understanding that the Ibadan chiefs were competent administrators. But on 29 April his Secretary, J.A. Maybin, reported that 'His Excellency no longer suffers from this illusion.'[150] Bourdillon had reached this view during the course of his meeting with *Bale* Abasi and the Ibadan Council on 22 April when he noted: 'I am uneasy as to the efficacy of a system which depends on promotion by seniority.'[151] As an alternative he suggested:

[145] NAI, Iba. Prof. 3/4: Dickenson, Intelligence Report on Ibadan Town (1938), p. 61.
[146] NAI, Oyo Prof. 1/1997: Findlay, Inspection Notes, Oyo Province, 14 March 1936.
[147] Order No. 25, *Nigeria Gazette*, 15 November 1917.
[148] R.K. Home, 'Urban Growth and Urban Government: Contradictions in the Colonial Political Economy', in Williams, *Nigeria: Economy and Society*, p. 67.
[149] NAI, MLG (W) 1/9924 Vol. I: Burns to Shute, 18 June 1934.
[150] NAI, Iba Div. 1/4 /CD1: Maybin to Dickins, 29 April 1936.
[151] NAI, Oyo Prof. 2/3 C. 54: Governor Bourdillon, Inspection Notes, 22 April 1936.

Photo 6.6 Governor Bourdillon and the Ibadan Native Authority at Mapo Hall, Ibadan, 20 April 1936. Standing second in front row from left to right: E. B. Ogunlade (interpreter), I. B. Akinyele, *Otun Bale*, *Balogun*, *Bale Ibadan*, Governor Bourdillon, Resident Ward Price, *Ataoja Oshogbo*, *Bale Ogbomoso*, *Oluwo Iwo*, *Timi Ede*
(*RH, Mss. Afr. S.1863/6 Vol. II/11: Papers of I.F.W. Schofield. Reproduced by permission of the Bodleian Library, University of Oxford*)

Photo 6.7 Resident Ward Price in 'native dress' on his departure from Ibadan, December 1936. Seated front row, left to right: Salami Agbaje (far left), District Officer Sumner (second from left), Bishop Akinyele (third from left), Resident Ward Price (fourth from left), *Bale* Abasi (sixth from left)
(*RH, Mss. Afr. S.2225/3 Vol. II/11: Papers of H.L. Ward Price. Reproduced by permission of the Bodleian Library, University of Oxford*)

A system … by which the facade of the Native Authority could be maintained while the actual administration of municipal affairs was efficiently conducted by a separate body under the nominal authority of the Bale and his Council.[152]

Subsequently, between May and December 1936, Resident Ward Price endeavoured to put this administrative scheme into practice, inadvertently sowing the seeds of fifteen years of recurrent chieftaincy disputes.

His first step was to address a special meeting of the Full Council, numbering over fifty chiefs. He suggested the elderly chiefs 'should content themselves with the dignity of their rank' and that the members of the Executive Council would be better chosen according to their personal qualities.[153] He later informed his District Officer that this arrangement was intended 'to satisfy the chiefs as regards their prestige; and at the same time improve the Executive Council'.[154] Significantly, the Resident then incorporated the proposal to change the name of Ibadan's head chief into the new administrative scheme. 'There are signs of a new spirit among the educated men in the town, which is badly needed', he wrote, 'and it is hoped that this change of title might also mark a change from apathy to activity among both literate and illiterate.'[155]

Despite reservations that the claim for a new title was prompted by rivalry between Ibadan and Oyo, Findlay approved the change on 18 June. However, five days on, Ward Price asked that notification in the *Nigeria Gazette* be delayed. He later explained that 'trouble might arise' in future because 'the present Bale's family might claim to have a right to supply his successors'. Alternatively, a group opposing the *Bale* could accuse him of usurping this right, even if it was not his actual intention. The Resident acknowledged that the Ibadan chiefs 'do not agree that my fears are justified' but he wanted time to reconsider.[156] On 7 July Findlay urged that the matter should drop.[157]

The next day, the Ibadan chiefs approved significant reforms to the membership of the Executive Council.[158] In August 1924, Resident Ross had decreed it to consist of four chiefs – the *Bale*, the *Balogun* and their immediate deputies. He had legalized this political body as a Native Authority in October 1925. Importantly, although the Gazette Notice of April 1934 had established the Ibadan N.A.'s independence from Oyo, excepting the addition of Councillors in 1933, the Executive Council had not changed. From 8 July 1936, it was expanded to nine members – the *Bale*, the *Balogun*, the two Councillors, the current member of the Legislative Council and his predecessor, the N.A. Treasurer, as well as 'Two chiefs selected for

[152] NAI, Iba Div. 1/4 /CD1: Maybin to Dickins, 29 April 1936.
[153] NAI, CSO 26/28775 Vol. III: *Ijoba Ibile Marun*, 1 June 1936.
[154] NAI, Oyo Prof 1/999 Vol. III: Ward Price to Sumner, 30 May 1936.
[155] NAI, CSO 26/28775 Vol. III: Ward Price to Findlay, 5 June. Chief Commissioner Hunt submitted a report (hereafter, Hunt Report) dated 15 October 1936 on the *Olubadan* title controversy, in which he quoted relevant correspondence. Since some of the original documents are missing I have relied upon it for a chronology of the debate.
[156] NAI, CSO 26/28775 Vol. III: Ward Price to Findlay, 29 June, Hunt Report.
[157] Hunt Report.
[158] NAI, Oyo Prof 1/999 Vol. III: Ward Price to Findlay, 8 July 1936.

their intelligence and loyalty and not according to rank'. The Executive Council was to be responsible to the Full Council; each would continue to meet weekly.[159]

'For some time', it was later reported, no one was clear about who was to attend Executive Council meetings and who was not. Neither the N.A. Treasurer nor the current Legislative Council member, N.D. Oyerinde, (from Ogbomoso) signed Council correspondence in the ensuing months. It appears that former Councillors *Asaju Balogun* Akinyele and *Ayingun Olubadan* Aboderin served in their places. The selected chiefs were Adebisi Giwa and Folarin Solaja, whilst Salami Agbaje joined in his capacity as ex-Legislative Council Member.[160] *Balogun* Akanmu, (of *ile* Ogunmola) who was a grandson of *Basorun* Apanpa and a brother of *Balogun* Kongi, was thus left as the only Council member who belonged to a military household. During the course of the next six months, his marginalisation was to become entrenched.

On 9 July, fifty-seven Ibadan chiefs signed a petition soliciting the aid of Ward Price 'to bring about the desired change that we all long for'.[161] The previous day, Rev. Williams had attended a meeting where the new 'Olubadan' title was discussed; he praised 'diplomacy shown by chiefs'.[162] Precisely when the post became a conflation of the words *olu* (town head) and Ibadan, rather than '*Olu* of Ibadan' is unclear; the petitioners insisted it was 'a mere nomenclature'. The proposal implied no alteration to the constitution of Ibadan, they claimed, which was 'a Republican Government and we wish that it will ever remain so'. They confirmed that titles in Ibadan were not hereditary and finally concluded:

> That this title 'Olubadan' does not confer upon the holder the right to wear a beaded crown, and it is hoped that no holder of it in future shall have such aspirations.
> [...] If we had cared for the beaded crown, we would have assumed one before the advent of the British Government. We have been democratic since the establishment of the third Ibadan, and we like our constitution to continue so.[163]

The petition reassured Ward Price. He immediately sent a telegram to the Chief Commissioner, informing that he 'had no further objection and gazetting might proceed'.[164] On 10 July, Obisesan recorded that his family had supplied hunters to participate in a gun salute to *Olubadan* Abasi. 'Warmest congratulations', he wrote, 'to the Olubadan & the IPU who originated the idea of this change.'[165] Subsequently, all *Bale* chiefs took on the name change.

In the political practice of colonial governing, the *Olubadan* title was a strategic institutional entanglement of modern administration and modern tradition. The precise sequence of negotiation suggests that *Bale* Abasi allied with Ward Price to push through the reconstitution of the Executive Council on condition that he gained a title that was not 'too commonplace'. 'The Alafin', as Schofield put it, 'did

[159] *Ibid.*
[160] NAI, Iba. Prof. 3/4: Dickenson, Intelligence Report (1938), p. 60.
[161] NAI, Oyo Prof. 2/3 C.42: Ibadan Chiefs to Ward Price, 9 July 1936.
[162] KDL, WD: 1936, 8 July.
[163] *Ibid.*
[164] NAI, CSO 26/28775 Vol. III: Ward Price to Dickins, 10 July, Hunt Report.
[165] KDL, OP/48: 1936, 11 July.

not much care for this development.'[166] Nonetheless, it was not until September that protests reached senior colonial administrators in Enugu and Lagos.

Ward Price claimed to have 'no hesitation' in accepting blame for supporting the change of title, 'because, in my opinion, the matter was one of little political importance.' The problem, he insisted, was the result of ambiguity about the relationship of the *Alaafin* to Ibadan and he requested that 'that relations to be adopted in future … be clearly defined in writing'.[167] The Ibadan chiefs, assisted by the IPU, readily offered their views in a 29-page petition. They exhaustively reviewed the relationship between their city and Oyo and also recounted mythical narratives of Ibadan's founding. They claimed that the *Olubadan* title had originally been assumed by Lagelu, but was abandoned by those who founded 'the third settlement … because Ibadan had then become democratic'. The chiefs now wished to re-assume it because that of *Bale* was 'too common'. As well as extracts from the 1886 and 1893 treaties, their document incorporated quotes from speeches given by various British administrators and Burns's *History of Nigeria*, Talbot's *The Peoples of Southern Nigeria*, Johnson's *The History of the Yorubas* and Hinderer's *Seventeen Years in the Yoruba Country*.[168]

From a contemporary perspective, the text demonstrates the great capacity of 'colonial subjects' to intellectually appropriate and re-present colonial discourse.[169] It was just what Ward Price needed. He forwarded the lengthy analysis to the Enugu authorities, emphasising, 'I knew nothing of it until it was already typed.'[170] On 5 October, Commissoner Hunt met with the entire Ibadan Native Administration Council, including the crowned rulers of Ede, Ogbomosho, Iwo, Oshogbo and Ejigbo and discussed 'the Olubadan question' for over two hours.[171] Ten days later, he presented a 14-page report on the matter. 'In my view', he wrote, 'never before as far as I can ascertain has 'Olu' been used in a democratic or non-hereditary sense'. He dismissed the Resident's assertion that there was 'no indication that the Ibadan people want to raise their status'. Concurring with Governor Bourdillon, he suggested that the new title was intended to emphasise the independence of Ibadan.[172]

The Resident retaliated, Hunt recalled, with the view that the *Alaafin* of Oyo was 'merely a "museum piece"'. Against his predecessor, Ward Price asserted that the treaty which Governor Carter signed with *Alaafin* Adeyemi on 3 June 1893: 'ought never to have been made … Carter was misled by the interpreter, Samuel Johnson, the author of the History of Yoruba [*sic*] which is notoriously pro-Alafin'.[173] Hunt argued that this view was mistaken but nevertheless recommended that the Government recognise the *Olubadan* title. As he later put it: 'I am a realist in politics

[166] *Ibid.*
[167] NAI, Oyo Prof. 2/3 C. 42: Ward Price to Secretary, Southern Provinces, 14 September 1936.
[168] NAI, Oyo Prof. 2/3 C. 42: Ibadan Native Authority to Hunt, 10 September 1936.
[169] This is a central theme in the analyses of 'mimicry' and 'hybridity' put forward by Homi Bhabha, a postcolonial theorist. See his *The Location of Culture* (London, 1994). For a useful critique of his work see Nicolas Thomas, *Colonialism's Culture: Anthropology, Travel and Government* (Cambridge, 1994), pp. 39–58.
[170] NAI, Oyo Prof. 2/3 C. 42: Ward Price to Hunt, 15 September, 1936.
[171] NAI, Oyo Prof. 1/1997: Hunt, Inspection Notes, Oyo Province, 5 October 1936.
[172] NAI, CSO 26/28775 Vol. III: Hunt Report, 15 October 1936.
[173] NAI, CSO 26/28775 Vol. III: Hunt Report, 15 October 1936. In fact, Johnson was not Carter's interpreter

as well as a theorist; the mischief was already done.'[174] He feared that if recognition was refused, Abasi would possibly commit suicide and would certainly be 'disgraced and mocked at by many of his people, and would not hold up his head again'.[175]

Evidently, a potential for Ibadan people to reject their *Bale* was a more threatening scenario than a chief's appropriation of greater prestige. All the same, Hunt urged: 'The approval needs to be qualified in some way as the Bale and Council require to be taken down a peg.'[176] So it was that the *Nigeria Gazette* gave official recognition, with the rejoinder that the Ibadan chiefs had failed to show the *Alaafin* 'the courtesy and consideration which they should properly have accorded him'.[177]

Ward Price was due for leave at the end of 1936. In November, it became public knowledge that he would not return to Ibadan – he was to be posted to Onitsha in Eastern Nigeria. The Ibadan chiefs and councillors petitioned against his transfer, presenting over fifty reasons against it. 'He has shown us a new value of life', they wrote, 'and has pointed out to us how to look at things from the right perspective.'[178] However, in senior administrative circles, it is clear that the controversy over the *Olubadan* title caused Ward Price to lose credibility. Commissioner Hunt reported that he believed the Resident had encouraged Ibadan people to 'reach out for more' and that he held a bias against *Alaafin* Ladugbolu.[179] There was further evidence in Ward Price's personal attack on the monarch, written before his departure on furlough in 1934. He described *Alaafin* Ladugbolu as 'obsessed with his importance' and as having 'no interest in the progress of the Native Administration'.[180]

Although these remarks were probably justified, British administrators were still coming terms with 'the mistake of trying to give the Alafin real executive power over Ibadan'. In Hunt's view, recent events revealed that Ward Price 'was now making the mistake of trying to show that there is not even a sentimental connexion'.[181] Acting Chief Secretary Whiteley concurred that the incident was badly handled.[182] This, it would appear, was the justification for Ward Price's transfer after only five years as Resident of Oyo Province. Captain Ross had held the post for seventeen years. For Ward Price, returning to Onitsha 'was not altogether agreeable [and] rather a waste of my long experience with the Yorubas'.[183] He resigned the Colonial Service. However, as we have seen, he returned briefly to Nigeria in 1945.

Before he left, the Resident had one more triumph – the successful completion of

---

[173] (cont.) during 1893, although he was engaged by Governor Moloney during 1886. However, it is significant that Ward Price appropriates Johnson as his evidence. See Chapter 3.

[174] NAI, CSO 26/32309 Vol. I: *The Nigerian Daily Times*, 24 July 1937. The paper reprinted the full text of an address by Chief Commissioner Hunt at Mapo Hall on 21 July.

[175] NAI, CSO 26/28775 Vol. III: Hunt Report, 15 October 1936.

[176] *Ibid.*

[177] *Nigeria Gazette*, Notice No. 1424, 29 October 1936.

[178] NAI, Oyo Prof. 1/1768: *Petition of the Ibadan Native Authority*, Appendix K., 1937. This document reprinted the original petition.

[179] NAI, CSO 26/28775 Vol. III: Hunt Report, 15 October 1936.

[180] NAI, Oyo Prof. 2/3 C. 189 Vol. I: Ward Price to Hunt, 8 December 1934.

[181] NAI, CSO 26/28775 Vol. III: Hunt Report, 15 October 1936.

[182] NAI, CSO 26/28775 Vol. III: Minute by Whiteley, 20 October 1936.

[183] Ward Price, *Dark Subjects*, p. 283.

Photo 6.8 Opening of Bower Tower, 16 December 1936. Seated left to right: District Office Sumner, Resident Ward Price, Miss Bower, *Bale* Abasi. Note the *Akoda* (policeman) holding the wreath (*RH, Mss. Afr. S.2225/3/24: Papers of H.L. Ward Price. Reproduced by permission of the Bodleian Library, University of Oxford*)

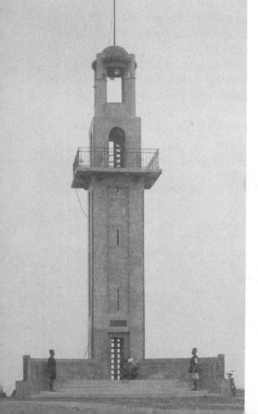

Photo 6.9 Postcard of Bower Tower, 1936 (*RH, Mss. Afr. S.2223/3/17: Papers of H.L. Ward Price. Reproduced by permission of the Bodleian Library, University of Oxford*)

Photo 6.10 *Ibadan Dun Adhire*. Note the icon of Mapo Hall (columns of the building [see photo 6.5] interspersed with spoons) in the lower right-hand corner

(*Photograph by the author*)

142

Bower Memorial. This purely decorative tower, located on a hill one mile from Mapo Hall, 'can be seen from almost every part of Ibadan'.[184] In stark contrast to the Council building, there were no labour shortages during its construction and it was financed by public subscription. The largest donation of £75 came from the Ibadan chiefs. Commander and Miss Bower, son and daughter of Ibadan's first British Resident, visited Nigeria especially for its unveiling on 16 December 1936. According to *The Nigerian Daily Times*, the ceremony was watched by over 30,000 people, 'amidst scenes of unrivalled pageantry'.[185]

It was Ward Price's ultimate civic Ibadan/imperial ritual. Once back in London, he reported it to *The Times*.[186] In Ibadan, he ordered the construction of an airtight case to contain a scroll listing the names of those who had subcribed to the erection of the Memorial, the December edition of *Ijoba Ibile Marun* and the 15 December issue of *The Nigerian Daily Times*, as well as a copy of the inscription to be mounted on a brass plate: 'To the memory of Sir Robert Lister Bower ... whose Fine Character, Courage and Administrative Ability won the universal and lasting esteem of the Yorubas and firmly established the loyalty of the people to the Imperial Crown.'[187]

This case was buried under the Memorial as part of the unveiling ceremony. During his speech for the occasion, Ward Price explained that if the Memorial was destroyed by war in the future, the archive would ensure that 'the invaders would know something of what was now going on in our time and the reason why that Tower was erected'.[188] Miss Bower then laid a wreath whilst numerous schoolchildren marched past, to songs composed by Ward Price and played by the I.N.A. Band. The ceremony concluded with the Resident and his guests ascending the tower to the tune of 'God Save the King'.[189]

Significantly, this ritual also embodied a marginalisation of the Oyo throne. As Ward Price recalled: 'It was Capt. Bower who fired a shell at the Afin at Oyo and a splinter hit the Alafin of those days on the knee!'[190] Nevertheless, *Alaafin* Ladugbolu and his chiefs contributed £25 to the cost of the Memorial and his son, *Aremo* Adeyemi came to the unveiling. Returning to Oyo after the opening of the Memorial, Adeyemi's car was stoned as it passed *ile* Latosisa, the burial place of *Bale* Situ. The windscreen and two windows were smashed and the *Aremo* himself was hit.[191] Three months later, District Officer Sumner regretted that the Council 'do not appear to have taken adequate steps to bring the culprits to justice.'[192]

The stoning incident did not dampen festivities. After the unveiling of the tower: 'The second program was a non-stop dance at Mapo Hall from 9 p.m.... At about 12.10 a.m. Commander Bower accompanied by Mr Ward Price entered the Hall and

---

[184] NAI, Oyo Prof. 1/1686 Vol. 1: Ward Price to Chadwick, 14 October 1936.

[185] RH, Mss. Afr. s. 2225/2/6, *The Nigerian Daily Times*: 17 December 1936, p. 6.

[186] RH, Mss. Afr. s. 2225/2/12, *The Times*: 19 January 1937.

[187] RH, Mss. Afr. s. 2225/2/9, *The Nigerian Daily Times*: 29 December 1936.

[188] *Ibid.*

[189] RH, Mss. Afr. s. 2225/2/6, *The Nigerian Daily Times*: 17 December 1936, p. 6.

[190] NAI, Oyo Prof. 1/1686 Vol. 1: Ward Price to Chadwick, 14 October 1936.

[191] NAI, Oyo Prof 1/55 Vol. III: Outram to Ward Price, 17 December 1936.

[192] NAI, Oyo Prof 1/55 Vol. III: Sumner to Findlay, 10 March 1937.

was received with a tremendous ovation. The all-night merriment concluded at 4 a.m'.[193] Three days on, *Olubadan* Abasi hosted a grand reception to farewell the Bowers and Ward Price and welcome Resident Findlay. The IPU 'rendered the occasion very lively by the staging of a drama entitled "Bower arresting Ogedemgbe"'.[194] The cast comprised pupils from the Ibadan Grammar School. Finally, ceremonies concluded with the installation of Commander Bower as *Seriki Olubadan*. 'Invested with gown and cap', reported *The Nigerian Daily Times*, 'the Hon. gentleman in his gorgeous native dress danced to the rhythmic time of the Native drums.'[195]

The cultural appropriations and entanglements which made civic Ibadan pageantry were vividly performed for the inauguration of the Bower Memorial. In the next chapter, I will investigate the symbolism of another material object – a cloth which threatened to cause a riot. But first, I return to the problem which began this one.

'An accomplished object'

'Ibadan – a model of historical facts.'[196] Mapo Hall embodies this assertion *par excellence*. Resident Ross laid the foundation stone of the council building on 14 July 1925. Just over four years later, he declared it open. Yet, this is not what Ibadan people remember. Since at least 1945, 'the architect of that symbol' has been Resident Ward Price. Today, Mapo Hall's columns are an icon on *Ibadan Dun*, an *adire* (indigo-patterned cloth) whose name means 'Ibadan is sweet.'

The building was originally intended as a material realisation of the city's political subordination to Oyo. However, its scale – 'magnificently ugly' in one official's view – made it amenable to alternative appropriations.[197] For Rev. Akinyele, it represented 'the Lift and good Name given us'.[198] For Ward Price, it was the obvious emblem for 'the largest civic community of negroes in the whole of Africa'.[199] For contemporary citizens, it is 'the permanent symbol of Ibadan'.[200]

Ideologically, they are correct. The building is not what it was made to be, but what it has become.[201] Resident Ward Price *was* one of its architects. As the 'Ibadan Chiefs and People' put it: 'The interested part which you played in making this great edifice – this Mapo Town Hall – an accomplished object was well known.'[202]

---

[193] RH, Mss. Afr. s. 2225/2/6, *The Nigerian Daily Times*: 17 December 1936, p. 6.

[194] RH, Mss. Afr. s. 2225/2/13, *Ijoba Ibile Marun*, January–February 1937, p. 17. Ogedemgbe was originally an Ibadan war-boy before he established the *Ekitiparapo* military alliance against Ibadan in 1877.

[195] RH, Mss. Afr. s. 2225/2/11, *The Nigerian Daily Times*: 21 December 1936.

[196] *Ibadan Mementoes*, p. 19.

[197] NAI, Oyo Prof. 1/1603: Anonymous minute, 20 May 1954.

[198] KDL, BAP/11: 1926–32, 8 October 1929.

[199] Ward Price, *Dark Subjects*, p. 231.

[200] Chief Ayorinde, *Asipa Olubadan*, interviewed 16 September 1995.

[201] Nicholas Thomas, *Entangled Objects. Exchange, Material Culture, and Colonialism in the Pacific* (Cambridge, MA., 1991), p. 4.

[202] RH, Mss. Afr. S.656: 'An Address Presented to H.L. Ward Price by the Ibadan Chiefs and People', 19 December 1945.

7

The Cloth of Field of Gold
Material Cultures & Civic Power

On 21 October 1936, Governor Bourdillon sanctioned Notice No. 1424 in the *Nigeria Gazette*, thus granting official recognition to the *Olubadan* title. He noted: 'I hope that we shall now be able to write R.I.P. on the grave of a controversy which should never have been allowed to arise.'[1]

Three years later, the contentious matter threatened to rise from the dead. In May 1939, the Conference of Yoruba Chiefs was to be held at Ibadan. This annual political forum had been convened since 1937 and was a legacy of the reforms to colonial administration that had been introduced by Governor Cameron. In the view of Acting Chief Commissioner Shute, the event encouraged 'a growing readiness among all classes to co-operate in a wider scheme of local government which will in no way undermine, but will rather support, acknowledged tribal authority'.[2] However, on the occasion of the third conference at Ibadan, there was a potential for this objective to be greatly undermined. This potential first came to the attention of Resident Kelly just a fortnight before the Conference was to open, when he received a sample of cloth and a letter from *Alaafin* Ladugbolu.

In response to this communication, Resident Kelly contacted Chief Commissioner Whiteley. Both men agreed that it was 'a matter of grave political importance that the sale of the cloth should be stopped'.[3] On 15 May 1939, the Ibadan Native Authority passed the 'Restriction of the use of certain kinds of cloth Order'. The law ruled that no person was allowed to expose the cloth in any public place; neither could they wear, buy, sell or even offer it for sale. These restrictions also applied to 'any garment of any description fashioned from the said cloth'.[4]

If these rules were ignored, the cloth or garment would be confiscated and the offender liable to a fine of £5, imprisonment for one month, or both. The Order was

---

[1] NAI, CSO 26/28775 Vol. III: Governor Bourdillon, 21 October 1936.
[2] NAI, CSO 26/12723 Vol. XIV: Comments by Shute, 18 May 1938.
[3] NAI, CSO 26/35943: E.G. Hardesworth, Secretary, Western Provinces to C.C. Wooley, Chief Secretary, 16 May 1939.
[4] Public Notice No. 21, *Nigeria Gazette*, 20 May 1939.

Photo 7.1 The *Olubadan* damask, 1939 This cloth was banned on suspicion that wearing it would cause a riotous 'civil disorder' (*NAI, CSO 26/35943. Photograph by the author*)

printed up in a Public Notice and copies were posted around the city of Ibadan. It was further advertised through the Ibadan chiefs' messengers.[5]

Five days later, the Order was published in the *Nigeria Gazette*. Copies were also sent for publication in the Lagos newspapers, since it was feared that the cloth had been widely sold there. The Order was made under a section of the 1933 Native Authority Ordinance 'Prohibiting any act or conduct which in the opinion of the Native Authority might cause a riot or a disturbance or a breach of the peace'.[6] Captain Kelly feared that if the cloth was worn at the forthcoming pageant, just such a disturbance would take place.

On 20 May, Alakija and Alakija, a law firm representing two political societies and Aladayemi Adeoba Stores, all of whom opposed the Order, petitioned the Chief Secretary in Lagos. They denied that the wearing of the cloth would cause a riot and asked that Governor Bourdillon revoke the Order.[7] Their plea was rapidly dismissed.

---

[5] NAI, CSO 26/35943: Hardesworth to Wooley.
[6] Native Authority Ordinance 1933, Section 8, Subsection (d).
[7] NAI, CSO 26/35943: Alakija and Alakija to Wooley, 20 May 1939.

The Lagos administrators were as convinced as Resident Kelly that the cloth was liable to provoke unrest:

> The wearing of this damask with crown and wording is simply asking for trouble and will revive in its bitter form all the troubles we are trying to forget. Mr Alakija knows this as well or better than I do and I certainly think it would be wise to grant him an interview and tell him in the plainest language Govt's attitude. I also consider this cloth should be a prohibited import otherwise it is certain to get worn and will always be liable to give rise to a breach of the peace.[8]

The Chief Secretary, C.C. Wooley, concurred and informed Governor Bourdillon: 'Nothing could be more calculated to rekindle past ill-feeling and precipitate trouble than this.'[9] Replying, the Governor wrote: 'I fully agree. The cloth should be declared a prohibited import.'[10]

On 23 May Chief Secretary Wooley met Mr Alakija and 'told him in no uncertain terms of the serious view which the Govt. took of this matter', suggesting 'he must surely be aware of the serious consequences which would follow if distribution of this cloth were allowed'.[11] Three days later, the cloth was declared a prohibited import under Order-in-Council No. 20 of 1936, promulgated under the Customs Ordinance.[12] This Order made unlawful the importation of 'Material of any description with a design which, considering the purpose for which the material is intended to be used, is likely in the opinion of the Governor in Council to create a breach of the peace'.[13] Action under this Order could only be taken against importers and not against retailers. For one official, this marked 'a weakness in the law' and he urged that the Customs Ordinance be amended.[14]

A few days after the prohibition was publicised in the *Nigeria Gazette*, J.C. Ticehurst contacted the Criminal Investigations Department (C.I.D.) on behalf of his client, Mr Karl Stark. An importer, Mr Stark admitted that he possessed a large stock of the cloth, having not initially appreciated 'the political significance of the words written on the design'.[15] Mr Ticehurst informed the C.I.D. that his client was 'Ready to give you any information you may require as to the circumstances of the ordering of the goods and as to certain sales which have already taken place'.[16] Indeed, people had arrived from Ibadan asking to take delivery of the goods that very day, Mr Ticehurst stated, and Mr Stark had refused them.[17] However, Mr Stark had nothing to fear. It was decided that 'prosecution of the importer of cloth already imported would serve no useful purpose' and consequently, the Chief Secretary advised that the Commissioner of Police 'should take no action on Mr Ticehurst's letter'.[18]

[8] NAI, CSO 26/35943: T. Hoskyns Abrahall, 23 May 1939.
[9] NAI, CSO 26/35943: C.C. Wooley, 23 May 1939.
[10] NAI, CSO 26/35943: Governor Bourdillon, 23 May 1939.
[11] NAI, CSO 26/35943: C.C. Wooley, 23 May 1939.
[12] NAI, CSO 26/35943: Clerk of Legislative Council, 26 May 1939.
[13] NAI, CSO 26/35943: Order in Council No. 20 of 1936, *Nigeria Gazette*, 23 March 1936.
[14] NAI, CSO 26/35943: G.H. Clifford, 30 May 1939.
[15] NAI, CSO 26/35943: J.C. Ticehurst to Superintendent, Criminal Investigations Department, 5 June 1939.
[16] *Ibid.*
[17] *Ibid.*
[18] NAI, CSO 26/35943: C.C. Wooley, 7 June 1939.

When Aladayemi Adeoba Stores petitioned the government in July, they were not similarly ignored. Their manager, Situ Adeoba, claimed that they had imported the cloth 'in good faith' through a German firm; their only consideration was 'to satisfy the need of their customers ... in these days when a cloth must be particularly appealing before it could capture the market'.[19] Adeoba complained that out of the 3,000 yards of the damask they had acquired, about 1,600 yards was unable to be sold and this represented a loss of £400, which could ruin their 'small Company'. To save them 'from being sacrificed at the altar of political expediency' Adeoba requested permission to sell the remaining 1,600 yards.[20] Finally, he asked that Governor Bourdillon point out 'the offensive matter on this Damask cloth'.[21]

The Lagos authorities debated how to reply. One officer acknowledged: 'I think we shall have to do something more than merely state that the cloth is considered by the Gov-in-Council to be likely to cause a breach of the peace; we shall have to indicate why. The main objection is the inscription but I'm not sure how much there is in the actual picture itself.'[22] He suggested that the Chief Commissioner of the Western Provinces, G.C. Whiteley, be consulted. His colleague agreed.[23]

Subsequently, J.A. Mackenzie, the Acting Secretary of the Western Provinces, replied: 'His Honour suggests that they might be informed that the whole design of the medallion depicted suggests that the *Olubadan* of Ibadan has been raised to the position of an *Oba*, a position to which he is not entitled by Yoruba custom and which the people of Ibadan have no wish that he should occupy.'[24] There the matter rested. Aladayemi Adeoba Stores was strictly forbidden to sell the cloth, despite the fact that there was actually no provision in the law for this ruling to be enforced. The issue remained on the Ibadan Council minutes in 1941, when Councillor Obisesan referred to a discussion on the 'vexed question of *Olubadan's* damask cloth which evoked sharp comment by the Senior District Officer'.[25] The discussion reportedly ended with the Council promising to enforce the ban. As late as 1950, Aladayemi Adeoba Stores was still requesting permission to sell the cloth and they were still being refused.[26]

Objects, representation and meaning

The *Olubadan* Damask is a commodity which embodies a 'social life'.[27] At the same time, it is an object of colonial material culture. Extending a theoretical analysis proposed by Annette Weiner, we can read the *Olubadan* Damask as an object with an acquired charisma and 'symbolic density'. For such objects, Weiner suggests: 'The most important goal is to keep them out of circulation in the face of their potential or

[19] NAI, CSO 26/35943: Situ Adeoba to Governor Bourdillon, 13 July 1939.
[20] *Ibid.*
[21] *Ibid.*
[22] NAI, CSO 26/35943: H. Clifford, 24 July 1939.
[23] NAI, CSO 26/35943: Hoskyns Abrahall, 25 July 1939.
[24] NAI, CSO 26/35943: J.A. Mackenzie to Wooley, 8 August 1939.
[25] KDL, OP/48: 1941, 3 March.
[26] NAI, CSO 26/35943: A.A. Williams to Messrs Aladayemi Adeoba & Son, 20 March 1950.
[27] Arjun Appadurai, (ed.) *The Social Life of Things. Commodities in Cultural Perspective* (Cambridge, 1986), p. 3.

Photo 7.2 *Olubadan* Abasi, 1936
(*Reproduced from the* Daily Times)

actual movements from one social or economic encounter to another.'[28] In colonial south-western Nigeria during 1939, British officials insisted that specific legislation be passed to prevent the *Olubadan* Damask from being circulated. This chapter will investigate why and how a piece of cloth could be so dense with cultural meaning and political symbolism that it was able to generate this reaction. By doing so, my exploration weaves together the multiple threads of change and continuity in Ibadan political culture through the course of a century.

To begin, we need to understand the process of signification that the *Olubadan* Damask engaged. The obvious place to begin this analysis is to describe the cloth. On the Public Notices displayed around Ibadan in May 1939, it was identified as follows:

> A representation in black and white on a coloured ground of an African clothed in Mohammedan robes and wearing a turban and decorated slippers and leading a leopard by a cord, the whole surrounded by a decorated border in black and white also on a coloured ground bearing at the top, a crown, and in the border the words 'OLUBADAN D'OBA ABUSE BUSE'.[29]

This description is censored. First, to all viewers of the cloth in 1939, it was evident that the human figure in the design was *Olubadan* Abasi, not simply an anonymous 'African'. Praising the workmanship, Governor Bourdillon wrote: 'The likeness to the Olubadan has been done extraordinarily well!'[30] It appears that the cloth designers had copied a photograph of Abasi in a similar pose which was often published to accompany

[28] Annette B. Weiner, 'Cultural Difference and the Density of Objects', *American Ethnologist* 21 (1), 1994, pp. 394–5.
[29] Public Notice No. 21, *Nigeria Gazette* No. 31, 20 May 1939.
[30] NAI, CSO 26/35943: Governor Bourdillon, 23 May 1939.

articles about him in newspapers of the period. Apart from the position of the leopard, which is more dominant in the cloth, the two depictions of *Olubadan* Abasi are remarkably similar. Second, the official Damask description failed to identify that the 'coloured ground' of the cloth was a deep royal blue. Third, since the Public Notice was printed in English, most residents of Ibadan were unlikely to be able to read it. However, the Yoruba inscription on the cloth: '*OLUBADAN D'OBA ABUSE BUSE*' was not translated. It means roughly, 'The *Olubadan* has become King, Everything is Finished.'

A descriptive analysis indicates what was represented on the *Olubadan* Damask. It does not explain why this representation was seen as subversive to the point that its exhibition had to be banned. Instead, it reveals that any process of signification which an object might engage is not inherent to the material structure of the object itself. As we have seen in the case of Mapo Hall, the identity and meaning of an object is not stabilised in a fixed and founded material form. Rather, meanings are embodied by entangled layers of cultural, social and political histories. Entangled histories allow what the anthropologist Nicholas Thomas has called 'creative recontextualisation'.[31]

The tale of the *Olubadan* Damask exemplifies this point very clearly. Otherwise, it seems absurd that a piece of cloth could be held causally responsible for a riot. Recall that Mackenzie, the Acting Secretary of the Western Provinces, explained that it was what the cloth suggested, in other words its *potential meanings*, that was politically dangerous. If we are to untangle why the *Olubadan* Damask threatened such powerful meanings and further, what these meanings were, we must explore the particular histories which the cloth embodied.

Civic material cultures in Ibadan

For readers of this book, these embodied histories are clear. First, chieftaincy in Ibadan was not royal. Second, the contestation inherent in Ibadan chieftaincy created difficulties for colonial governing. Related to this was the development of antagonism between Ibadan and Oyo, a consequence of Ibadan chiefs being made subject to the *Alaafin*. Third, colonial governmentality required a material culture and, when ideologically necessary, it recontextualised its objects.

In the specific case of Ibadan, Residents Ross and Ward Price developed material cultures of colonial governmentality as part of reforming Ibadan chieftaincy – or, put another way, as a means for envisioning a social transformation of Ibadan civic politics. Although both men held strikingly different political visions, self-consciously constituting a *civic* material culture was part of each governing project. For Ross, Mapo Hall was a material expression of the *Alaafin's* civic jurisdiction over Ibadan chiefs. For Ward Price, the material presence of Mapo Hall 'bred civic pride' and he embellished his recontextualisation with further projects such as the Jubilee Celebrations and the Bower Memorial.

This effort was a practical response to the ideological problems presented by Ibadan chieftaincy. However, the obsessive requirement of colonial governmentality

---

[31] Thomas, *Entangled Objects*, p. 5.

for indigenous aristocracy masked a view of a more long-standing civic Ibadan institution. Its origins were in the political culture of the nineteenth century. To bring it into focus, we return momentarily to the years of military empire.

At the commencement of a war campaign, an Ibadan chief and his followers would go off to battle, ostensibly in the name of their city. If successful, they would return in triumph with captured people and loot from conquered towns. The greater each chief's hoard of war booty and consequent wealth, the greater appeared his civic power, as people flocked to him in social acknowledgement. This phenomenon was the subject of *oriki* or praise poetry belonging to *Balogun* Ajobo, an Ibadan warrior chief in 1871:

> There are four hundred and twenty plates in Awututu's house.
> There are four hundred and forty bowls there too.
> The bowls made of local pottery number almost
> two thousand in Awututu's house.
> If you find two thousand plates there,
> You'll find that each contained meat stew;
> There's always something to eat in Olominrin Ajobo's house.[32]

'Plates', textually linked with *Balogun* Ajobo's 'house', were in this *oriki* a material culture of a civic Ibadan. This institution was also embodied by the followers who ate from the thousands of plates; they constituted the social base from which *Balogun* Ajobo built his political acknowledgement as a chief in the city.[33]

Importantly, cloth was also used as a material expression of civic Ibadan power. According to both oral and written histories, *Basorun* Oluyole restricted the use of silk velvet in Ibadan town.[34] As Johnson retold it: 'Silk velvet was then very rare and of a high value; he allowed no one but himself alone to use a velvet robe; the chiefs might use velvet caps only, but this no common man dared to do.'[35] Johnson maintains that this practice was necessary to prevent less well-off Ibadan residents from impoverishing those dependent upon them by aspiring 'to what they could not easily obtain'.[36] Thus, implicitly, the more velvet one was able to display in Ibadan, the higher was one's political rank.

The assistant Colonial Secretary Alvan Millson, who visited Ibadan in 1890, also commented on the high cost of imported textiles. Although he estimated that over 95 per cent of the cloth consumed was locally produced, he did identify a demand for manufactured fabrics: 'The richer cloths alone, such as silks, velvets, velveteens, sateens, and damasks are purchased from Lagos ... by the wealthier slave owners and chiefs of the interior at most exorbitant rates.'[37] This market for European textiles and the importance of cloth for assertions of political status was of long standing. Apart from the silk velvet restriction imposed in Ibadan during the 1840s, Johnson

---

[32] Quoted in Morgan, *Akinyele's Outline: Part Two*, p. 111. Awututu is another name for *Balogun* Ajobo.
[33] See more discussion of this text in Barber, 'Money, Self-Realization', p. 213.
[34] Johnson, *History*, pp. 306–7, Morgan, *Akinyele's Outline (Part One)*, p. 83; Ayo Fasoro, *Verdict of God*, p. 29; Chief Akanbi interview, 14 February 1996.
[35] Johnson, *History*, p. 306.
[36] *Ibid.*
[37] Millson, 'The Yoruba Country,' p. 586.

recounts an incident of diplomacy in the Old Oyo Empire, where the *Elewi-odo* and the *Alaafin* endeavoured to outdo each other in the garments they wore.[38]

After 1897, the cessation of wars made it difficult for chiefs to sustain large followings and meet the expense of maintaining an ebullient social status in the city. Heightened intrigue and political rivalry was in part a consequence of this. Nonetheless, the material expression of civic Ibadan power, embodied by a chief's followers, his lavish spending for them and his elaborate self-display, remained vitally important in city politics.

Conspicuous materialism was especially evident in Ibadan's commercial arena during the 1920s and 1930s. No man personified this trend more than Adebisi Giwa.[39] Obisesan enviously noted the merchant's attire in his diary during June 1921: 'Heard news of gorgeous robes with which Adebisi dressed himself today in attending Mohammedan service.'[40] On another occasion, Obisesan wrote about the final Ramadan prayer [id ul-fitr]: 'Mr. Adebisi and friends dressed like mighty men & put out a very decent appearance, Adebisi himself being like a king amongst his nobles.'[41]

Thus, as a type of imported cloth, the *Olubadan* Damask was a commodity with a particular cultural significance in Ibadan politics and society. At the same time, it was an object which simultaneously entangled and politically mobilised different civic material cultures. The final section of this chapter will investigate how it did so.

Embodying civic power

In October 1938 Resident Kelly requested permission to build a wall and gates around Mapo Hall so as to control the huge crowds of spectators expected to gather for the Conference of Yoruba Chiefs.[42] About the same time, the Ibadan Patriotic Association ordered the *Olubadan* Damask.[43] This political society had been established two years earlier in the midst of the political fallout surrounding *Bale* Abasi's assumption of the *Olubadan* title. The Yoruba name of the association was *Egbe Omo Ibile*, meaning 'Society of Sons of the Soil'. Unlike the IPU, its constituents were mostly Muslim and illiterate; they comprised over thirty trade and craft guilds, credit organisations and dancing societies. The IPA stated that their prime objective was to assist their members 'to find out how they can become good and useful citizens of Ibadan'.[44] Importantly, a key mover behind the association was Belo Abasi, who aimed to muster popular support for his father, *Olubadan* Abasi.[45]

The Conference of Yoruba Chiefs was a forum invented by the Nigerian colonial

[38] Johnson, *History*, p. 179.

[39] Chief Adebisi, *Abese Olubadan*, interviewed 16 December 1995, Ibadan; Lawuyi Ogunniran, local historian, interviewed 19 October 1995, Ibadan.

[40] KDL, OP/55: 1921, 10 June.

[41] KDL, OP/55: 1924, 6 May.

[42] NAI, Oyo Prof. 1/790 Vol. IV: Kelly to Secretary, Southern Provinces, 20 October 1938.

[43] Akande interview.

[44] KDL, OP/30/2: IPA to Executive Council, 19 October 1936.

[45] Bello Abasi (now deceased), interviewed by Gavin Williams, Ibadan, 14 November 1971.

administration – there had been no comparable event in the pre-colonial period. Although such 'Conferences' were intended to present chiefs as having a voice in colonial policy-making and as being accountable to their subjects, the actual policy contribution of each Conference was minimal. In practice, they performed a theatre of colonial politics. The important role of costume in this theatre did not escape the attention of the IPA, as their lawyers later admitted:

> Since the announcement that the next Yoruba Conference of Chiefs will be held at Ibadan, different Societies composed of Yoruba descendants agreed that a special design of Damask containing the photograph of Olubadan with suitable inscription should be ordered from Europe to be used on the occasion. The cloth was ordered and sales have been made to individual members of the several Societies and Unions as well as non-natives of Ibadan who desire to attend the Show at Ibadan.[46]

The characterisation of the Conference as a 'Show' exemplifies its performative aspect. Furthermore, given the cultural significance of cloth in Ibadan political practice, a suggestion that a unique style of damask be designed and imported for the event was wholly appropriate.

Yet, the damask did not only symbolise long-standing indigenous notions of status and power. The opening ceremonies of Mapo Hall and Bower Memorial demonstrated that material display was also part of the politics of imperial rule. This display, especially its colours, embodied colonial hierarchies. So much is evident from a description of the Oyo Conference Hall in 1937:

> At the eastern end was the red-carpeted carved dais where the chairs of His Excellency and His Honour were placed; down each side and facing it were the chairs of the Chiefs and behind them those of their followers; the gorgeous robes of the Chiefs and the white uniforms of the Officers sitting behind the dais contrasted vividly with the huge red and blue carpets which covered the floor of the Hall, and made a scene of great dignity.[47]

Within the political space of the Chiefs' Conference, cloth was a material symbol of power.[48] Following Weber, one might say it was representative of a 'style of life … expected from all those who wish to belong to the circle'.[49] 'The circle,' in this particular context, was an eclectic group of people striving for power within a colonial political culture that was imperial and indigenous *at the same time*. After all, not only chiefs went to Chiefs' Conferences – members of the IPU and IPA went as well. It was partly their cloth which assured that they belonged; quite literally, it legitimated their material presence. No wonder then, that Akinpelu Obisesan paid such attention to his dress when reporting on his trip to the 1937 Oyo Conference: 'In our journey the dirt packed my face & spoiled my white garment.'[50]

---

[46] NAI, CSO 26/35943: Alakija and Alakija to Wooley, 20 May 1939.

[47] NAI, Oyo Prof. 2 OD. 213: Anonymous, 'The Conference of the Yoruba Chiefs,' 1937.

[48] C.A. Bayly has made a similar argument in the Indian context. See his 'The Origins of Swadeshi (home industry): Cloth and Indian Society, 1700–1930' in Arjun Appadurai (ed.) *The Social Life of Things: Commodities in Cultural Perspective* (Cambridge, 1986), pp. 286–321.

[49] Max Weber, 'Class, Status, Party,' in *From Max Weber: Essays in Sociology* (London, 1991 [1948]), translated and edited by H.H. Gerth and C. Wright Mills, p. 187.

[50] KDL, OP/48: 1937, 31 March.

The Cloth of Field of Gold

At the 1939 Conference, *Olubadan* Abasi and the IPA tried to go further. They attempted, for their own political objectives, to harness the cultural symbolism of cloth in a strategic way. Imagine the entire Ibadan chiefs and their followers attending this 'Show', in Ibadan, clothed in a royal blue shining damask which proclaimed: 'The *Olubadan* has become King, Everything is Finished.' Suddenly, not only the Ibadan chiefs, but also the damask itself, have a tangible political agency.

Crowns, tigers and diplomacy

Colonial officialdom became aware of the existence of the *Olubadan* Damask when *Alaafin* Ladugolu sent a piece of the cloth to Resident Kelly. He explained:

> These, you know too well, are truly the emblems of Obaship. The general design is too meaning-ful to average Yoruba man and child.
>
> I must tell you, My Good Friend, this action on the part of the Bale of Ibadan and his people is a direct and deliberate insult and abuse to the Alafin apart from the fact that it is offensive to my brother Obas of Yorubaland.[51]

The first of the damask's 'emblems of Obaship' was the crown. Crucially, this emblem was a precise appropriation of the material culture of indirect rule. It was not a Yoruba beaded crown; it was the St Edward crown, a most strategic choice. In 1917, Resident Ross might have relegated Ibadan to the ranks of the 'second-class', but he could not prevent the *Olubadan* Damask claiming and recontextualising the staff-of-office-crown in order to promote Ibadan civic grandeur.[52] This was enhanced by the deep royal blue colour of the cloth, a feature which the official damask description later attempted to neutralise by referring to it as a 'coloured ground'. To use the phrase 'royal blue' would give material legitimacy to a symbolic meaning that the colonial authorities were vigorously attempting to deny.

Second, apart from *Olubadan* Abasi, the damask's dominant motif was the leopard, whose significance mystified the Lagos authorities. Abasi's driver recently explained: 'Abasi was holding a tiger, that signifies Oyo under Ibadan because that tiger sign belongs to *Alaafin*. He had a rope tied around that tiger's neck, it was pulled tight.'[53] The leopard/tiger thus encapsulated a particular assertion of Ibadan hegemony. It was a reversal of those bitter years from 1914 until 1933 when 'Political theory emanated from Oyo that people of Royal parentage are tigers and must feed on the flesh of the common people.'[54] Finally, the inscription: 'The *Olubadan* has become King, Everything is Finished', implies a somewhat rude subtext of: 'So there! And you [the *Alaafin*] can't do anything about it!' Thus the *Olubadan* Damask appropriated and entangled symbols of two regal material cultures – the English and the Oyo. In doing this, it was a political image which served to undermine the power of both the colonial authorities and the *Alaafin*.

---

[51] NAI, CSO 26/35943: *Alaafin* Ladugbolu, quoted in Hardesworth to Wooley, 16 May 1939.

[52] I am indebted to J.D.Y. Peel for making this point.

[53] Akande interview. The translation of *ekùn* as tiger is incorrect, for there are no tigers in south-western Nigeria. However, the mistake is not significant because the translation is common among present-day Yoruba speakers. I am grateful to Karin Barber for her advice on this.

[54] NAI, CSO26/28775: Ibadan Native Administration to Governor Bourdillon, 11 October 1936.

154

Photo 7.3 *Olubadan*
Abasi. Note the staff of
office, three of which can
also be seen in Photo 6.8
(*RH, Mss. Afr. S.225/3/19:*
Papers of H.L. Ward Price.
Reproduced by permission of
the Bodleian Library,
University of Oxford)

This capacity of the damask did not arise solely from its iconography. Otherwise, one might have expected a similar image to have been banned. This was the photograph of *Olubadan* Abasi which was most likely the basis of the damask design – Abasi stands in an identical pose and holds a leopard by a leash (Photo 7.2). Although the photograph lacked the damask's crown and inscription, the presence of the leopard made it embody a political statement. However, it was often printed in locally-read newspapers after 1936 and there were no protests from either the *Alaafin* or the colonial authorities.

In this context, it is important to note that portrait photographs were another example of colonial material culture. They were (and still are) displayed in the reception rooms of Ibadan households to connote social status. Perhaps Abasi had the photograph taken when he assumed the title of *Olubadan* in 1936 and, afterwards, provided it to the press as a suitable portrait. Its transfer to the damask is significant, revealing the role of certain technologies in the production of material culture.[55]

Moving from colonial photography to imported textiles, we see that the most distinctive and crucial feature of the damask was that it could be *worn*, a potential that

[55] I thank John Iliffe for making this observation.

caused great alarm to the colonial authorities. For, should the *Olubadan* damask be worn by swarming crowds of Ibadan people at the 1939 Conference of Yoruba Chiefs, its symbolic meanings would be mobilised politically on Ibadan bodies. The material density of this embodied symbolic display would make an object – a piece of cloth – have an agency in itself. The 1939 Conference would become dominated by a body politic which appropriated and entangled the multiple civic material cultures of Ibadan history.[56] This body politic would be a new form of civic power in Ibadan – its apex was the figure of *Olubadan* Abasi.

The powerful agency of the worn *Olubadan* damask was such that Resident Kelly had no doubts that if it was displayed at the 1939 Conference, the result could be a riot. There was a precedent for such violence: just after the unveiling of the Bower Memorial in December 1936, the car carrying *Aremo Adeyemi* had been stoned when it was leaving Ibadan.[57] Two and a half years later, antagonism between Ibadan and Oyo remained high. Even if violence was averted, Kelly was sure that 'the atmosphere of the conference would be ruined'.[58]

In response to the *Alaafin's* letter about the damask, Resident Kelly contacted Chief Commissioner Whiteley who drew up the 'Restriction of the use of certain kinds of cloth Order'. When the Order was presented to *Olubadan* Abasi and the Ibadan chiefs, they were said by Kelly to be 'unanimous in condemning any suggestion that the Olubadan should be made an Oba'.[59] The chiefs duly signed the Order, claiming that they had never before seen the damask. *Olubadan* Abasi, on the other hand, admitted that 'one bale' of the cloth had been sold to his house. However, he stated that: 'He did not notice the crown on the cloth and he did not enquire the meaning of the inscription.' To this claim of innocent ignorance, a colonial officer annotated: 'Stuff!'[60]

The same handwriting features on a subsequent petition against the Order from Alakija and Alakija, lawyers employed by the Ibadan Patriotic Association. They wrote to Chief Secretary Wooley on 20 May, nine days before the Chiefs' Conference was to open. Maintaining that the Order was 'an encroachment on the liberty and freedom of His Majesty's protected subjects', Alakija and Alakija engaged in an innovative discursive strategy to have the Order revoked:

It can hardly do less.   5. Our Clients respectfully beg to submit that the wearing of such
                              a cloth on the day of the Conference *cannot create a breach of the*
                              peace or disturbance nor cause a riot; on the contrary, they believe
                              and they are of the opinion that it would lend grandeur to an
Quite! More Ibadan   occasion of such an historic nature just similar to Henry VIII's
Megalomania.   Cloth of Field of Gold.

---

[56] Weiner makes a similar argument, describing the practice of bedecking a Fijian chief with vast quantities of bark cloth at his inauguration. Annette B. Weiner, 'Cultural Difference and the Density of Objects', *American Ethnologist* 21 (1994), p. 399.

[57] NAI, Oyo Prof 1/55 Vol. III: Outram to Ward Price, 17 December 1936.

[58] NAI, CSO 26/35943: Kelly, quoted in Hardesworth to Wooley, 16 May 1939.

[59] *Ibid.*

[60] *Ibid.*

6. We venture to send along for His Excellency's inspection a
sample of the said cloth, and we would humbly suggest to His
Excellency to invite expert opinion on the propriety of the use of
such a cloth which we say does not in any way offend the
Quite untrue   susceptibility of any Native Ruler or detract any iota from their
& he knows it.   royal position and greatness.[61]

In their petition, Alakija and Alakija made clear that they realised what was at stake
for the colonial authorities if the *Olubadan* damask was circulated and worn: the
'royal position and greatness' of any Native Ruler. If the political status of '*any*
Native Ruler' was threatened, so too was the legitimacy of colonial governmentality.
However, the lawyers boldly suggested that this view was incorrect. They advised
Governor Bourdillon to seek 'expert opinion' on the significance of the worn
Olubadan damask and implied that if he did so, he would find an explanatory
precedent in his own nation's history. For their own political purposes, Alakija and
Alakija aligned colonial pageantry with a lavish diplomatic theatre of the European
sixteenth century – just as the damask itself was culturally entangled, so too was the
attempt to make it lawful.

The meeting of the Field of Cloth of Gold between Henry VIII of England and
Francis I of France was a final act of reconciliation arising from the Anglo–French
peace of 1514. The name of the meeting is thought to derive from its location 'in the
palm of a shallow dip called Val d'Or', which lay exactly halfway between the towns
of Guines and Ardres near Calais.[62] Equally, the name could also be a reflection of the
grand pomp of the event. Described by contemporaries as 'the eighth wonder of the
world', the Field of Cloth of Gold was notable for the fantastic lengths to which both
French and English went in displaying a material culture of power. On the English
side:

> Over five thousand persons made up the suites of Henry and his queen. Hundreds of pounds'
> worth of velvet, sarcenet, satin, cloth of gold and doublets, bonnets, shirts and boots were
> supplied for them.
> … [On 31 May 1520] The twenty-odd miles of sea between Dover and Calais was filled with a
> great concourse of ships carrying the king and queen and their suites to France – leaving
> England emptied of most of its nobility, hierarchy, courtiers, precious stuffs, jewels and high-
> born women. All were shipped to France.[63]

It would seem that the act of generating a body politic through the material/
symbolic display of people and cloth was not unique to embodiments of civic power
in colonial Ibadan. It was also crucial to early Tudor diplomacy.

In a brilliant discursive move, Alakija and Alakija appropriated these cultural
resonances to rewrite the Field of Cloth of Gold into Ibadan history. Their
recontextualisation shifted the order of the nouns, Field and Cloth, so as to
transform the *Olubadan* Damask into the Cloth of Field of Gold, a cloth that 'would
lend grandeur to an occasion of such an historic nature'. Aligning the showy

---

[61] NAI, CSO 26/35943: Alakija and Alakija to Wooley, 20 May 1939. Colonial officer's annotations in left-hand
column, in italics.

[62] J.J. Scarisbrick, *Henry VIII* (London, 1968), p. 77.

[63] *Ibid.*

Conference of Yoruba Chiefs with the 'huge, expensive game'[64] of sixteenth-century European diplomacy was something of an elevation for colonial pageantry. It was not appreciated. This inspired historical imagination was simply dismissed by colonial officialdom as 'More Ibadan Megalomania'.

Historians, however, should not blithely ignore this discursive strategy. Recall that Alakija and Alakija opened their case against the 'Restriction of the use of certain kinds of cloth Order' on the grounds that it encroached on the rights of their clients as colonial subjects. Their subsequent argument and appropriation of the Field of Cloth of Gold was predicated on an assumption that the symbolic object of colonial subjecthood had a material life which, in this particular case, they asserted was embodied by the *Olubadan* damask. Reminding the colonial authorities of their obligation to uphold the rights of colonial subjects, Alakija and Alakija sought to enable the *Olubadan* damask to be worn, in Ibadan, at the 1939 Conference of Yoruba Chiefs.

In Ibadan politics, this discourse of subjecthood was not as innovative as it might first appear. Throughout this book, I have demonstrated how deeply both Ibadan chieftaincy and colonial governmentality assumed their symbolic conceptions of power as already and always material. Histories entangled in the Olubadan damask provide a particularly explicit example of this mutually constitutive relationship. Further, the damask's exposé of symbolic-as-material made it have a potential political agency. The threat posed by this agency was so real that British colonial officials were compelled to generate legislation against it.

The *Olubadan* damask was thus kept out of circulation and it was not worn, as intended, at the 1939 Conference of Yoruba Chiefs. Since its agency was never realised there was not much material for living social memory to document. Consequently, the story of the damask is generally absent in Ibadan oral histories.[65] What it might have become remains embodied in its archive.

[64] *Ibid.*

[65] Apart from Alhaji Akande, a resident of the Abasi compound, the only other interviewee who knew of the damask was Chief Ayorinde, a prominent oral historian.

8

Weighty Words
The Material Form of Civic Discourse in Colonial Ibadan

By 1939, just over a century after its establishment as a war camp, Ibadan was the most populous city in Nigeria. As District Officer Schofield reminisced at the time of his 1931 posting there, it was 'usually called "the largest native town in Africa"'.[1] For British officials, describing Ibadan as a 'native town' distinguished it from a 'colonial town' such as Nairobi, whose origins were in the consolidatation of British imperial control in East Africa. Like Accra by the mid-colonial period, Ibadan was still unequivocally an 'African town'.[2]

Notwithstanding this continuity, Ibadan and its residents had lived through a period of significant political, social and cultural change. The regional wars of the nineteenth century, which had led directly to the foundation of Ibadan and its subsequent rise as a military polity, ended in 1893 with the imposition of British colonial rule. Up until this time, male residents had proved themselves worthy Ibadan citizens through their activities on the battlefield. Female residents ranked as citizens through their commercial and manufacturing enterprises and through their influential roles as wives and mothers.

Both men and women strove to maintain the honour of membership of a civic Ibadan by attracting the social gaze of followers and by achieving a chieftaincy title. The relationship between a material body of supporters and the symbolic status of political office was both interdependent and highly unstable. This instability gained its fullest expression in the endemic competition for chieftaincy titles – the disease of civil disorder – which was itself a struggle between chiefs to assert civic power. Such competition maintained a rapid turnover of titles and continually reconstituted a civic Ibadan.

The cessation of regional warfare challenged the institution of Ibadan chieftaincy. Nevertheless, British officials recognised military men as political actors and strove to govern through and with them, excluding women in the process. These social interactions between colonial officers and warrior chiefs reconfigured the contentious

---

[1] RH, Mss. Afr. S.1863/4/1, Memoirs, p. 68.
[2] John Parker, *Making the Town: Ga State and Society in Early Colonial Accra* (Portsmouth NH, 2000).

159

processes of making and allocating constitutional forms of power in the city. From an external perspective, this reconfiguration appeared to be political chaos. However, an internal view suggests that this contest was not only a manifestation of 'traditional' civil disorder; it was also a demonstration of the innovative capacity of chiefs to adapt and integrate the administrative tools of the colonial state for their own political purposes. Consequently, Ibadan chieftaincy was institutionalised and the symbolic civic status embodied by chieftaincy titles was maintained.

This institutionalisation, expressed in political discourse and in political practice, was particularly explicit during the administrations of Resident Ross and Resident Ward Price. The policy of indirect rule, which they both implemented in different ways, required legitimate institutions to exercise political authority as well as cooperation from competing local constituencies. Ibadan people could collaborate with or resist their administrative models. At the same time, they could also pursue their political objectives by selectively rejecting and appropriating imperial symbols of status and power. In turn, colonial officers could be equally strategic in their manipulation of local political interests.

It was these complex social layers of collusion and alliance that generated the discursive field of the civic Ibadan. A crucial feature of this discursive field was that it could take a material form. For example, Mapo Hall and the *Olubadan* Damask were physical objects that embodied civic discourses. But, most importantly, there was the ongoing disease of civil disorder – British administrators were never able to eradicate this constitutive feature of the civic Ibadan.

The disease of civil disorder *c.* 1937–51

Two years before the controversy over the *Olubadan* Damask, Ibadan was gripped by a serious civil crisis 'threatening the whole fabric of the Ibadan Native Administration'.[3] It began a few days after Resident Ward Price left Oyo Province in December 1936, accompanied to his port of departure at Lagos by *Olubadan* Abasi.

A group of chiefs, led by the grandson of *Basorun* Ogunmola, *Balogun* Akanmu, presented a petition to the recently appointed Resident Findlay. 'We are very much against,' they wrote, 'the Land Court Book being in the Custody of the present Chief *Asipa Olubadan*.'[4] This 'Book' was the judicial record of all land cases brought before the Ibadan chiefs and it had been given over to *Asipa Olubadan* Adebisi when he was appointed President of the new Lands Court. The establishment of this Court was another aspect of the municipal reforms introduced by Resident Ward Price. Previously, land cases had been heard by the four senior chiefs who comprised the Executive Council. After October 1936, control over these cases passed to the Lands Court judges who, apart from Adebisi, were *Asaju Balogun* Akinyele and *Ekarun Balogun* Solaja.

Combined with the changes in the membership of the Executive Council introduced during July 1936, these administrative reforms represented a significant loss of civic status for the chiefs from military households. As Samuel Layode put it,

[3] NAI, CSO 26/12723 Vol. XIV: Resident Kelly, Oyo Province Annual Report, 1938, para. 32.
[4] KDL, HMP/28/3: Akanmu and chiefs to Sumner, 19 December 1936.

The Material Form of Civic Discourse in Colonial Ibadan

Olubadan Abasi's reign was characterised by 'common men of the time becoming chiefs for the first time without doing any significant thing. These newly created common men helped Olubadan greatly.'[5] Chiefs like *Balogun* Akanmu thus found themselves cut off from the profitable returns they had previously gained from land cases and simultaneously, they realised that their access to chieftaincy titles was challenged by men outside their ranks, men whom the British authorities were actively supporting. It was clear that these circumstances would ultimately threaten their own and their descendants' claims to a monopoly of political titles in the city, as well as their control of a lucrative patronage network.

Consequently, at the end of 1936, *Balogun* Akanmu and his supporters turned against the 'newly created common men'. They petitioned for Chief Adebisi to be suspended for six months, on the grounds that he had publicly insulted them. However, Resident Findlay refused to authorise their request. *Olubadan* Abasi suggested that Adebisi be fined but, at a meeting on 30 January 1937, *Balogun* Akanmu and his allies stated that they would not be satisfied unless Adebisi was deposed altogether. *Olubadan* Abasi refused to sanction their ultimatum and the aggrieved chiefs then would not 'render him the necessary salutations and respect due to office,' reported Resident Findlay, 'with the result that there is now a feud in the town'.[6]

The subsequent constitutional crisis spawned copious documents and extensive press coverage – far more than any previous political conflict in the city. But this was only the beginning. Between 1941 and 1942 Ibadan was again torn by dissent over the promotion of *Osi Balogun* Solaja and the continuing rule of *Olubadan* Abasi.[7] The British authorities responded by attempting to reduce competition for chieftaincy titles through creating alternative municipal institutions. These political bodies, known successively as the 'advisory board' and the 'advisory committee', were intended to govern Ibadan in tandem with chieftaincy. However, the scheme failed.[8]

Ultimately, the Ibadan chiefs' suspension of *Otun Balogun* Agbaje in 1950 brought an end to the continuing civil unrest. Neither Agbaje nor the local colonial officials would accept his dismissal and the chiefs absolutely refused to back down. Their leader was *Olubadan* Oyewusi – a key player in the 1937–38 dispute. His grandfather was *Bale* Fijabi, the chief who had headed the signatories of the 1893 Ibadan Agreement and whose skeleton had mysteriously disappeared from King George V Avenue in 1935.

'The Ibadan boil has now been lanced and it can only be hoped that there will be some permanent relief.'[9] So commented a senior British administrator on the 1950 Oyo Province Annual Report. After a year of non–cooperation, on 11 January 1951 an official administrative inquiry was set up to investigate allegations of 'misconduct' against Salami Agbaje and of 'inefficiency and maladministration' against the Native

---

[5] Layode Mss.

[6] NAI, CSO 26/32309 Vol. I: Findlay to Secretary, Southern Provinces, 4 March 1937.

[7] See NAI, Iba. Div. 1/1/18 Vol. VIII; Oyo Prof. 2/1/2573 Vol. III.

[8] See NAI, Oyo Prof. 2/1/3131; Iba. Div. 1/1/2285.

[9] NAI, CSO 26/12723 Vol. XVII: Resident Whiting, Oyo Province Annual Report, 1950. Comments by Hoskyns Abrahall, undated.

Authority.[10] It resulted in far-reaching reforms that marginalised the civic authority of Ibadan chiefs. Simultaneously, it provided a political forum for the emergence of a nationalist consciousness in the city.[11]

The war of pen

In Chapter 3, I argued that civil disorder constituted a pre-colonial civic Ibadan. Under colonial rule, the disease remained. But it changed. It moved from the battle-field of Ibadan military compounds to a 'war of pen' – a discursive field of petitions, press articles and written histories. Illiterate successors of warrior chiefs were aware that they were not very well equipped for this type of conflict. In 1937, having employed a letter-writer to produce a petition to District Officer Ward, they complained that their literate opponents 'always give out or say some weighty words against our saying nothing'.[12]

Given this context, it is not surprising that one of the main grievances of *Balogun* Akanmu and his supporters in 1937 was the confiscation of their official stamps into the hands of *Asipa Olubadan* Adebisi. These 'special stamps' were first proposed by District Officer Dew in 1927, when he discovered that *Bale* Oyewole's messengers were in the habit of dictating letters to judicial clerks. He correctly discerned that the *Bale* might be unaware of 'the contents of all letters bearing his name'. In Dew's view, the use of personalised metal stamps would reduce the potential for forgeries.[13] Resident Ross was enthusiastic about the idea – he ordered no less than twenty-seven for the Ibadan Native Administration. Of these, four were given to members of the Executive Council.[14]

Although the stamps were intended solely for judicial duties, they were generally used for all correspondence. They enabled illiterate chiefs to associate themselves with the paraphernalia of writing – even if they could not read the letters they were signing. As Hofmeyr argues, by appropriating such things, 'chiefs announced themselves entitled and authorised to participate in a documentary culture'.[15] These objects were literally the markers of bureaucratic power. Put another way, stamps were weapons in the discursive field of a civic Ibadan and a manifestation of its material form. No wonder, then, that, in 1937 the discontented chiefs wanted them

---

[10] H.L.M. Butcher, *Report of the Commission of Inquiry into Allegations of Misconduct Made against Chief Salami Agbaje, Otun Balogun of Ibadan and Allegations of Inefficiency and Maladministration on the Part of Ibadan and District Native Authority* (Lagos, 1951).

[11] 'The Agbaje Affair' was a focus of conflict between political parties in the 1951 elections to the Western Regional House of Assembly. Scholars have generally analysed the incident ahistorically, without considering its connection to the administrative reforms implemented by Ward Price and subsequent chieftaincy disputes. The main works to examine the Agbaje Affair are: Justin Labinjoh, *Modernity and Tradition in the Politics of Ibadan* (Ibadan 1991); Post and Jenkins, *Price of Liberty*; Olufemi Vaughan, *Nigerian Chiefs: Traditional Power in Modern Politics, 1890s–1990s* (Rochester, NY, 2000).

[12] NAI, Oyo Prof. 1/1960: Oyekola and chiefs to Ward, 11 October 1937.

[13] NAI, Iba. Div. 1/1/231: Dew to Ross, 27 July 1927.

[14] NAI, Oyo Prof. 5/1/916/27–28: Indent for Chiefs Stamps, undated.

[15] Hofmeyr, *We Spend Our Years*, p. 62.

back. 'These officious official stamps', they complained, 'are lying within easy reach of both the Bale and his Councillors to our detriment.'[16]

This book has explored how the making of a civic Ibadan shifted to this 'war of pen'. In this war, political discourse and political practice were not only historically constitutive, they were often identical. Today, the consequence of this relationship is that when one asks a *mogaji* or chief about the history of chieftaincy politics in Ibadan, he claims that he can only speak about his compound. But when one asks about the history of the city, he recounts the Ibadan past in terms of competing political narratives of chieftaincy. Thus we return to the statement with which we began: 'Ibadan – a model of historical facts'.

[16] NAI, Oyo Prof. 1/1960: Oyekola and chiefs to Ward, 11 October 1937.

Appendix I

Chieftaincy Titles in Ibadan History

c. 1851[1]

Bale	Balogun	Seriki	Iyalode	HEREDITARY TITLES
Otun Bale	Otun Balogun	Sarunmi		Oluwo: Priest of Moremi
Osi Bale	Osi Balogun	Areagoro		Apena: Ogboni title
Ekefa Bale	Ekefa Balogun	Asaju		Aboke: Priest of Okebadan
Ekerin Bale	Ekerin Balogun			
Ajiya Bale				

c. 1893[2]

Bale	Balogun	Seriki	Iyalode	HEREDITARY TITLES
Otun Bale	Otun Balogun	Otun Seriki		Oluwo: Priest of Moremi
Osi Bale	Osi Balogun	Osi Seriki		Apena: Ogboni title
Ekerin Bale	Asipa	Ekerin Seriki		Aboke: Priest of Okebadan
Areagoro Bale	Ekerin Balogun	Sarunmi		
Are Alasa	Ekarun Balogun	Maye		
Agbakin	Ekefa Balogun	Abese		
	Asaju			

c. 1937[3]

Olubadan	Balogun	Seriki	Iyalode	HEREDITARY TITLES
Otun Olubadan	Otun Balogun	Otun Seriki	Otun Iyalode	Oluwo: Priest of Moremi
Osi Olubadan	Osi Balogun	Osi Seriki	Balogun Iyalode	Apena: Ogboni title
Asipa Olubadan	Asipa Balogun	Ekerin Seriki	Osi Iyalode	Aboke: Priest of Okebadan
Ekerin Olubadan	Ekerin Balogun	Asipa Seriki		
Ekarun Olubadan	Ekarun Balogun	Ekerin Seriki		
Abese Olubadan	Abese Balogun	Ekarun Seriki		
Maye Olubadan	Maye Balogun	Abese Seriki		
Ekefa Olubadan	Ekefa Balogun	Ekefa Seriki		
Agbakin Olubadan	Agbakin Balogun			
Arealasa Olubadan	Arealasa Balogun			
Ikoloba Olubadan	Ikoloba Balogun			
Asaju Olubadan	Asaju Balogun			
Ayingun Olubadan	Ayingun Balogun			
Areago Olubadan	Areago Balogun			
Lagunna Olubadan	Lagunna Balogun			
Ota Olubadan	Ota Balogun			
Aregbeomo Olubadan	Aregbeomo Balogun			
Gbonka Olubadan	Gbonka Balogun			
Areonibon Olubadan	Areonibon			

---

[1] CMSB, CA2/049/104: Hinderer Journal, 23 October 1851 and Johnson, *History*, p. 310.

[2] Johnson, *History*, p. 637.

[3] NAI, Iba Prof 3/4: Dickenson, Intelligence Report (1938), p. 39.

Appendix II

Senior Title-Holders in the Bale *&* Balogun *Lines* 1902–14[1]

	1902	1904	1907	1910	1912	1914
Bale	Mosaderin	Dada	Apanpa	Akintayo✥	Irefin	Situ
Otun Bale	Dada	Apanpa♣	Olafa	Irefin	Akinwale	Akinwale
Osi Bale	Olafa	Olafa	Irefin	Akinwale	Ola	Oyewusi
Asipa Bale	Oyebode	Oyebode	Oyebode	Oyebode✚	Oyewusi✩	Amida
Ekerin Bale	Irefin	Irefin	Ola✩	Ola✩	Adeaga✳	Adeaga
Maye Bale	Akinwale	Akinwale	Akinwale	Ajala	Ajala✳	Bola

♣ Shift from *Balogun*.
✩ Shift from *Maye Balogun*.
✥ Shift from *Balogun* (due to paralysis of *Otun Bale* Olafa, who died shortly after Akintayo's installation, enabling promotions of Irefin and Akinwale)
✚ Oyebode was from *ile* Osuntoki and his predecessor had been *Bale* of Ibadan between 1895 and 1897; this probably explains why Oyebode's promotion was consistently blocked.
✩ Ola became *Asipa Bale* in 1912 after the death of Oyebode; Oyewusi became *Ekerin*. His previous title (if any) is unknown. Both chiefs were promoted when *Bale* Irefin was installed.
✳ For unknown reasons, these chiefs were not signatories to 'The Native Chiefs' Complaints against Commissioner Ross' dated 14 January 1914.

	1902	1904	1905	1907	1910	1912	1914
Balogun	Apanpa	Apanpa	Omiyale	Akintayo	Situ	Situ	Ola✩
Otun Balogun	Bamgbegbin	Akintayo	Akintayo	Situ	Idowu	Idowu	Idowu
Osi Balogun	Akintayo	Situ	Situ	Suberu	Suberu	Oyewole	Oyewole
Asipa Balogun	Situ♦	Suberu	Suberu	Idowu	Oyewole	Fagbemi	Fagbemi
Ekerin Balogun	Suberu	Oyewole✥	Oyewole	Oyewole	Sanusi	Sanusi	Sanusi
Maye Balogun	Ola	Ola✩	Ola	Sanusi	Fagbemi	Aminu✦	Aminu

♦ Shitu was promoted from *Areago* in 1902.
✥ The death of Bamgbegbin (after signing the Judicial Agreement in August 1904) enabled *Ekefa Balogun* Oyewole to enter the senior ranks.
✩ Ola signed the Judicial Agreement as *Maye Balogun*; Omiyale is absent. Historian Akinyele states that *Bale* Dada promoted Omiyale from *Ekarun* in 1905.
✦ Aminu was *Areago Balogun* on the 1914 petition.
✩ *Bale* Situ installed *Osi Bale* Ola as his *Balogun*.

[1] The rules of succession to Ibadan's highest chieftaincy title were agreed on 19 August 1946; after the death of *Olubadan* Abasi. It was then decided that the *Balogun* and *Otun Olubadan* would take the post alternately. NAI, CSO 26/3457: Acting Secretary, Western Provinces to Chief Secretary, 8 November 1946.

Bibliography

Manuscript Sources

Nigerian National Archives, Ibadan

Chief Secretary's Office Series
CSO 1/3 Vol.6
CSO 16/3
CSO 16/4
CSO 16/5
CSO 16/6
CSO 16/7
CSO 26

Ibadan Province Series
Iba. Prof. 1/1
Iba. Prof. 3/1
Iba. Prof. 3/4
Iba. Prof. 3/6
Iba. Prof. 3/10

Ministry of Local Government
(Western Region) Series
MLG (W) 1

Oyo Province Series
Oyo Prof. 1
Oyo Prof. 2/1
Oyo Prof. 2/3
Oyo Prof. 4/5
Oyo Prof. 4/7
Oyo Prof. 4/11
Oyo Prof. 4/13
Oyo Prof. 5/1
Oyo Prof. 6/1
Oyo Prof. 8/3

Ibadan Division Series
Iba. Div. 1/1
Iba. Div. 1/4
Iba. Div. 4

Maps and Manuscripts Collection, Kenneth Dike Library, University of Ibadan

Rev. Akingbehin Papers.
I.B. Akinyele Papers: Personal diaries of nineteenth-century missionaries.
  William Stephen Allen, 1880, 1882, 1886, 1895.
  Daniel Olubi, 1884.
  Robert Scott Oyebode, 1877, 1878.
Bishop A.B. Akinyele Papers.
Akinpelu Obisesan Papers.
Herbert Macaulay Papers.
Rev. D.A. Williams Diaries.

Private Collection of Professor Bolanle Awe

Samuel Layode, 'Rebirth of Ibadan Town History'.

Special Collections, Main Library, The University of Birmingham

Church Missionary Society, Yoruba Mission, Original Papers.
CA 2/O49/ 94–114:   Hinderer, Rev. David, Quarterly Journal Extracts, 1849–51.

Rhodes House Library, Oxford

Mss. Afr. S.1169:   E.H. Elgee, 'The Evolution of Ibadan'.

Bibliography

Mss. Afr. S.1379:	Papers of Selwyn Macgregor Grier.
Mss. Afr. R. 63:	Ronald Martin Leslie, A History of Ibadan, West African History Notebook, *c.* 1944, 2 Vols.
Mss. Brit. Emp. S.76:	Lugard Papers.
Mss. Afr. S.656:	Papers of H.L. Ward Price.
Mss. Afr. S. 2225:	Papers of H.L. Ward Price
Mss. Afr. S.1863:	Papers of I.F.W. Schofield.
Mss. Afr.S.538:	Papers of L.R.C. Sumner.

Interviews (with the assistance of Mr Raufu Yesufu)

Interviews by Gavin Williams

Delesolu Alabelahon, *Itan* (translated English text), 1970.
Bello Abasi (deceased), 14 November 1971.
Chief Akinbiyi (deceased), *Otun Olubadan*, 25 April 1971.

Interviews by Ruth Watson

Chief Ayorinde, *Asipa Olubadan*, 16 September and 20 September 1995.
Alhaji Ekanoye (*ile* Delesolu), 2 October 1995.
Ibadan Founding Fathers' Descendants Union, 5 October 1995.
Chief Adeyemo, *Olubadan*, 6 October 1995.
Archdeacon Alayande, 6 October 1995.
Bale Adabale, 9 October 1995.
Chief Adedibu, *Lagunna Olubadan*, 11 October 1995.
Chief Omiyale, *Ekerin Balogun* (*Mogaji* Opeagbe), 14 October 1995.
Mogaji Ojuolape, 15 October 1995.
Mr Lawuyi Ogunniran and *Mogaji* Olugbode, 19 October 1995.
Mr Ogundeji (Delesolu family lawyer), 21 October 1995.
Chief Ajani, *Ekarun Balogun* (*Mogaji* Jenrinyin), 21 October 1995.
Chief Olunloyo, *Otun Balogun* (*Mogaji* Olunloyo) 26 October 1995.
Chief Ladimeji (Secretary to the *Olubadan*-in-Council), 27 October 1995.
Chief Akande, *Asipa Balogun*, 31 October 1995.
Chief Fijabi, *Mogaji* Babalola, 4 November 1995.
Chief Durosaro, *Osi Olubadan*, 7 and 11 November 1995.
Chief Ogundipe, *Balogun*, 9 November 1995.
Chief Amoo, *Ekarun Iyalode*, 11 November 1995.
Mogaji Oderinlo, 20 November 1995.
Mogaji Ibikunle, 24 November 1995.
Mogaji Ogunmola,15 December 1995.
Chief Ojerinola, 16 December 1995.
Chief Adebisi, 16 December 1995.
Alhaji Giwa (*ile* Aliwo), 29 December 1995.
Mogaji Kofo, 6 January 1996.
Mogaji Irefin, 9 January 1996.
Mogaji Fadaya, 16 January 1996.
Alhaji Raji (*ile* Delesolu), 18 January 1996.
Chief Adisa (Delesolu family lawyer), 20 January 1996.
Mogaji Kure, 21 January 1996.
Mogaji Latosisa, 23 January 1996.
Mrs Mabel Akinyele (Isaac Akinyele's daughter-in-law), 23 January 1996.
Mogaji Ogboriefon, 24 January 1996.
Chief Lanlehin, *Osi Balogun*, 5 February 1996.
Mogaji Foko, 28 January 1996.
Mogaji Agbaje, 29 January 1996 and 12 April 1997.
Chief Adetunji, *Ekefa Balogun*, 4 February 1996.
Chief Akanwo, *Oluwo* of Ibadan, 6 February 1996.
Chief Akintola, *Iyalode*, 6 February 1996 and 20 April 1997.
Chief Akanbi, *Lagunna Balogun* (*Mogaji* Oluyole), 14 February 1996.

Bibliography

Alhaji Akande (*ile* Alesinloye), 12 April 1997 and 7 May 1997.
Mogaji Kobomoje, 13 April 1997.
Chief Lana, 2 May 1997.
Chief Obisesan, 3 May 1997.
Mr Yekinni Agbaje, 9 May 1997.
Raufu Yesufu (*iIe* Delesolu), 10 May 1997.
Mogaji Solaja, 25 May 1997.

Printed sources

Official documents

Lagos Annual Report, 1899.
Lagos Government Gazette, 1905.
Nigeria Gazette, 1917–1939.
Butcher, H.L.M. *Report of the Commission of Inquiry into Allegations of Misconduct Made against Chief Salami Agbaje, Otun Balogun of Ibadan and Allegations of Inefficiency and Maladministration on the Part of Ibadan and District Native Authority* (Lagos, 1951).
Kirk-Greene, A.H.M. (ed.) *The Principles of Native Administration in Nigeria: Selected Documents, 1900-1947* (London, 1965).
Kirk-Greene, A.H.M. (ed.) *Political Memoranda*, London, 1970 (1919).
Ward Price, H.L. *Land Tenure in the Yoruba Provinces* (Lagos, 1933).

Newspapers

The Yoruba News, 1924–43.
Daily Times of Nigeria, 1935–37
Lagos Daily News, 1925–37
Southern Nigeria Defender, 1945.

Contemporary works

Akinyele, I.B. *Iwe Itan Ibadan* (Exeter, 1951 [1916]).
Akinyele, I.B. *The Outlines of Ibadan History* (Lagos, 1946).
Bowen, T.J. *Central Africa: Adventures and Missionary Labours in the Interior of Africa, 1849-1856* (London, 1857).
Hinderer, A. *Seventeen Years in the Yoruba Country* (London, 1872).
Hopkins, A.G. 'A Report on the Yoruba, 1910', *Journal of the Historical Society of Nigeria* 5 (1969), pp. 67–100.
Johnson, S. *The History of the Yorubas from the Earliest Times to the Beginning of the British Protectorate* (London, 1921).
Millson, A.W. 'The Yoruba country, West Africa,' *Proceedings of the Royal Geographical Society* 13 (1891), pp. 577–91.
Perham, M. *West African Passage: a Journey Through Nigeria, Chad and the Cameroons*, ed. A.H.M. Kirk-Greene (London, 1983).
Ward Price, H.L. *Dark Subjects* (London, 1939).

Recent works

Adebiyi, T.A. *The Beloved Bishop* (Ibadan, 1969).
Adedeji, S. *Metamorphosis of a Kid Trader* (Ibadan, 1995).
Adedibu, L. *What I Saw on the Politics and Governance of Ibadanland and the Issue of June 12, 1993* (Ibadan, 1997).
Ademakinwa, J.A. *Ife, Cradle of the Yoruba Part II* (Lagos, n.d.).
Adeyemo, A. *Oluyole: an Epic History of the Yorubas* (Ibadan, 1989).
Aofolaju, B. *Landmarks in the History of Ibadan* (Ibadan, 1996).
Ayorinde, J.A. *Oba Akinyele* (Ibadan, 1974).
Fabunmi, M.A. *An Anthology of Historical Notes on Ife City* (Lagos, 1985).
Fasoro, A. *Verdict of God: a Biography of his Royal Highness Oba Emmanuel Adegboyega Adeyemo Operinde I,*

Bibliography

Olubadan of Ibadanland (Ibadan, 1995).
Ibadan Mementoes: Oba Adeyemo's Noble Past, Glorious Present and Progressive Future X-Rayed. Historical Perspective on Ibadanland (Ibara, 1995).
Ibadan Progressive Union, *50 Years of Its Founding 1930–1980: Exhibition Programme* (Ibadan, 1983).
Latunde v. Olajinfin, Supreme Court of Nigeria, 1989. This court record was loaned to me by Raufu Yesufu of *ile* Delesolu, Oje, Ibadan.
Matches, Bro. W.R.D. *Ibadan Lodge 5316, 1931–1966* (Ibadan, 1967).
Morenikeji v. Adegbosin, Court of Appeal, 1994. This court record was loaned to me by Raufu Yesufu of *ile* Delesolu, Oje, Ibadan.
Morgan, K. *Akinyele's Outline History of Ibadan, Revised and Enlarged (Part One)* (Ibadan, n.d.).
Morgan, K. *Akinyele's Outline History of Ibadan, Revised and Enlarged (Part Two)* (Ibadan, n.d.).
Morgan, K. *Akinyele's Outline History of Ibadan, Revised and Enlarged (Part Three)* (Ibadan, n.d.).
Ogundipe, Y.B. *Eto Oye Jije, Mogaji Ati Asa Wa Ni Ilu Ibadan* (Ibadan, n.d)
Ogunranti, A. *I Know a Man, a Saint* (Ibadan, 1964).

Published Secondary Sources

Abraham, R. C. *Dictionary of Modern Yoruba* (London, 1958).
Adeniran, A. 'Benevolent Neutrality?: The Ijebu and the Kiriji/Ekitiparapo War, 1877–1892', *Ife: Annals of the Institute of Cultural Studies* 4 (1993), pp. 62–71.
Adeleye, R.A. *Power and Diplomacy in Northern Nigeria, 1804–1906: The Sokoto Caliphate and its Enemies* (London, 1971).
Adewoye, O. 'The Judicial Agreements in Yorubaland, 1904–1908', *Journal of African History* 12 (1971), pp. 607–27.
Afigbo, A.E. *The Warrant Chiefs* (London, 1972).
Afigbo, A. *Ropes of Sand: Studies in Igbo History and Culture* (Nsukka, 1981).
Agiri, B.A. 'Early Oyo History Reconsidered', *History in Africa* 2 (1975), pp. 1–16.
Akinjogbin, I.A. 'A Chronology of Yoruba History, 1789-1840', *Odu* 2 (1966), pp. 81–86.
Ajayi, J.F.A. and Smith, R. *Yoruba Warfare in the Nineteenth Century* (Cambridge, 1964).
Ajayi, J.F.A. 'Professional Warriors in Nineteenth-Century Yoruba Politics', *Tarikh* 1 (1965), pp. 72–81.
Ajayi, J.F.A. *Christian Missions in Nigeria 1841-1891: the Making of a New Elite* (Ibadan, 1965).
Ajayi, J.F.A. and Ikora, B. (eds) *Evolution of Political Culture in Nigeria: Proceedings of a National Seminar organised by the Kaduna State Council for Arts and Culture* (Ibadan, 1985).
Akintoye, S.A. *Revolution and Power Politics in Yorubaland 1840-1893: Ibadan Expansion and the Rise of Ekitiparapo* (New York, 1971).
Albert, I. 'The Growth of an Urban Migrant Community: the Hausa Settlements in Ibadan, c.1830–1979', *Ife: Annals of the Institute of Cultural Studies* 4 (1993), pp. 1–15.
Alliance Francaise, *Adire: Indigo Dyed Cloth of the Yoruba* (Ibadan, 1987).
Almond, G. and Verba, S. *The Civic Culture: Political Attitudes and Democracy in Five Nations* (London, 1989 [1963]).
Appadurai, A. (ed.) *The Social Life of Things: Commodities in Cultural Perspective* (Cambridge, 1986).
Appiah, K.A. *In My Father's House: Africa in the Philosophy of Culture* (London, 1992).
Apter, A. '*Que Faire?* Reconsidering Inventions of Africa', *Critical Inquiry* 19 (1992), pp. 85–104.
Apter, A. *Black Critics and Kings: the Hermeneutics of Power in Yoruba Society* (Chicago, 1992).
Aronson, D. 'Capitalism and Culture in Ibadan Urban Development', *Urban Anthropology* 7 (1978), pp. 253–67.
Aronson, D. *The City is Our Farm: Seven Migrant Ijebu Familes* (Boston, 1978).
Asiwaju, A.I. *Western Yorubaland under European Rule 1889–1945* (London, 1976).
Atanda, J.A. *The New Oyo Empire: Indirect Rule and Change in Western Nigeria, 1894–1934* (London, 1973).
Awe, B. 'The *Ajele* System: A Study of Ibadan Imperialism in the Nineteenth Century', *Journal of the Historical Society of Nigeria* 3 (1964), pp. 47–71.
Awe, B. 'Ibadan, Its Early Beginnings', in *The City of Ibadan*, (eds) P.C. Lloyd, A.L. Mabogunje and B. Awe (Cambridge, 1967), pp. 11–25.
Awe, B. 'Some Ibadan Place-Names: a Source of Historical Evidence', *African Notes* 6 (1970–71), pp. 85–93.
Awe, B. 'Militarism and Economic Development in Nineteenth Century Yoruba Country: the Ibadan Example', *Journal of African History* 14 (1973), pp. 65–77.
Awe, B. 'The *Iyalode* in the Traditional Yoruba Political System', in *Sexual Stratification: a Cross-Cultural View*, (ed.) A. Schlegel (New York, 1977), pp. 144–160.
Awe, B. '*Iyalode* Efunsetan Aniwura (Owner of Gold)' in *Nigerian Women in Historical Perspective* (ed.) B. Awe (Ibadan, 1992), pp. 55–71.
Ayandele, E.A. *The Missionary Impact on Modern Nigeria, 1842–1914* (London, 1966).
Ayandele, E.A. *The Educated Elite in the Nigerian Society* (Ibadan, 1974).
Ayandele, E.A. *Nigerian Historical Studies* (London, 1979).

Bibliography

Barber, K. and de Moraes Farias, P.F. (eds) *Discourse and Its Disguises: the Interpretation of African Oral Texts* (Birmingham, 1989).

Barber, K. 'Interpreting *Oriki* as History and as Literature' in *Discourse and Its Disguises: the Interpretation of African Oral Texts*, (eds) K. Barber and P.F. de Moraes Farias, (Birmingham, 1989), pp. 13–23.

Barber, K. *I Could Speak Until Tomorrow: Oriki, Women and the Past in a Yoruba Town* (Edinburgh, 1991).

Barber, K. '*Oriki* and the Changing Perception of Greatness in Nineteenth-Century Yorubaland' in *Yoruba Historiography*, (ed.) T. Falola (Madison, 1991), pp. 31–41.

Barber, K. 'Money, Self-Realization and the Person in Yorùbá Texts', in *Money Matters: Instability, Values and Social Payments in the Modern History of West African Communities*, (ed.) J.I. Guyer (London, 1995), pp. 205–24.

Barber, K. (ed.) *Readings in African Popular Culture* (Oxford, 1997).

Barnes, S.T. *Patrons and Power: Creating a Political Community in Metropolitan Lagos* (Manchester, 1986).

Barnes, S.T. 'The Urban Frontier in West Africa: Mushin, Nigeria' in I. Kopytoff (ed.) *The African Frontier: the Reproduction of Traditional African Societies* (Bloomington, 1987), pp. 257–81.

Barnes, S.T. 'Political Ritual and the Public Sphere in Contemporary West Africa' in *Politics of Cultural Performance* (eds) D. Parkin, L. Caplan and H. Fisher (Oxford, 1996), pp. 19–40.

Bascom, W. 'Urbanization Among the Yoruba', *The American Journal of Sociology* 60 (1955), pp. 446–54.

Bascom, W. 'Urbanism as a Traditional African Pattern', *The Sociological Review* 7 (1959), pp. 29–43.

Bascom, W. *Ifa Divination* (Bloomington, 1969).

Bayart, J.F. *The State in Africa: the Politics of the Belly* (Harlow, 1993).

Bayly, C. 'The Origins of Swadeshi (Home Industry): Cloth and Indian Society, 1700–1930' in *The Social Life of Things: Commodities in Cultural Perspective* (Cambridge, 1986) (ed.) A. Appadurai, pp. 286–321.

Beer, C.E.F. *The Politics of Peasant Groups in Western Nigeria* (Ibadan, 1976).

Beer, C.E.F. and Williams, G. 'The Politics of the Ibadan Peasantry' in *Nigeria: Economy and Society*, (ed.) G. Williams (London, 1976), pp. 135–58.

Berry, S. 'The Concept of Innovation and the History of Cocoa Farming in Western Nigeria', *Journal of African History* 15 (1974), pp. 83–95.

Berry, S. *Cocoa, Custom and Socio-economic Change in Rural Western Nigeria* (Oxford, 1975).

Berry, S. *Fathers Work for Their Sons: Accumulation, Mobility and Class Formation in an Extended Yoruba Community* (Berkeley, 1985).

Berry, S. 'Social Institutions and Access to Resources', *Africa* 59 (1989), pp. 41–55.

Berry, S. 'Hegemony on a Shoestring: Indirect Rule and Access to Agricultural Land', *Africa* 62 (1992), pp. 327–56.

Berry, S. 'Unsettled Accounts: Stool Debts, Chieftaincy Disputes and the Question of Asante Constitutionalism', *Journal of African History* 39 (1998), pp. 39–62.

Bhabha, H. K. *The Location of Culture* (London, 1994).

Brown, S. (ed.) *The Pressures of the Text: Orality, Texts and the Telling of Tales* (Birmingham, 1995).

Calhoun, C. 'Introduction: Habermas and the Public Sphere', in *Habermas and the Public Sphere* (ed.) C. Calhoun (Cambridge, MA, 1993).

Calvocoressi, D. and David, N. 'A New Survey of Radiocarbon and Thermoluminescence Dates for West Africa', *Journal of African History* 20 (1979), pp. 1–29.

Casely-Hayford A. and Rathbone R. 'Politics, Families and Freemasonry in the Colonial Gold Coast' in *People and Empires in African History: Essays in Memory of Michael Crowder*, (eds) J.D.Y. Peel and J.F.A. Ajayi (London, 1992), pp. 143–60.

Chakrabarty, D. 'Of Garbage, Modernity and the Citizen's Gaze', *Economic and Political Weekly* 28 (1992), pp. 541–7.

Chokor, B.A. 'External European Influences and Indigenous Social Values in Urban Development and Planning in the Third World: The Case of Ibadan, Nigeria', *Planning Perspectives* 8 (1993), pp. 283–306.

Cohen, A. *Custom and Politics in Urban Africa. A Study of Hausa Migrants in Yoruba Towns* (London, 1969).

Cole, P. *Modern and Traditional Elites in the Politics of Lagos* (Cambridge, 1975).

Coleman, J.S. *Nigeria: Background to Nationalism* (Berkeley, 1963).

Crowder M. and Ikime O. (eds) *West African Chiefs: Their Changing Status Under Colonial Rule and Independence* (Ile-Ife, 1970).

Danmole, H.O. 'The Abortive Peace Missions: Intervention of Lagos Muslims in Anglo-Ilorin Boundary Dispute, 1894–96', *Journal of the Historical Society of Nigeria* 13 (1985–86), 67–82.

de Moraes Farias, P.F. and Barber, K. (eds) *Self-Assertion and Brokerage: Early Cultural Nationalism in West Africa*. (Birmingham, 1990).

de Moraes Farias, P.F. '"Yoruba Origins" Revisited by Muslims', in *Self-Assertion and Brokerage: Early Cultural Nationalism in West Africa*, (eds) P.F. de Moraes Farias and K. Barber (Birmingham, 1990), 109–47.

de Moraes Farias, P.F. 'History and Consolation: Royal Yorùbá Bards Comment on Their Craft', *History in Africa* 19 (1992), pp. 263–97.

de Polignac, F. *Cults, Territory, and the Origins of the Greek City-State*, (trans.) Janet Lloyd (Chicago, 1995).

Bibliography

Doortmont, M.R. 'The Invention of the Yorubas: Regional and Pan-African Nationalism versus Ethnic Provincialism', in *Self-Assertion and Brokerage: Early Cultural Nationalism in West Africa*, (eds) P.F. de Moraes Farias and K. Barber (Birmingham, 1990), pp. 101–8.

Doortmont, M.R. 'The Roots of Yoruba Historiography: Classicism, Traditionalism and Pragmatism' in *African Historiography: Essays in Honour of Jacob Ade Ajayi*, (ed.) T. Falola (Harlow, 1993), pp. 52–63.

Duncan, J.S. *The City as Text: The Politics of Landscape Interpretation in the Kandyan Kingdom* (Cambridge, 1990).

Eades, J.S. *The Yoruba Today* (Cambridge, 1980).

Fadipe, N.A. *The Sociology of the Yoruba*, (eds) F.O. Okediji and O.O. Okediji (Ibadan, 1970).

Falola, T. *The Political Economy of a Pre-Colonial African State: Ibadan, 1830–1900* (Ile-Ife, 1984).

Falola, T. and Oguntomisin, D. *The Military in Nineteenth Century Yoruba Politics* (Ile-Ife, 1984).

Falola, T. 'The Political System of Ibadan in the 19th Century', in *Evolution of Political Culture in Nigeria*, (eds) J.F.A. Ajayi and B. Ikora (Ibadan, 1985), pp. 104–16.

Falola, T. 'From Hospitality to Hostility: Ibadan and Strangers, 1830–1904', *Journal of African History* 26 (1985), pp. 51–68.

Falola, T. 'Brigandage and Piracy in Nineteenth Century Yorubaland', *Journal of the Historical Society of Nigeria* 13 (December 1985–June 1986), pp. 83–105.

Falola, T , 'A Research Agenda on the Yoruba in the Nineteenth Century', *History in Africa* 15 (1988), pp. 211–27.

Falola, T. and Doortmont, M.R. '*Iwe Itan Oyo*: a Traditional Yoruba History and its Author', *Journal of African History* 30 (1989), pp. 301–29.

Falola, T. *Politics and Economy in Ibadan 1893–1945* (Lagos, 1989).

Falola, T. 'The Yoruba Toll System: Its Operation and Abolition', *Journal of African History* 30 (1989), pp. 69–88.

Falola, T. (ed.) *Yoruba Historiography*. (Madison, 1991).

Falola, T. 'Kemi Morgan and the Second Reconstruction of Ibadan History', *History in Africa* 18 (1991), pp. 93–112.

Falola, T. 'Ibadan Power Elite and the Search for Political Order, 1893–1939', *Africa: Rivista Trimestrale di studi e documentozione dell'Istituto Italo-Africano* 68 (1992), pp. 336–54.

Falola, T.(ed.) *African Historiography: Essays in Honour of Jacob Ade Ajayi* (Harlow, 1993).

Falola, T. 'Ade Ajayi on Samuel Johnson: Filling the Gaps' in *African Historiography: Essays in Honour of Jacob Ade Ajayi*, (ed.) T. Falola (Harlow, 1993), pp. 80–9.

Falola, T. 'Slavery and Pawnship in the Yoruba Economy of the Nineteenth Century', *Slavery and Abolition* 15 (1994), pp. 221–45.

Fatton, R. *Predatory Rule: State and Civil Society in Africa* (London, 1992).

Filani, M.O., Akintola, F.O. and Ikporukpo, C.O. *Ibadan Region* (Ibadan, 1994).

Flint, J.E. *Sir George Goldie and the Making of Nigeria* (London, 1960).

Gbadamosi, T.G.O. *The Growth of Islam Among the Yoruba, 1841–1908* (London, 1978).

Goheen, M. 'Chiefs, Sub-Chiefs and Local Control: Negotiations Over Land, Struggles Over Meaning', *Africa* 62 (1992), pp. 389–412.

Guyer, J.I. 'Wealth in People and Self-Realization in Equatorial Africa', *Man* n.s. 28 (1993), pp. 205–24.

Guyer, J.I. 'The Spatial Dimensions of Civil Society in Africa: an Anthropologist Looks at Nigeria', in *Civil Society and the State in Africa* (eds) J.W. Harbeson, D. Rothchild and N. Chazan (London, 1994).

Guyer, J.I. 'Wealth in People, Wealth in Things – Introduction', *Journal of African History* 36 (1995), pp. 83–90.

Guyer, J.I. and Belinga S.M.E. 'Wealth in People as Wealth in Knowledge: Accumulation and Composition in Equatorial Africa', *Journal of African History* 36 (1995), pp. 91–120.

Guyer, J.I. (ed.) *Money Matters: Instability, Values and Social Payments in the Modern History of West African Communities* (London, 1995).

Guyer, J.I. *An African Niche Economy. Farming to Feed Ibadan, 1968-88* (Edinburgh, 1997).

Hannerz, U. *Exploring the City. Inquiries toward an Urban Anthropology* (New York, 1980).

Harbeson, J.W., Rothchild, D. and Chazan, N. (eds) *Civil Society and the State in Africa* (London, 1994).

Harvey, D. *The Urban Experience* (Oxford, 1989).

Haynes, D.E. *Rhetoric and Ritual in Colonial India: the Shaping of a Public Culture in Surat City, 1851–1928* (Berkeley, 1991).

Heap, S. '"*Jaguda* Boys": Pickpocketing in Ibadan, 1930–1950', *Urban History* 24 (1997), pp. 323–43.

Hecht, D. and Simone, M. *Invisible Governance: The Art of African Micropolitics* (New York, 1994).

Hofmeyr, I. *We Spend Our Years as a Tale That Is Told: Oral Historical Narrative in a South African Chiefdom* (London, 1993).

Holston, J. and Appadurai, A. 'Cities and Citizenship', *Public Culture* 19 (1996), pp. 187–204.

Home, R. K. 'Urban Growth and Urban Government: Contradictions in the Colonial Political Economy', in *Nigeria: Economy and Society*, (ed.) G. Williams (London, 1976), pp. 55–75.

Idowu, E. B. 'Religion in Ibadan: Traditional Religion and Christianity', in *The City of Ibadan*, (eds) P.C. Lloyd, A.L. Mabogunje and B. Awe (Cambridge, 1967), pp. 235–47.

171

Bibliography

Inden, R. 'Embodying God: from Imperial Progresses to National Progress', *Economy and Society* 24 (1995), pp. 245–78.

Jacobs, J.M. *Edge of Empire: Postcolonialism and the City* (London, 1996).

Jenkins, G. 'Government and Politics in Ibadan', in *The City of Ibadan*, (eds) P.C. Lloyd, A.L. Mabogunje and B. Awe (Cambridge, 1967), pp. 213–33.

Jewsiewicki, B., and Newbury, D. *African Historiographies: What History for Which Africa?* (Beverly Hills, 1986).

Joyce, R.B., *Sir William MacGregor* (Melbourne, 1971).

Kopytoff, I. (ed.) *The African Frontier: the Reproduction of Traditional African Societies* (Bloomington, 1987).

Krapf-Askari, E. *Yoruba Towns and Cities. An Enquiry into the Nature of Urban Social Phenomena* (Oxford, 1969).

Labinjoh, J. *Modernity and Tradition in the Politics of Ibadan 1900–1975* (Ibadan, 1991).

Law, R. 'The Chronology of the Yoruba Wars of the Early Nineteenth Century: a Reconsideration', *Journal of the Historical Society of Nigeria* 5 (1970), pp. 211–22.

Law, R. 'Early Yoruba Historiography', *History in Africa* 3 (1976), 69–89.

Law, R. *The Oyo Empire, c. 1600–c.1836: A West African Imperialism in the Era of the Slave Trade* (Oxford, 1977).

Law, R. *The Horse in West African History: The Role of the Horse in the Societies of Pre-Colonial West Africa* (Oxford, 1980).

Law, R. 'How Truly Traditional Is Our Traditional History? The Case of Samuel Johnson and the Recording of Yoruba Oral Tradition', *History in Africa* 11 (1984) pp. 195–221.

Law, R. 'How Many Times Can History Repeat Itself? Some Problems in the Traditional History of Oyo' *International Journal of African Historical Studies* 18 (1985), pp. 33–51.

Law, R. 'Constructing "a Real National History": A Comparison of Edward Blyden and Samuel Johnson', in *Self-Assertion and Brokerage: Early Cultural Nationalism in West Africa*, (eds) P.F. de Moraes Farias and K. Barber (Birmingham, 1990), pp. 78–100.

Law, R. (ed.) *From Slave Trade to 'Legitimate' Commerce: The Commercial Transition in Nineteenth-Century West Africa* (Cambridge, 1995).

Lloyd, P.C. 'The Yoruba Lineage', *Africa* 25 (1955), pp. 235–51.

Lloyd, P.C. 'The Yoruba Town Today', *The Sociological Review* 7 (1959), pp. 45–63.

Lloyd, P.C. 'Sacred Kingship and Government Among the Yoruba', *Africa* 30 (1960), pp. 221–37.

Lloyd, P.C. *Yoruba Land Law* (London, 1962).

Lloyd, P.C. 'Agnatic and Cognatic Descent Among the Yoruba', *Man* n.s. 1 (1966), pp. 484–500.

Lloyd, P.C., Mabogunje, A.L. and Awe, B. (eds) *The City of Ibadan: A Symposium on its Structure and Development* (Cambridge, 1967).

Lloyd, P.C. 'Conflict Theory and Yoruba Kingdoms', in *History and Social Anthropology* (ed.) I.M. Lewis (London, 1968), pp. 25–61.

Lloyd, P.C. *The Political Development of Yoruba Kingdoms in the Eighteenth and Nineteenth Centuries* (London, 1971).

Lloyd, P.C. 'The Yoruba: An Urban People?' in *Urban Anthropology. Cross-Cultural Studies of Urbanization*, (ed.) A. Southall (New York, 1973), pp. 107–23.

Lloyd, P.C. *Power and Independence: Urban Africans' Perception of Social Inequality* (London, 1974).

Lovejoy, P.E. 'The Ibadan School of Historiography and its Critics', in *African Historiography: Essays in Honour of Jacob Ade Ajayi* (ed.) T. Falola (Harlow, 1993), pp. 195–202.

Low, D.A. and Pratt, R.C. *Buganda and British Overrule, 1900–1955: Two Studies* (London, 1960).

Mabogunje, A.L. *Yoruba Towns* (Ibadan, 1962).

Mabogunje, A.L. 'The Morphology of Ibadan', in *The City of Ibadan*, (eds) P.C. Lloyd, A.L. Mabogunje and B. Awe (Cambridge, 1967), pp. 35–56.

Mabogunje, A.L. *Urbanization in Nigeria* (London, 1968).

Mabogunje, A.L. and Omer-Cooper, J.D. *Owu in Yoruba History* (Ibadan, 1971).

Mabogunje, A.L. *Cities and Social Order* (Ibadan, 1974).

Mamdani, M. *Citizen and Subject: Contemporary Africa and the Legacy of Late Colonialism* (Princeton, 1996).

Mann, K. and Roberts, R. *Law in Colonial Africa* (London, 1991).

McCaskie, T.C. 'Asantesem: Reflections on Discourse and Text in Africa' in *Discourse and Its Disguises: The Interpretation of African Oral Texts*, (eds) K. Barber and P.F. de Moraes Farias (Birmingham, 1989), pp.70–86.

McCaskie, T. C. 'Inventing Asante' in *Self-Assertion and Brokerage: Early Cultural Nationalism in West Africa*, (eds) P.F. de Moraes Farias and K. Barber (Birmingham, 1990), pp. 55–67.

McCaskie, T.C. *State and Society in Pre-Colonial Asante* (Cambridge, 1995).

Mitchel, N.C. 'Yoruba Towns', in *Essays on African Population* (eds) K.M. Barbour and R.M. Prothero (London, 1961), pp. 279–301.

Mitchell, J.C. *Cities, Society, and Social Perception: A Central African Perspective* (Oxford, 1987).

Mitchell, L.G. *Greeks Bearing Gifts: The Public Use of Private Relationships in the Greek World, 435–323 BC* (Cambridge, 1997).

Morgan, W.B. 'The Influence of European Contacts on the Landscape of Southern Nigeria,' *The Geographical*

Bibliography

Journal 125 (1959), pp. 48–64.

Mudimbe, V. Y., and Jewsiewicki, B. (eds) *History Making in Africa. History and Theory: Studies in the Philosophy of History* 32 (1994).

Offer, A. 'Between the Gift and the Market: The Economy of Regard', *Economic History Review* 50 (1997), pp. 450–76.

Ogunbiyi I.A. and Reichmuth, S. 'Arabic Papers from the *Olubadan* Chancery I: A Rebellion of the Ibadan Chieftains Or, At the Origins of Yoruba Arabic Prose', *Sudanic Africa: A Journal of Historical Sources* 8 (1997), pp. 109–35.

Ojo, G.F.A. *Yoruba Culture: a Geographical Analysis* (London, 1966).

Oldenburg, V. *The Making of Colonial Lucknow, 1856–1877* (Princeton, 1984)

Onibokun, A. and Faniran, A. (eds) *Urban Research in Nigeria* (Ibadan, 1995).

Otite, O. *The Presence of the Past* (Ibadan, 1974).

Ottenberg, S. 'Further Light on W.R. Bascom and the Ife Bronzes', *Africa* 64 (1994), pp. 561–68.

Paden, J.N. *Religion and Political Culture in Kano* (Berkeley, 1973).

Pallinder-Law, A. 'Aborted Modernization in West Africa? The Case of Abeokuta', *Journal of African History* 15 (1974), 65–82.

Park, E. 'Taffy Jones: First Town Engineer of Ibadan', *Nigerian Field* 28 (1963), pp. 103–14.

Parker, J. *Making the Town: Ga State and Society in Early Colonial Accra*, (Portsmouth NH, 2000)

Parkin, D., Caplan, L. and Fisher, H. (eds) *Politics of Cultural Performance* (Oxford, 1996).

Parrinder, G. 'Ibadan's Annual Festival', *Africa* 21 (1951), pp. 54–8.

Parrinder, G. *Religion in an African City* (London, 1953).

Peel, J.D.Y. 'Kings, Titles and Quarters: a Conjectural History of Ilesha. I: The Traditions Reviewed', *History in Africa* 6 (1979), pp. 109–53.

Peel, J.D.Y. '*Olaju*: A Yoruba Concept of Development', *Journal of Development Studies* 14 (1978), pp. 135–65.

Peel, J.D.Y. *Ijeshas and Nigerians: the Incorporation of a Yoruba Kingdom, 1890s–1970s* (Cambridge, 1983).

Peel, J.D.Y. 'Making History: the Past in the Ijesha Present', *Man* n.s. 19 (1984), pp. 111–22.

Peel, J.D.Y. 'The Cultural Work of Yoruba Ethnogenesis' in *History and Ethnicity*, (eds) E. Tonkin, M. McDonald and M. Chapman (London, 1989), pp. 198–215.

Peel, J.D.Y. and Ajayi, J.F.A. (eds) *People and Empires in African History: Essays in Memory of Michael Crowder* (London, 1992).

Peel, J.D.Y. 'Between Crowther and Ajayi: the Religious Origins of the Modern Yoruba Intelligentsia', in *African Historiography: Essays in Honour of Jacob Ade Ajayi*, (ed.) T. Falola (Harlow, 1993), pp 64–79.

Peel, J.D.Y. 'Historicity and Pluralism in Some Recent Studies of Yoruba Religion', *Africa* 64 (1994), pp. 150–66.

Peel, J.D.Y. 'For Who Hath Despised the Day of Small Things? Missionary Narratives and Historical Anthropology', *Comparative Studies in Society and History* 37 (1995), pp. 581–607.

Peel, J.D.Y. 'Two Pastors and their Histories: Johnson and Reindorf', *Basler Afrikanische Bibliographie*, forthcoming.

Peil, M. *Cities and Suburbs: Urban Life in West Africa* (New York, 1981).

Perham, M. *Native Administration in Nigeria* (Oxford, 1937).

Pred, A. *Lost Words and Lost Worlds: Modernity and the Languages of Everyday Life in Late-Nineteenth Century Stockholm* (Cambridge, 1990).

Post, K.W.J. and Jenkins, G. *The Price of Liberty: Personality and Politics in Colonial Nigeria* (Cambridge, 1973).

Putnam, R.D. *Making Democracy Work: Civic Traditions in Modern Italy* (Princeton, 1993).

Quayson, A. *Strategic Transformations in Nigerian Writing. Orality and History in the Work of Rev. Samuel Johnson, Amos Tutuola, Wole Soyinka & Ben Okri* (Oxford, 1997).

Rathbone, R. 'A Murder in the Colonial Gold Coast: Law and Politics in the 1940s', *Journal of African History* 30 (1989)

Rathbone, R. *Murder and Politics in Colonial Ghana* (New Haven, 1993).

Ranger, T. and Kirk-Greene, A.H.M. (eds) *Legitimacy and the State in Twentieth-Century Africa: Essays in Honour of A.H.M. Kirk-Greene* (London, 1993).

Richards, P. 'Landscapes of Dissent – Ikale and Ilaje Country, 1870–1950', in *People and Empires in African History: Essays in Memory of Michael Crowder*, (ed.) J.D.Y. Peel and J.F.A. Ajayi (London, 1992), pp. 161–83.

Scarisbrick, J.J. *Henry VIII* (London, 1968).

Schwab, W. 'Kinship and Lineage Among the Yoruba', *Africa* 25 (1955), pp. 352–74.

Schwab, W. 'The Terminology of Kinship and Marriage Among the Yoruba', *Africa* 28 (1958), pp. 301–13.

Schwab, W.B. 'Oshogbo – An Urban Community?', in *Urbanization and Migration in West Africa*, (ed.) Hilda Kuper (Berkeley, 1965), pp. 85–109.

Schwerdtfeyer, F.W. *Traditional Housing in African Cities: a Comparative Study of Houses in Zaria, Ibadan and Marrakech* (Chichester, 1982).

Simpson, G.E. *Yoruba Religion and Medicine in Ibadan* (Ibadan, 1991 [1980]).

Sklar, R. *Nigerian Political Parties: Power in an Emergent African Nation* (Princeton, 1963).

Sjoberg, G. *The Preindustrial City* (New York, 1960).

Bibliography

Smith, R. 'Yoruba Armament', *Journal of African History* 8 (1967), pp. 87–106.
Smith, R. *Warfare and Diplomacy in Pre-colonial West Africa* (London, 1976).
Smith, R. *Kingdoms of the Yoruba* (London, 1976).
Southall, A. *Social Change in Modern Africa* (Oxford, 1961).
Stoller, P. *Embodying Colonial Memories: Spirit Possession, Power and the Hauka in West Africa* (New York, 1995).
Strathern, M. *After Nature: English Kinship in the Late Twentieth Century* (Cambridge, 1992).
Sudarkasa, N. *Where Women Work: A Study of Yoruba Women in the Marketplace and in the Home* (Ann Arbor, 1973).
Tamuno, T.N. *The Evolution of the Nigerian State. The Southern Phase, 1898–1914* (London, 1972).
Thomas, N. *Entangled Objects: Exchange, Material Culture, and Colonialism in the Pacific* (Cambridge, MA., 1991).
Thomas, N. *Colonialism's Culture: Anthropology, Travel and Government* (Cambridge, 1994).
Thomas, N. *Out of Time: History and Evolution in Anthropological Discourse* (Ann Arbor, 1996 [1989]).
Thompson, L.A. *Democracy, Democratization and Africa* (Ibadan, 1994).
Tignor, R.L. 'Bascom and the Ife Bronzes', *Africa* 60 (1990), pp. 425–34.
Vaughan, O. *Nigerian Chiefs: Traditional Power in Modern Politics, 1890s–1990s* (Rochester, NY, 2000).
Weber, M. *The City*, (trans. and eds) D. Martindale and G. Neuwirth (Glencoe, 1958).
Weber, M. 'Class, Status, Party', in *From Max Weber: Essays in Sociology* (London, 1991 [1948]), (trans. and eds) H.H. Gerth and C. Wright Mills, pp. 180–95.
Weiner, A.B. 'Cultural Difference and the Density of Objects', *American Ethnologist* 21 (1994), pp. 391–403.
Wheatley, P. 'The Significance of Traditional Yoruba Urbanism', *Comparative Studies in Society and History* 12 (1970), pp. 393–433.
Williams, G. (ed.). *Nigeria: Economy and Society* (London, 1976).
Williams, G. 'Political Consciousness among the Ibadan Poor', in *State and Society in Nigeria* (Idanre, 1980), pp. 110–34.
Williams, G. 'Garveyism, Akinpelu Obisesan and His Contemporaries: Ibadan, 1920-22', in *Legitimacy and the State in Twentieth-Century Africa: Essays in Honour of A.H.M. Kirk-Greene*, (eds) T. Ranger and O. Vaughan (London, 1993), pp. 112–32.
Willett, F. *Ife in the History of West African Sculpture* (London, 1967).
Wirth, L. 'Urbanism as a Way of Life', *The American Journal of Sociology* 44 (1938), pp. 1–24.
Wolpe, H. *Urban Politics in Nigeria: a Study of Port Harcourt*. (Berkeley, 1974).
Wright, G. *The Politics of Design in French Colonial Urbanism* (Chicago, 1991).
Young, R. *White Mythologies: Writing History and the West* (London, 1990).

Unpublished Secondary Sources

Adeboye, O.A. '*Egbe Agba O'tan* of Yorubaland: an Educated Elite Organisation, 1914–1944', paper presented in the Department of History, University of Ibadan, 14 December 1995.
Adeboye, O.A. 'The Ibadan Elite, 1893–1966' (Ibadan University Ph.D. thesis, 1996).
Alo, L.K. 'The Native Courts in Ibadan, 1901–1960' (Ibadan University M.A. thesis, 1995).
Awe, B. 'The Rise of Ibadan as a Yoruba Power' (Oxford University D.Phil. thesis, 1964).
Dawes, G.H.C. 'The Politics of Militarism in Ibadan, 1819–1905' (Ibadan University M.A. thesis, 1982).
Denzer, L. 'The *Iyalode* in Ibadan Politics and Society: A Preliminary Study', Paper presented at the Oluyole Club Seminar on Ibadan, 13 February 1997.
Doortmont, M.R. 'Recapturing the Past: Samuel Johnson and the Construction of Yoruba History' (Erasmus University Ph.D. thesis, 1994).
Jenkins, G. 'Politics in Ibadan' (Northwestern University Ph.D. thesis, 1965).
Ojo, O.A. 'The Life and Times of Chief Salami Agbaje' (Ibadan Univ. B.A. long essay, 1988).
Ojo, O.A. 'The Changing Status of the *Olubadan* of Ibadan, 1893–83' (Ibadan University M.A. thesis 1990)
Vaughan, O. 'The Impact of Party Politics and Military Rule on Traditional Chieftaincy in Western Nigeria' (Oxford University D.Phil. thesis, 1989).
Williams, G. 'Social Conflict in Rural Ibadan Division', unpublished paper, University of Durham, 1972.

Index

Index

Index

177

Index

John Holt (company) 121
Johnson, Horatio 78
Johnson, Obadiah 40n, 97, 100, 103
Johnson, Samuel 10-11, 17, 21-2, 29-36, 39-40, 43-53, 65, 75, 97, 105, 140, 151
Jones, Robert 117-18, 129, 131
Jubilee Celebrations (1935) 131-2, 133, **134**, 150

Kaduna 123
Kelly, Resident 145-7, 152, 154, 156
kinship 7-8, 26-7
Kipling, Rudyard 133
kola-nuts 61, 104
Kongi 61-3, 71-3, 75, 82, 86, 88, 96, 139
Kudeti Girls' Training College 133
Kure 27

Labosinde 12, 17
labour 42, 108, 118
Ladugbolu, Shiyanbola 89-90, 95, 107, 111-13, 115-16, 119-20, 122, 128-9, 141-2, 145, 154, 156
Lagelu 12-14, 17, 140
Lagos 52, 54, 55-6, 60, 76, 80, 90, 102-3, 107, 117, 140, 146-8, 151, 160; *Eleko* 119; police 78; trade 42
Lagos Colony 98-9
Lagos Protectorate 69
Lagos Railway 64n, 79, 87n, 105, 107-8
Lagos Supreme Court 79, 81
Lakanle 17-18, 29, 34, 48, 105
land 24-5, 27-8, 52, 79-80, 108, 110, 160-1
Land Court 160
Lanipekun *see* Adebisi, Sanusi
Lanlatu 23n, 90, 130
Latosisa 22, 30, 36-8, 41, 43, 62, 88; *ile* 115, 143
Latunde 19, 26
law 79-81, 92, 96, 125, 145, 147-8, 158; courts 15, 22, 24, 33, 51, 59, 70-2, 79-81, 96, 126, 160; inheritance 19
Law, R. C. C. 40-1
Lawoyin 32, 36
Lawton, District Officer 118
Layode, Samuel 64, 75, 78, 92, 97-8, 101, 103, 105, 108, 113, 160
leaves, sacred 91 *see also akoko* tree

leopards 149-50, 154-5
Leslie, Police Superintendent 92
libraries 130
licences 77
lineages 7-8, 19-20, 23-8
Lloyd, Peter 7, 27
Lugard, Frederick 10, 79n, 90, 92-7, 100-4, 106
Lyttleton, Alfred 81, 84

Mabogunje, A. L. 40
Macaulay, Herbert 100-1
MacGregor, William 69, 76, 79-80, 115
Mackenzie, J. A. 148, 150
Mackie, J. R. and Mrs **133**
Mahomedans *see* Islam
Mapo Hall 112-13, 117-20, **119**, 123-4, 130-2, **134-5**, 133-6, **137**, **142**, 143, 144, 150, 152-3, 160
markets 13, 32, 64
Mason, H. **133**
materialism 152
Maybin, J. A. 136
Maye 16, 34
McCallum, Governor 95
men 5, 25, 159
Menasara 60, 66-70, 72-3, 76
Methodists 113
migration 80
militarism *see* warfare
Miller Brothers (company) 87, 111
Millson, Alvan 5, 151
missionaries 31, 39, 45, 101n, 113-14, 132
Mogaji title 19-23, 163
Molete 27
Moloney, Governor 141n
Moma, Emir 49, 53
money 107-8, 116 *see also* cowries
Moody, Mr 108
Morenikeji family 24
Morgan, Kemi 17
Mosaderin 59, 62-3, 67-70, 80, 82, 84
Moseley, Harley 63, 84
murder 37, 59-60, 64-5, 67-8, 70, 72-3, 75-6, 79-82, 108
Muslims *see* Islam
mythology 140

Nabham, H. **133**
Nairobi 159
nationalism 39-40, 101n, 162
Native Authority 124, 146 *see also under name*
Native Authority Ordinance (1916) 104

Native Authority Ordinance (1933) 146
Native Chiefs' Complaints 94-5, 100-1
Native Council Ordinance (1901) 69-70, 83, 115
Native Courts Ordinance (1933) 127
Newboldia laevis see akoko tree
newspapers 100, 110, 113, 120, 122-3, 129, 142, 144, 146, 150, 155 *see also Nigeria Gazette*
Niger Mission 101n
Nigeria 4, 6, 10, 39, 131, 141, 152; Bauchi Province; Court of Appeal 24; Criminal Investigations Department 147; Legislative Council 88n, 91n, 123, 126-7, 138-9; Northern and Southern Protectorates 94; northern emirates 93; Northern Provinces 128; Oyo Province 103, 110, 123-4, 126, 128, 136, 141, 160-1; Southern Provinces 94, 104, 106, 128; Supreme Court 15; Western Regional House of Assembly 88n, 162n; Western Provinces 148, 150
Nigeria Gazette 112, 128, 138, 141, 145-7
Nigerian Co-operative Movement 87n
Nigerian Daily Times 143, 144
Nupe people 54

oaths 106
oba see chiefs and chieftaincy
Obasa, Daniel 97, 99-100, 110
Obisesan, Akinpelu 86-7, 91, 96, 100, 107-8, 110-16, 117, 119-22, 124, 126-8, 130, 139, 148, 152-3
Oderinlo 17-19, 25, 34-5; *ile* 74, 76, 81
Odo Otin 54
Ogbomosho 16, 19, 25, 27, 140; Native Authority 128
Ogboriefon, Ajayi 36-7, 46, 48, 62
Ogun (god) 17
Ogunbiyi, T. A. J. 99
Ogunfemun, Mr 129
Ogunlade 89
Ogunlade, E. B. **137**
Ogunmola 36, 45-6, 61-3, 160; *ile* 73, 76, 139
Ogunniran, Lawuyi 1-2, 6

Index

Index